Many Circles

Other Books by Albert Goldbarth

POETRY

Coprolites

Jan. 31

Opticks

Keeping

A Year of Happy

Comings Back

Different Fleshes

Who Gathered and Whispered Behind Me

Faith

Original Light: New & Selected Poems 1973–1983

Arts & Sciences

Popular Culture

Heaven and Earth: A Cosmology

The Gods

Across the Layers: Poems Old and New

Marriage, and Other Science Fiction

A Lineage of Ragpickers

Adventures in Ancient Egypt

Beyond

Troubled Lovers in History

Saving Lives

PROSE

A Sympathy of Souls

Across the Layers

Great Topics of the World

Dark Waves and Light Matter

Many Circles

New & Selected Essays

by

Albert Goldbarth

Graywolf Press

SAINT PAUL, MINNESOTA

Publication of this volume is made possible in part by a grant provided by
the Minnesota State Arts Board through an appropriation by the Minnesota
State Legislature, and by a grant from the National Endowment for the Arts.
Significant support has also been provided by the Bush Foundation; Dayton's
Project Imagine with support from Target Foundation; the McKnight Foundation; a grant made on behalf of the Stargazer Foundation; and other generous
contributions from foundations, corporations, and individuals. To these organ-
izations and individuals we offer our heartfelt thanks.

Published by Graywolf Press
2402 University Avenue, Suite 203
Saint Paul, Minnesota 55114

www.graywolfpress.org

Published in the United States of America

ISBN 1–55597–321–3

2 4 6 8 9 7 5 3 1
First Graywolf Printing, 2001

Library of Congress Catalog Number: 00–105088

Cover design: Julie Metz

Cover photograph: NASA, "Composition Differences within Saturn's Rings"

Acknowledgments

My gratitude to the editors of the following publications, where these essays first appeared:

"After Yitzl": originally in *The Georgia Review*; collected in *A Sympathy of Souls* (Coffee House Press) © 1990 by Albert Goldbarth

"Parade March from *That Creaturely World*": originally in *The Georgia Review*; collected in *A Sympathy of Souls* (Coffee House Press) © 1990 by Albert Goldbarth

"Dual": originally in *The Georgia Review*; collected in *Across the Layers* (The University of Georgia Press) © 1993 by Albert Goldbarth

"Calling Up": originally in *The New Virginia Review*; collected in *A Sympathy of Souls* (Coffee House Press) © 1990 by Albert Goldbarth

"The Lake": originally in *The Georgia Review*; collected in *Dark Waves and Light Matter* (The University of Georgia Press) © 1999 by Albert Goldbarth

"Fuller": originally in *The Kenyon Review*; collected in *A Sympathy of Souls* (Coffee House Press) © 1990 by Albert Goldbarth

"Farder to Reache": originally in *The Ohio Review*

"The Space": originally in *The Georgia Review*; collected in *A Sympathy of Souls* (Coffee House Press) © 1990 by Albert Goldbarth

"Ellen's": originally in *The Kenyon Review*; collected in *A Sympathy of Souls* (Coffee House Press) © 1990 by Albert Goldbarth

"Many Circles": originally in *Quarterly West*

"Worlds": originally in *New England Review*; collected in *Great Topics of the World* (David R. Godine) © 1994 by Albert Goldbarth

"Parnassus": originally in *Parnassus*

Special appreciation to the good people at Coffee House Press and the University of Georgia Press; and to John Gallaher for his generous discography. Thanks to Fiona McCrae, Jeffrey Shotts, and Anne Czarniecki, leaders of the pack.

Additionally, "After Yitzl" was included in the 1988 editions of both *The Pushcart Prize: The Best of the Small Presses* and *The Best American Essays*; "Parade March from *That Creaturely World*" was included in the 1989 edition of *The Best American Essays*; "The Lake" was reprinted in *Harper's* and listed under Notable Essays in the 1997 edition of *The Best American Essays*; and "Farder to Reache" was anthologized in *In Short* (eds. Kitchen and Jones). Deep thanks to the editors of these.

Contents

After Yitzl / 1

Parade March from *That Creaturely World* / 17

Dual / 27

Calling Up / 47

The Lake / 69

Fuller / 93

Farder to Reache / 123

The Space / 125

Ellen's / 141

Many Circles / 175

Worlds / 237

Parnassus / 305

Notes / 307

Look for miracles, find history; look for history, run headlong into the blunt edge of a miracle.

—Robert Charles Wilson, *Darwinia*

# After Yitzl

It is not for nothing that a Soviet historian once remarked
that the most difficult of a historian's tasks is to predict
the past. —Bernard Lewis, *History*

1.

This story begins in bed, in one of those sleepy troughs between the crests of sex. I stroke the crests of you. The night is a gray permissive color.

"Who do you think you were—do you think you were anyone, in an earlier life?"

In an earlier life, I think, though chance and bombs and the salt-grain teeth in ocean air have destroyed all documents, I farmed black bent-backed turnips in the hardpan of a shtetl compound of equally black-garbed bent-backed grandmama and rabbinic Jews.

My best friend there shoed horses. He had ribs like barrel staves, his sweat was miniature glass pears. (I'm enjoying this now.) On Saturday nights, when the Sabbath was folded back with its pristine linens into drawers for another week, this Yitzl played accordion at the schnapps-house. He was in love with a woman, a counter girl, there. She kept to herself. She folded paper roses in between serving; she never looked up. But Yitzl could tell: she tapped her foot. One day the cousin from Milano, who sent the accordion, sent new music to play—a little sheaf with American writing on it. *Hot* polka. Yitzl took a break with me in the corner—I was sipping sweet wine as dark as my turnips and trying to write a poem—and when he returned to his little grocer's crate of a stand, there was an open paper rose on his accordion. So he knew, then.

In this story-*in*-my-story they say, "I love you," and now I say it in the external story, too: I stroke you slightly rougher as I say it, as if under-lining the words, or reaffirming you're here, and I'm here, since the gray in the air is darker, and sight insufficient. You murmur it back. We say it like anyone else—in part because our death is bonded into us meiotically, from before there was marrow or myelin, and we know it, even as infants our scream is for more than the teat. We understand the wood smoke in a tree is aching to rise from the tree in its shape, its green and nutritive damps are readying always for joining the ether around it—any affirming clench of the roots in soil, physical and deeper, is preventive for its partial inch of a while.

So: genealogy. The family tree. Its roots. Its urgent suckings among the cemeterial layers. The backsweep of teat under teat. The way, once known, it orders the Present. A chief on the island of Nios, off Sumatra, could stand in the kerosene light of his plank hut and (this is on tape) recite—in a chant, the names sung out between his betel-reddened teeth like ghosts still shackled by hazy responsibility to the living—his ancestral linkup, seventy generations deep; it took over an hour. The genealogical record banks of the Mormon Church contain the names and relationship data of 1½ to 2 billion of the planet's dead, "in a climate-controlled and nuclear-bomb-proof repository" called Granite Mountain Vault, and these have been processed through the Church's IBM computer system, the Genealogical Information and Names Tabulation, acronymed GIANT.

Where we come from. How we need to know.

If necessary, we'll steal it—those dinosaur tracks two men removed from the bed of Cub Creek in Hays County, using a masonry saw, a jackhammer, and a truck disguised as an ice-cream vendor's.

If necessary (two years after Yitzl died, I married his schnapps-house sweetie: it was mourning him that initially drew us together; and later, the intimacy of hiding from the Secret Police in the burlap-draped back corner of a fishmonger's van. The guts were heaped to our ankles and our first true sex in there, as we rattled like bagged bones over the countryside, was lubricated—for fear kept her dry—with fishes' slime: and, after . . . but that's another story) we'll make it up.

2.

Which is what we did with love, you and I: invented it. We needed it, it wasn't here, and out of nothing in common we hammered a tree house into the vee of a family tree, from zero, bogus planks, the bright but invisible nailheads of pure will. Some nights a passerby might spy us, while I was lazily flicking your nipple awake with my tongue, or you were fondling me into alertness, pleased in what we called bed, by the hue of an apricot moon, in what we called our life, by TV's dry-blue arctic light, two black silhouettes communing: and we were suspended in air. If the passerby yelled, we'd plummet.

Because each midnight the shears on the clock snip off another twenty-four hours. We're frightened, and rightfully so. Because glass is, we now know, a "slow liquid"; and we're slow dust. I've heard the universe howling—a conch from the beach is proof, but there are Ears Above for which the spiral nebulae must twist the same harrowing sound. Because pain, in even one cell, is an ant: it will bear a whole organ away. And a day is so huge—a Goliath; the tiny stones our eyes pick up in sleeping aren't enough to confront it. The marrow gives up. We have a spine, like a book's, and are also on loan with a due date. And the night is even more huge; what we call a day is only one struck match in an infinite darkness. This is knowledge we're born with, this is in the first cry. I've seen each friend I have, at one time or another, shake at thinking how susceptible and brief a person is: and whatever touching we do, whatever small narrative starring ourselves can bridge that unit of emptiness, is a triumph. "Tell me another story," you say with a yawn, "of life back then, with—what was her name?" "With Misheleh?" "Yes, with Misheleh." As if I can marry us backward in time that way. As if it makes our own invented love more durable.

3

The Mormons marry backward. "Sealing," they call it. In the sanctum of the temple, with permission called a "temple recommend," a Mormon of pious state may bind somebody long dead (perhaps an ancestor of his own, perhaps a name provided by chance from a list of cleared names in the computer)—bind that person to the Mormon faith, and to the flow of Mormon generations, in a retroactive conversion good "for time and all eternity." (Though the dead, they add, have "free agency" up in Heaven to accept this or not.) A husband and wife might be "celestially married" this way, from out of their graves and into the spun-sugar clouds of a Mormon Foreverness . . . from out of the Old World sod . . . from sand, from swamp water. . . . Where does ancestry *stop*?

To pattern the present we'll fabricate the past from before there *was* fabric. Piltdown Man. On display in the British Museum. From 65 million years back—and later shown to be some forgery of human and orangutan lockings, the jawbone stained and abraded. Or, more openly and jubilant, the Civilization of Llhuros "from the recent excavations of Vanibo, Houndee, Draikum, and other sites"—in Ithaca, New York. Norman Daly, professor of art at Cornell and current "Director of Llhurosian Studies," has birthed an entire culture: its creatures (the Pruii bird, described in the article "Miticides of Coastal Llhuros"), its rites ("the Tokens of Holmeek are lowered into the Sacred Fires, and burned with the month-cloths of the Holy Whores"), its plaques and weapons and votive figurines, its myths and water clocks, its poems and urns and a "nasal flute." An elephant mask. An "early icon of Tal-Hax." Wall paintings. "Oxen bells." Maps. The catalogue I have is 48 pages—135 entries. Some of the Llhuros artifacts are paintings or sculpture. Some are anachronismed, a five-and-dime on-sale orange juicer becomes a *trallib,* an "oil container . . . Middle Period, found at Draikum." A clothes iron: "Late Archaic . . . that it may be a votive of the anchorite Ur Ur cannot be disregarded." Famous athletes. Textiles. "Fornicating gods."

Just open the mind, and the past it requires will surface. "Psychic archaeologists" have tranced themselves to the living worlds of the pyramids or the caves—one chipped flint scraper can be connection enough. When Edgar Cayce closed his eyes he opened them (inside his head, which had its eyes closed) in the undiluted afternoon light of dynastic Egypt: wind was playing a chafing song in the leaves of the palm and the persea, fishers were casting their nets. "His findings and methods tend to be dismissed by the orthodox scientific community," but Jeffrey Goodman meditates, and something—an invisible terra-form diving bell of sorts—descends with his eyes to fully twenty feet below the sands of Flagstaff, Arizona, 100,000 B.C., his vision Brailling happily as a mole's nose through the bones set in the darkness there like accent marks and commas.

Going back . . . the darkness . . . closing your lids. . . .

A wheel shocked into a pothole. Misheleh waking up, wild-eyed. Torches.

"We needed certain papers, proof that we were Jews, to be admitted to America. To pass the inspectors there. And yet if our van was stopped by the Secret Police and we were discovered in back, those papers would be our death warrant. Such a goat's dessert!—that's the expression we used then."

"And . . . ?"

"It comes from when two goats will fight for the same sweet morsel—each pulls a different direction."

"No, I mean that night, the escape—what *happened*?"

"The Secret Police stopped the van."

3.

Earlier, I said, "in a trough between crests"—sea imagery. I mean in part that dark, as it grows deeper, takes the world away, and a sleepless body will float all night in horrible separation from what it knows and where it's nurtured. Freedom is sweet; but nobody wants to be flotsam.

Ruth Norman, the eighty-two-year-old widow of Ernest L. Norman, is Uriel, an Archangel, to her fellow Unarian members and is, in fact, the "Cosmic Generator," and head of all Unarius activities on Earth (which is an applicant for the "Intergalactic Confederation" of thirty-two other planets—but we need to pass a global test of "consciousness vibration"). In past lives, Uriel has been Socrates, Confucius, Henry VIII, and Benjamin Franklin—and has adventured on Vidus, Janus, Vulna, and other planets. All Unarians know their former lives. Vaughn Spaegel has been Charlemagne. And Ernest L. himself has been Jesus (as proved by a pamphlet, *The Little Red Box*) and currently is Alta; from his ankh-shaped chair on Mars he communicates psychically and through a bank of jeweled buttons with all the Confederation. Everyone works toward the day Earth can join. The 1981 Conclave of Light, at the Town and Country Convention Center in El Cajon, California, attracted over 400 Unarians, some from as far as New York and Toronto. Neosha Mandragos, formerly a nun for twenty-seven years, was there; and George, the shoe-store clerk, and Dan, assistant manager of an ice-cream parlor.

Uriel makes her long-awaited entrance following the *Bolero*-backed procession of two girls dressed as peacocks, led by golden chains, then two nymphs scattering petals from cornucopias, someone wearing a feathered bird's head, and various sages. Four "Nubian slaves . . . wearing skin bronzer, headdresses, loincloths and gilded beach thongs" carry a palanquin adorned with enormous white swans, atop which . . . Uriel! In a black velvet gown falling eight feet wide at the hem, with a wired-up universe of painted rubber balls representing the thirty-two worlds and dangling out to her skirt's edge. According to Douglas Curran, "the gown, the painted golden 'vortex' headdress, and the translucent elbow-length gloves with rapier nails have tiny light bulbs snaked through the fabric. The bulbs explode into volleys of winking. Waves of light roll from bodice to fingertips, Infinite Mind to planets." People weep. Their rich remembered lives are a sudden brilliance over their nerves, like ambulance flashers on chicken wire, like . . . like fire approaching divinity. Nobody's worrying here over last week's sales of butter-pecan parfait.

We'll sham it. We need it. It's not that we lie. It's that we *make* the truth. The Japanese have a word especially for it: *nisekeizu,* false genealogies. Ruling-class Japan was obsessed with lineage and descent, and these connived links to the Sewangezi line of the Fujiwaras qualified one—were indeed the only qualification at the time—for holding office. "High birth." "Pedigree." It's no less likely in Europe. In the seventeenth century, Countess Alexandrine von Taxis "hired genealogists to fabricate a descent from the Torriani, a clan of warriors who ruled Lombardy until 1 3 1 1 ."

European Jews, who by late in the 1 7 0 0 s needed to take on surnames in order to cross a national border, often invented family names that spoke of lush green woods and open fields—this from a people traipsing from one cramped dingy urban ghetto to another. Greenblatt. Tannenbaum. Now a child born choking on soot could be heir to a name saying miles of mild air across meadows. Flowers. Mossy knolls.

Misheleh's name was Rosenblum. I never asked but always imagined this explained the trail of paper roses she'd left through Yitzl's life. My name then was Schvartzeit, reference to my many-thousand-year heritage of black beets. The name on our papers, though, was Kaufman—"merchant." This is what you had to do, to survive.

I remember: they were rough with us, also with the driver of the van. But we pretended being offended, like any good citizens. It could have gone worse. This was luckily early in the times of the atrocities, and these officers—they were hounds set out to kill, but they went by the book. A hound is honest in his pursuit. The rat and the slippery eel—later on, more officers were like that.

They might have dragged us away just for being in back of the van at all. But we said we were workers. In this, the driver backed us up. And the papers that shouted out *Jew*? My Misheleh stuffed them up a salmon. Later, after the Secret Police were gone and we had clumped across the border, we were on our knees with a child's doll's knife slicing the bellies of maybe a hundred fish until we found it! Covered in pearly offal and roe. We had it framed when we came to America. Pretty. A little cherrywood frame with cherubim puffing a trump in each corner. We were happy, then. A very lovely frame around an ugliness.

"And you loved each other."

Every day, in our hearts. Some nights, in our bodies. I'll tell you this about sex: it's like genealogy. Yes. It takes you back, to the source. That's one small bit of why some people relish wallowing there. A burrowing, completely and beastly, back to where we came from. It tastes and smells "fishy" in every language I know. It takes us down to when the blood was the ocean, down the rivers of the live flesh to the ocean, to the original beating fecundity. It's as close as we'll ever get.

And this I'll tell you, about the smell of fish: for our earliest years, when I was starting the dry-goods store and worrying every bolt of gabardine or every bucket of nails was eating another poem out of my soul—which I think is true—we lived over a fish store. Kipper, flounder, herring, the odors reached up like great gray leaves through our floorboards. And every night we lived there, Misheleh cried for a while. After the van, you see? She could never be around raw fish again, without panic.

But on the whole we were happy. There was security of a kind, and friends—even a social club in a patchy back room near the train tracks, that we decorated once a month with red and yellow crepe festoons and paper lanterns pouring out a buttery light.

Once every year she and I, we visited the cemetery. A private ritual: we pretended Yitzl was buried there. Because he'd brought us together, and we wanted him with us yet. For the hour it took, we always hired a street accordionist—it wasn't an uncommon instrument then. Like guitar now. Play a polka, we told him—*hot*. It drove the other cemetery visitors crazy! And always, Misheleh left a paper rose at the cemetery gates.

We heard that accordion music and a whole world came back, already better and worse than it was in its own time. Harsher. Gentler. Coarser. Little things—our shtetl dogs. Or big things too, the way we floated our sins away on toy-sized cork rafts once each spring, and everybody walking home singing. . . . All of that world was keeping its shape but growing more and more transparent for us. Like the glass slipper in the fairy tale. The past was becoming a fairy tale. In it, the slipper predicates a certain foot and, so, a certain future.

At night I'd walk in my store. The moon like a dew on the barrel heaped with bolts, and the milky bodies of lamps, and the pen nibs, and shovels . . . Kaufman. Merchant.

4.

Within a year after death we have what Jewish tradition calls "the un-veiling"—the gravestone dedication ceremony. September 14, 1986: I arrived in Chicago, joining my mother, sister, two aunts, and perhaps thirty others, including the rabbi, at the grave of my father Irving Goldbarth, his stone wrapped in a foolish square of cheesecloth. A stingy fringe of grass around the fresh mound. The burial had taken place in bitter city winter, the earth (in my memory) opening with the crack of axed oak. Now it was warmer, blurrier, everything soft. My mother's tears.

The rabbi spoke, his voice soft: to the Jews a cemetery is "a house of graves". . . but also a "house of eternal life." The same in other faiths, I thought. There are as many dead now as alive. A kind of balance along the ground's two sides. That permeable membrane. Always new dead in the making, and always the long dead reappearing over our shoulders and in our dreams. Sometimes a face, like a coin rubbed nearly smooth, in a photo. We're supposed to be afraid of ghosts but every culture has them, conjures them, won't let go. Our smoky ropes of attachment to the past. Our anti-umbilici. . . . My mind wandering. Then, the eldest and only son, I'm reciting the Kaddish. "*Yisgadahl v'yisgadosh sh'may rahbbo. . . .*" In back, my father's father's grave, the man I'm named for. Staring hard and lost at the chiseling, ALBERT GOLD-BARTH. My name. His dates.

In 1893 "Albert Goldbarth An Alien personally appeared in open Court and prayed to be admitted to become a Citizen of the United States. . . ."—I have that paper, that and a sad, saved handful of others: September 15, 1904, he "attained the third degree" in the "Treue Bruder Lodge of the Independent Order of Odd Fellows." Five days after, J. B. Johnson, General Sales Agent of the Southern Cotton Oil

Company, wrote a letter recommending "Mr. Goldbarth to whomsoever he may apply, as an honest and hardworking Salesman, leaving us of his own accord." That was 24 Broad Street, New York. In two years, in Cleveland, Ohio, John H. Silliman, Secretary, was signing a notice certifying Mr. Albert Goldbarth as an agent of The American Accident Insurance Company. And, from 1924, "$55 Dollars, in hand paid," purchasing Lot Number 703—this, from the envelope he labeled in pencil, "Paid Deed from Semetery Lot from Hibrew Progresif Benefit Sociaty." I'm standing there now. I'm reading this stone that's the absolute last of his documents.

There aren't many stories. Just two photographs. And he was dead before I was born. A hundred times, I've tried inventing the calluses, small betrayals, tasseled mantel lamps, day-shaping waves of anger, flicked switches, impossible givings of love in the face of no love, dirty jokes, shirked burdens, flowerpots, loyalties, gold-shot silk page markers for the family Bible, violin strings, sweet body stinks from the creases, knickknacks, lees of tea, and morning-alchemized trolley tracks declaring themselves as bright script in the sooted-over paving bricks—everything that makes a life, which is his life, and buried.

And why am I busy repeating that fantastical list . . . ? We're "mountain gorillas" (this is from Alex Shoumatoff's wonderful study of kinship, *The Mountain of Names*) who "drag around moribund members of their troop and try to get them to stand, and after they have died" (above my grandfather's grave, imagining bouts of passion with imaginary Misheleh over my grandfather's grave now) "masturbate on them and try to get some reaction from them." An offering, maybe. A trying to read life backward into that text of dead tongues. Give us any fabric scrap, we'll dream the prayer shawl it came from. Give us any worthless handful of excavated soil, we'll dream the scrap. The prayer. The loom the shawl took fragile shape on, in the setting shtetl hill-light. The immigrant ships they arrived in, the port, the year. We'll give that year whatever version of semen is appropriate, in homage and resuscitative ritual. We'll breathe into, rub, and luster that year.

1641: on a journey in Ecuador, a Portuguese Jew, Antonio de

Montezinos, discovered—after a weeklong, brush-clogged hell trek through the hinterlands—a hidden Jewish colony, and heard them wailing holy writ in Hebrew. Yes, there in the wild domain of anaconda and peccary—or so he told the Jewish scholar and eminent friend of Rembrandt, Menasseh ben Israel. Or so Menasseh claimed, who had his own damn savvy purposes; and based on his claim that the Ten Lost Tribes of Israel were now found in the New World, and their global equidispersion near complete—as the Bible foretells will usher in an Age of Salvation—Britain's Puritan leaders readmitted their country's exiled Jews, the better to speed the whole world on its prophesied way to Redemption. (Maybe Rembrandt was an earlier body of Ernest L. Norman? Maybe the massed Confederation planets were holding their astro-collective breath even then, as destiny wound like spool thread on the windmills. And maybe, in the same Dutch-sunset oranges and mauves he let collect like puddled honey in his painted-dusk skies, Rembrandt helped Menasseh finagle this plot on behalf of a troubled people, tipped a flagon of burgundy in a room of laundered varnish rags, and plotted as the radio-telescope Monitor Maids of planet Vidus lounged about in their gold lamé uniforms, listening. . . .)

Maybe. Always a maybe. Always someone forcing the scattered timbers of history into a sensible bridge. The Lost Tribes: China. The Lost Tribes: Egypt. The Lost Tribes: Africa. India. Japan. They formed a kingdom near "a terrible river of crashing stones" that roared six days a week "but on the Jewish Sabbath did cease." Lord Kingsborough emptied the family fortune, won three stays in debtor's prison, "in order to publish a series of sumptuously illustrated volumes proving the Mexican Indians. . . ." Ethiopians. Eskimos. The Mormons have them reaching America's shores as early as "Tower of Babylon times" and later again, about 600 B.C., becoming tipi dwellers, hunters of lynx and buffalo, children of Fire and Water Spirits. . . . Maybe. But today I think these caskets in Chicago soil are voyage enough. The moon's not that far.

We visit the other family graves: Auntie Regina (brain cancer) . . . Uncle Jake (drank; slipped me butterscotch candies). . . . Miles square and unguessably old, this cemetery's a city, districted, netted by streets and their side roads, overpopulated, undercared. Dead Jews dead Jews dead Jews. *Ruth Dale Noparstak *Age 2 Weeks* 1944*—death about the size of a cigar box.

My mother says to Aunt Sally (a stage whisper): "You'll see, Albert's going to write a poem about this." Later, trying to help that endeavor: "Albert, you see these stones on the graves? Jews leave stones on the graves to show they've visited." Not flowers? Why not flowers? . . . *I think I farmed black bent-backed turnips in the hardpan of a shtetl compound of equally black-garbed bent-backed grandmama and rabbinic Jews.*

My mother's parents are here in the Moghileff section, "Organized 1901." "You see the people here? They came from a town called Moghileff, in Russia—or it was a village. Sally, was Moghileff a town or a village?—you know, a little place where all the Jews lived. And those who came to Chicago, when they died, they were all buried here. Right next to your Grandma and Grandpa's graves, you see?—Dave and Natalie?—they were Grandma and Grandpa's neighbors in Moghileff, and they promised each other that they'd stay neighbors forever, here.

"Your Grandma Rosie belonged to the Moghileff Sisterhood. She was Chairlady of Relief. That meant, when somebody had a stillbirth, or was out of a job, or was beat in an alley, she'd go around to the members with an empty can and collect five dollars." Sobbing now. "Five dollars."

On our way out there's a lavish mausoleum lording it over this ghetto of small gray tenanted stones. My Uncle Lou says, still in his Yiddish-flecked English: "And *dis* one?" Pauses. "Gotta be a gengster."

5.

The Mormons marry backward. "Sealing," they call it.
   "Is that the end of your story of Misheleh and you?"
   The story of marrying backward never ends.

In Singapore not long ago, the parents of a Miss Cheeh, who had been stillborn twenty-seven years before, were troubled by ghosts in their dreams, and consulted a spirit medium. Independently, the parents of a Mr. Poon consulted her, too—their son had been stillborn thirty-six years earlier and, recently, ghosts were waking them out of slumber. "And the medium, diagnosing the two ghosts' problem as loneliness, acted as their marriage broker." The Poons and the Cheehs were introduced, a traditional bride price paid, and dolls representing the couple were fashioned out of paper, along with a miniature one-story house with manservant, car, and chauffeur, a table with teacups and pot, and a bed with bolster and pillows. Presumably, on some plane of invisible, viable, ectoplasmic endeavor, connubial bliss was enabled. Who knows?—one day soon, they may wake in their version of that paper bed (his arm around her sex-dampened nape, a knock at the door . . .) and be given the chance to be Mormon, to have always been Mormon, and everlastingly Mormon. They'll laugh, but graciously. She'll rise and start the tea. . . .

These ghosts. Our smoky ropes of attachment. And our reeling them in.

Eventually Misheleh and I prospered. The store did well, then there were two stores. We grew fat on pickled herring in cream, and love. I suppose we looked jolly. Although you could see in the eyes, up close, there was a sadness: where our families died in the camps, where I was never able to find time for the poetry—those things. Even so, the days and nights were good. The children never lacked a sweet after meals (but only if they cleaned their plates), or a little sailor suit, or Kewpie blouse, or whatever silliness was in fashion. Before bed, I'd tell them a story. *Once, your mother and I, we lived in another country. A friend introduced us. He was a famous musician. Your mother danced to his songs and a thousand people applauded. I wrote poems about her, everyone read them. Gentlemen flung her roses. . . .*

I died. It happens. I died and I entered the Kingdom of Worm and of God, and what happens then isn't part of this story, there aren't any words for it. And what I became on Earth—here, in the memory of the living . . . ?—it isn't over yet, it never ends, and now I'm me and I love you.

Because the ash is in this paper on which I'm writing (and in the page you're reading) and has been from the start. Because the blood is almost the chemical composition of the ocean, the heart is a swimmer, a very sturdy swimmer, but shore is never in sight. Because of entropy. Because of the nightly news. Because the stars care even less for us than we do for the stars. Because the only feeling a bone can send us is pain. Because the more years that we have, the less we have—the schools don't teach this Tragic Math but we know it; twiddling the fingers is how we count it off. Because because because. And so somebody wakes from an ether sleep: the surgeons have made him Elvis, he can play third-rate Las Vegas bars. And so someone revises the raven on top of the clan pole to a salmon-bearing eagle: now his people have a totem-progenitor giving them certain territorial privileges that the spirits ordained on the First Day of Creation. So. Because.

In *He Done Her Wrong,* the "Great American Novel—in pictures—and not a word in it" that the brilliant cartoonist Milt Gross published in 1930, the stalwart square-jawed backwoods hero and his valiant corn-blond sweetheart are torn from each other's arms by a dastardly mustachioed villain of oily glance and scowling brow, then seemingly endless deprivations begin: fistfights, impoverishment, unbearable loneliness, the crazed ride down a sawmill tied to one of its logs. . . . And when they're reunited, as if that weren't enough, what cinches it as a happy ending is uncinched buckskin pants: the hero suddenly has a strawberry birthmark beaming from his tush, and is known for the billionaire sawmill owner's rightful heir. . . .

Because it will save us.

The story-in-my-story is over: Misheleh and the children walk home from the cemetery. She's left a stone and a paper rose. We never would have understood it fifty years earlier, sweated with sex, but this is also love.

The story is over, too: the "I" is done talking, the "you" is nearly asleep, they lazily doodle each other's skin. We met them, it seems a long while ago, in what I called "a trough between crests." Let their bed be a raft, and let the currents of sleep be calm ones.

Outside of the story, I'm writing this sentence, and whether some-one is a model for the "you" and waiting to see me put my pen down and toe to the bedroom—or even if I'm just lonely, between one "you" and the next—is none of your business. The "outside" is never the proper business between a writer and a reader, but this I'll tell you: tonight the rains strafed in, then quit, and the small symphonic saws of the crickets are swelling the night. This writing is almost over.

But nothing is ever over—or, if it is, then the impulse is wanting to make it over: "over" not as in "done," but "again." "Redo." Re-synapse. Re-nova.

I need to say "I love you" to someone and feel it flow down the root of her, through the raw minerals, over the lip of the falls, and back, without limit, into the pulse of the all-recombinant waters.

I meet Carolyn for lunch. She's with Edward, her old friend, who's been living in the heart of Mexico all of these years:

> Our maid, Rosalita, she must be over seventy. She had "female troubles," she said. She needed surgery. But lis-ten: she's from the hills, some small collection of huts that doesn't even bear a name, so she hasn't any papers at all—absolutely no identification. There isn't a single professional clinic that can accept you that way. There isn't any means for obtaining insurance or public aid.

So we went to a Records Division. I slipped the agent *dinero*. He knew what I was doing. It's everywhere. It's the way Mexico works. And when we left, Rosalita was somebody else. She had somebody else's birth certificate, working papers—everything.

She had somebody else's life from the beginning, and she could go on with her own.

Parade March from
That Creaturely World

The halved ham, with its dipsy smile and majorette boots. The headdress-topped pineapple in its sleek-lined 1950s bowl like a chieftain in canoe. The dapper pepper mill. The jitterbugging celery and tomato. . . .

I would keep my father company on weekends. Mr. Penny-Insurance-Peddler. Mr. Shlep-and-Sell. He shmoozed, but he was honest. "Albie, you'll see. I'll joke but I won't lie." Mostly I didn't see, I stayed in the car while he labored up four floors with his enormously heavy leatherette case of waiting dotted lines, his promo giveaway cookbooks. I didn't want to go partners in this. 1956—I was eight, I was only eight, but already it was clear to me: the fiscal wasn't my world.

So I sprawled dreamy on the front seat with the reading at hand. It was there in the car when we all went on vacation every summer, and it was in the apartment like water or electricity, some natural phenomenon you didn't question: *The Metropolitan Life Insurance Cook Book.* There were days, I suppose, when I spent more time in its heavily stylized cosmos—with those leapfrogging muffins, barbershop-quartet condiment bottles, deckle-edged lettuces, troupes of onion acrobats—than I did with my neighborhood friends.

"Memory food," my mother called fish. Is that why the shad on page 11, his body so scaled it's artichoke-like, looks doleful? Would he like to forget? Carrots were "good for your eyes" though even then, I think I sensed that these ridiculous penile guys moved through their proper earthy domain by touch alone. What stayed with me most accurately was the final parade at the top of page 60, a marching pie with a pennant, a pear who's pouring his full rotundity into a trumpet blast. . . .

Once in a while I did go up. These were buildings, scant blocks out of some ghetto, where a brief shot at a foreman's job meant cheap-pink-gingham-curtained windows that might have been simply news-papered one year back. These were families ready to think *insurance*—Greek, Italian, Polish versions of the Jewish home I'd waked in that morning. Walking up the hallway—always to something like "Apartment 4D" in a courtyard building done in the thirties, its bricks a liver color . . . the smells of other-ethnic simmers wooed and unsettled me. Moussaka. Duck-blood soup.

I remember now: Mrs. Poniewiecz didn't know how to say it, coughed politely, roved her eyes. And it was true: I was trying to leave with 40 cents of *her* polite negotiations in my fist. *He* was so flustered; there was no joke for this. He built a rococo architecture of foot-shuffle and apology, and I was ashamed: for him, not for myself. To me, it hadn't really seemed thieving. Just as those cartoon foods were my natural environment—not the intricate, ordinary grown-ups' world of the kitchen—so, too, the winking small change making its way through the riffle of tens of dollars was *my* province. Anyway, it only happened the once; I wasn't inveterate.

Oh, but I could feel, I could *hear,* him turning red with embarrass-ment. Maybe that's why, all these years, I'd "remembered" a crimson lobster topping one page, a lobster in some unexplained dismay, al-though when I chanced on the book last week at a flea market . . . there's no lobster at all.

One of the luckless in the D.C. drug-trade wars, age twenty, was thrown in a motel bathtub filling with scalding water. This you don't forget: "As his skin was peeling off, they took turns urinating on him."

How ashamed would I have to feel for thinking *lobster,* for the tic that starts a joke from this scenario? But I did think that.

I read the story in *Time* that same afternoon I excavated the cook-book from its clutterbox of spotted farmer's almanacs and fifties "humor magazines" with teasing swimsuit cuties and titles like *Wink* and *Wow.*

He must have given out a terrible sound—even if it were silent, even if it only shrieked on the level of where his cellular chemistry broke, then altered.

Two texts, and I couldn't help think what I thought. It's night. I'm walking under stars we like to believe are stories or beam down influence over our lives, but how much here is ever seen in a nebulous "there?" I know the lettuce on 3 is frilled like a petticoated belle, the chickpea leaps arms out with cockamamie grace, the small soup-carrot rides its spoon as if some mermaid-costumed carnival queen in a Mardi Gras float. . . .

And these two disparate texts and their denizens are real and both exist in the same world. This can't be but is.

And it can't be I wasn't there to hear that sound he made, I remember it so distinctly.

And the sound my father made in Chicago when I was in Texas: an egg, a very tiny egg, of pain. Just the size of one period out of that cookbook. First he centered it on his tongue, in 1985, in the Edgewater Hospital cardiac ward, then swallowed until it filled him.

Is this a recipe?

I can taste it.

And I see now what I couldn't (maybe *looked* at, yes, but not with real *seeing*) in those lolling hours waiting for my father in the half-paid-for fedora-gray '48 Chevy: that some of the cookbook's normally uptempo population exhibits . . . well, twistedness.

A bowl of whites is being whipped by one of those handheld eggbeaters looking as spiked and aggressive as any medieval mace. Of course, it's a humanoid bowl, with two google-eyes near its rim peeking fearfully upward, and two spidery arms, the spidery hands of which fidget. Its brains, essentially, are being violently frothed. Its cranium is open to the skies while this crude instrument of torture whirs erratic, turbid circles through its silky insides.

Who drew a thing like that? Who gave the world page 37's dearly ambulatory sardine can—yes, with arms and legs, its oval lid keyed open, so we see its brains are three individual chartreuse fishlings in heavy oil? Whoever he is or was, he made certain the human condition was emblemized within an adequate range, some touch of its uttermost limits, before he drew the rest of his festive comforting crew: a momma teapot gaily pouring into a row of progeny cups, a group of sausages horsing around like the guys in the locker room, a single blissful layer cake as corpulent and knowing as a Buddha.

I grew up with these. Once, age thirty, I needed a word for a poem, some part a tractor drags, and tried describing it to Tony and Theo. "Draw it for us," Tony told me. It was natural, my tractor had these headlight eyes and a smiling mechanical snout. Theo laughed. But Tony, who knew me longer and better, shook his head and said to her, "No, it's not that funny. You don't understand: *he REALLY sees the world that way.*"

That angered me so much it had to be right. And it delighted me as well, in a way. I felt I'd been true to that eight-year-old boy and his beat, breadwinner father. I can see them tired, cross with each other, but bonded by being tired and cross, driving home through five o'clock Saturday traffic. There's no radio; the father sings some popular hit. He loves the boy, who he hopes will join in. The boy knows it and won't. It's a ritual—even this bonds them. Sweaty, lazy, they stop at a carhop shack, it might be Buns & Suds, and bask as well as they can in the feel of two giant root beers. Even the Chevy gets to bask, in the shade of the corrugated tin. It sighs, I hear it sigh, and it dips its overwrought grille to that shade and drinks deeply.

"We give a chair arms, legs, a seat and a back, a cup has its lip / and a bottle its neck"—this from a poem by Marvin Bell. Yes, and a potato its eyes. The mandrake we give an entire human body; if you tugged one from the soil in the year of our Lord 1500 it might squeal deafeningly, an infant being murdered. Just ask anyone.

In Elizabeth Bishop's persona monologue "Crusoe in England," the rescued speaker, old now, "bored too," back in a realm of courtesies and teatime, considers the knife that for so many years was his closest companion and (even following Friday's arrival) the fondled, talked-to, slept-with, absolutely unrelinquishable, major-causal object of his universe. It's a souvenir now. "The living soul has dribbled away."

That knife. The simple Mesopotamian oracle plate that held the watchful consciousness of a god in its glaze. Some thumb-long balsa doll a child has loved so nuzzlingly much the face is rubbed away inversely to the personality quickened inside it: "my Wubsie" (though why *Wubsie,* no one knows), you swear if you slipped that doll from her sleeping grip it would squeal like an infant being murdered. . . .

These come from what David Jones calls, in the preface to his novel *In Parenthesis,* "that creaturely world inherited from our remote beginnings." He wonders (this in 1937) if we'll come to see "newfangled technicalities as true extensions of ourselves, that we may feel for them a native affection." Maybe. Ten years after, men were tightening the last of the nuts of the Chevy they'd premiere that fall and my father would buy a year later, and curse, and coddle-coo, and intimately discourse with, in ways I wouldn't have with any woman for a long bleak while, not even a woman I'd claim I "loved."

And I've watched my father's mother hold such forthright conversation with her ancient foot-treadle sewing machine. The bobbin was all business, but, oh, the vines carved over the wooden side-drawers on the body were like a factory worker's secret descending tattoos. She didn't know I was there. She stitched all night alone with it, and while I only heard *her* voice—a kind of singing, really—I have no reason to say a kind of dialogue wasn't taking place.

I've seen her sing to the soup, low and Yiddish-guttural, seen her sing to the chicken she disemboweled, until the face of the man I was named for must have risen visibly in the soup steam for her. What came then was the everyday talking of woman to man. He was dead. She was holding the heart of a chicken. Now I know, thirty-two years later: if she whistled, an ancient Egyptian bowl would arrive to receive that slick purple thing, would walk in slightly tilted on its own two childlike feet.

The fries in their wire fryer, like goldfinches sleeking about a cage. The froufrou cabbage in her indigo chanteuse ruffles. All those frolicking Cub Scout olives, deviled eggs, radish rosettes: the Appetizer Troop, out on maneuvers. . . .

In the sixteenth century, somebody's grabbing a mandrake's gnarly top and yanking hard (her ears are beeswaxed closed to muffle its shrill of agony). . . . Somebody's curing a headache by smearing his scalp with a lard-based walnut paste; why? simple: the meat of the nut resembles the brain. . . . "Matter," Morris Berman says in *The Reenchantment of the World,* "possessed consciousness." And then goes on, after detailing much of alchemical versus Newtonian cosmologies, to a "conclusion . . . that will probably strike most readers as radical in the extreme. . . . It is not merely the case that men conceived of matter as possessing mind in those days, but rather that in those days, matter *did* possess mind, 'actually' did so."

When I was eight, wedges of cheese ran races around the fondue tureen, a Spanish onion promenaded hand-in-hand with a steak-sauce bottle whose black cap fit him snug as a derby. . . .

Morris Berman: "The animism implicit in quantum mechanics has been explored mathematically by the physicist Evan Harris Walker, who argues that every particle in the universe possesses consciousness."

. . . The cherry tomato, sighing with love for the urbane, professorly roast. . . .

And if they *are* a denatured version of such primacy? Still, they're a version.

Skyler and Babs collect lobsterania: ashtrays, serving platters, blotters, squeeze toys, stamps, you name it.

What a creature! From the major bones of dinosaur, or of Cro-Magnon man, we can, in a rational process of retro-extrapolation, construct the whole. But who could guess *this* whisker-sprouting jointed-castanet armory from its insides? When we eat one, overblooming its shell like a split couch pillow—all those buttersweet meat-feathers!

Lobster postcards are a specialty subgenre of postcard collecting. One, in high demand, is a photograph of The Lobsterettes: a chorine line in life-sized lobster costumes.

In a "fifties shop" in Kansas City, Skyler and I found a set of lobster salt-and-pepper shakers. They're standing up and might be rhumba partners or pugilists. Rarefied kitsch. They were screamingly fireplug-red on a shelf of pastel celadon and eggshell 1950s radios, whose round contours and unashamed dials and gawking or grinning station-bands easily give them the spirit of human faces.

In an African market, Skyler and Bobby Sue picked two apiece from wooden buckets and lugged them home by their antennae, giant specimens, a foot and a half. "They were lovely in their buckets—so many greens! They were . . . hazel." "Like eyes?" I ask her. "Yes, that many colors. Like hazel eyes."

Wasn't it Gérard de Nerval—some Symbolist poet—who in a fit of revel or breakdown walked a lobster on a leash?

And why am I doing this, talking around it? Here, let me say his name: *Patrick Monfiston.* Twenty years old, his skin heated past being skin, and the live piss eating him.

Babs owns an inflatable lobster and one that leaps when you press a small rubber bulb.

I know how comic they can be.

I know what salt means, too. I can't play with that shaker and not hear contents shifting—even if the shaker's empty.

Every year at the Passover holiday, Jews dip a token of what they're feasting on into a basin of salt water. To remind them of suffering.

Wine and honey and singing until the table is cleared. And that: to remind them of suffering.

I remember it this vividly: the dining-room light of that small apartment breaking into splinters on the knobules of the kiddush goblet. Passover, and my father conducting the ceremonial meal. Grandma Nettie (yes, alive then) with her hands still bright from the only emollient they ever knew, fresh chicken fat. Uncle Morrie (alive then) making subterfuge cracker boats in his soup while the service drones on around us in Hebrew—he winks at me, but slyly. My mother. Aunt Sally. My sister Livia. The carpet is the sickly color of moss from a tree's wrong side, and Cousin Beverly's overenthusiastic oil portrait of Tuffy the poodle is still on the wall. And my father is singing the High Tongue, my father is opening Time itself until the days of the Bible pull chairs up to the table, and goatstink and angel shadows attend us. My father, alive then. I remember: his voice a ladder to God.

I remember, he demystified the intricacy of a necktie. I remember, once, in search of some keys I lucked upon the girlie coin ("heads"/ "tails") under his handkerchiefs—that ripe clef of the body thereon. I remember his passion for home-pickling cukes. I remember his arm when he slammed on the brakes of the Chevy, instinctively bolting me safe from the windshield—do I really see it? Every hair, the cuff the day's stained gray.

And I can hear each lousy penny of that forty—one for each year of my life now—dropping out of my fingers, down the Grand Canyon, measured by Galileo himself for velocity, hitting the tin plate at the centermost magma of Earth and melting there to forty damp grains of salt.

I remember because I found them, in their camouflage of yellowed gazettes and palmistry tracts, and they're bringing it with them, all of it, and all of them, parading: the various eggs in their top hats and bonnets are here, and the drum-beating gourd, and the bread with his slices inching him along like the ribs of a snake, and the goof-off kidney and lima and chili beans like Shriners and Masons and lodge brothers everywhere marching and cavorting, and the burger gals are here, and the pear, and the phalanx of clown-nosed cookies. . . .

And my dear old friend, the melancholy fish of page 1 1 , isn't eaten.

Of course. Mr. Memory Food. Mr. Memory Food. Over time he'll consume himself.

Dual

The Wheel

I don't believe he did anything indifferently. That formulaic paint-by-number "winter woodland" scene, from my father's attempts to fill his retirement time, is no exception: every empty cusp and ganglion was filled to its perimeters exactly, as if a slip of his fussing brush might cause a similar slip in gravity or the seasons. I can see him double-checking that the tube of black in his hand was also "8," to match the number in some tiny blank arena—holding the tube to the living-room light, as if appraising the soul inside it.

They were all "black," "green," "white," "red," as I remember; there weren't dubious mixes, "salmon" or "rhubarb" or "gunmetal blue." And of course their borders never overlapped, an idea like "scumbling" was another universe's altogether. No, each flat patch held itself intact and separate, like the tiles of a mosaic or the coexistent shapes of a stained-glass window inside their leadings.

Still, the effect was uncanny: step back just enough, and the eye comprised them into a single seamless stretch of snowed-over landscape. It had depth, it could be entered.

When I walk there now, when I idly kick its fresh dry snow into quick white wings, or trace the serial commas of ice along a branch's belly, when I'm in it, I can see that no thing's one thing. Ice is water. The shadow that's gray is also lavender. My own face is and isn't my father's. Simple truths.

In twilight—twin light—anything can happen. One day, a bird—a winter bird, as edged as scrap metal—leisurely hung in that pallid winter sky. It was moving, of course, but distance gave it the look of a single black flaw in those turbidly milky heavens. And then it divided: two birds. They must have been mating. I thought of the story of Jacob, the moment his psyche divides the angel-part out of the man.

At Tabby Katt's Exotic Dancers, the women say one thing only, the way we *all* do, at our jobs. I guess I'm supposed to say "the humanities." What *they* say, in the terms of my father's regiment of tubes, is decidedly "scarlet." They're one supple muscle of sexual beckon, often coy in the first song; by the third, spread open like butterflied shrimp. I've seen sad clubs like this, but in the happy ones the dancers and their audience share a great raw camaraderie, and the money is good, a green river. People are pleased to pay, to be shouted that one scarlet thing.

And yet you know with another part of your brain—some of these women are mothers, and the five-year-old is mysteriously stippled with a painful rash; they're daughters, and somebody's father is signing the bankruptcy papers, somebody's father is shyly accepting the Engineer of the Year award; they're biker mamas and novice political activists and budding artists: somebody's wondering vaguely if the foreplane jade-and-amaranth swatch is dry yet. . . . Chantilly is also Elizabeth; Candy is also Maude.

Last August, Lady J, the manager, upgraded to a row of flashing strobes; a snazzy haze effect from a nozzle that sprays out talcum; and The Wheel, the size of a dashboard wheel but set in the ceiling over the stage, with which the dancers dizzyingly spin themselves into perfect columns of lickerish skin. When Neely uses The Wheel, she whirls so centrifugally fast, so long, I wonder if her blood is going to separate its cells, red, white. Or maybe she'll suddenly *stop!*—and both of her selves will be standing there, next to each other.

No Distinctions

There are no pews or benches yet; the prayerful bring cushions, or sit in the straw on the floor. It's draughty. You're seated next to someone disfigured badly by disease, whose skin is like a damp gray omelette. Ah, but when the choir beatifically gaggles in; and invisible, aural vaults of Gregorian chant are architected antiphonally in the air, complex yet lightsome; and the village's pride, its vaguely pomegranate-shaped censer, releases its billowy wafts . . . then a man or a woman can also be ascendatory, and rise in fumes, in a radiant plumage of fumes, to the foot of the throne of Heaven.

Our workaday world of salt in the eyes, and death in ambush around any corner, and voices whispering out of the empty dusk, of impossibly painful Solomonic choices that need declaring—this world is filled with mysteries. Surely the Church elucidates some of the murk: such-and-such is the one true path, while this-and-that is not. But when you enter the Church in an uplands British village in the year 1250— or anywhere, really; anytime—the mysteries you leave in the shadowy entrance hall, you simply trade for Mysteries, the Big Ones, including the twofold nature of Jesus the Christ.

For Jesus is the Son of the Lord God: "Lo, a voice from Heaven did say 'This is my beloved Son, in whom I am well pleased.'" But Jesus is also the "Son of man"—six times, this appellation is scattered throughout the New Testament, there, I suppose, at least in part as a reminder of the essentially *Homo sapiens* hurt and sinfulness and grandeur he shares or seemingly shares with the rest of us. Born of the seed of the Holy Spirit, from out of the rended smatters of mortal flesh, "I am Alpha," he says, "and Omega." We like this cosmic paradox, the encompass, in a Messiah.

We like it far less glimpsed amid the congregation. Here, the combination of opposite attributes bespeaks a horrible chaos. Mary Douglas says, "It is only by exaggerating the difference"—not embodying it—"between within and without, above and below, male and female, with and against, that a semblance of order is created.

"For example, when a monstrous birth occurs, the defining lines between humans and animals may be threatened. If a monstrous birth can be labelled an event of a peculiar kind the categories can be restored. So the Nuer treat monstrous births as baby hippopotamuses, accidentally born to humans and, with this labelling, the appropriate action is clear. They gently lay them in the river where they belong."

The religious lore of the world is rich in hermaphrodite deities (Jesus is often depicted with a pronunciation of "feminine" features). Mircea Eliade: "The ambivalence of the divinity is a constant theme to the whole religious history of humanity," and "the hermaphrodite (as a god) represented in antiquity an ideal condition which men endeavored to achieve spiritually; but if a child showed at birth any signs of hermaphroditism, it was killed by its own parents."

Much of the punch of Diane Arbus's photograph of "Alberto/ Alberta" comes from the fact that it isn't hoked up, it's an "everyday" portrait of somebody staring frankly at the camera. "Diane's deceptively simple approach leveled all of her subjects, and made both 'freak' and 'normal,' 'eccentric' and 'middle-class,' appear in some aspects the same. Diane made no distinctions." She'd do a mother-and-child sitting that was as sweetly composed as anyone's, but the mother was stripper Heaven Lee, agleam in titty sequins.

At a museum showing, visitors spit on her photographs.

It is only by exaggerating the difference. . . . But Arbus, snapping away in her flophouse, peep-show, loony-bin swirl, incorporates: "once they began talking to each other and she started clicking her camera, the gulfs that divided them—gulfs of race, age, expectation, craziness even—momentarily disappeared."

The incense smokily rises, aromatic, disembodied, a perfect symbol of transcendence. We don't want to be reminded it exists as much to mask the stink of packed-in, unwashed bodies, our bodies, our frail, empowered, aging, haunted, tumultuous human bodies, in the year 1250; or anytime.

Parallel Lines

This is what I remember: the light was *so* clear, everything seemed to be bordered as certainly as the black-line drawings in coloring books. My comprehension would "color"—would complete—the world. Each rumple in the sleeves on my jacket cast the shadows of foothills. Each elm leaf shimmered with the individual presence of a garden spade. Where my father's jaw was stubbled it was the neat gray of a helmet strap, and then the pink and sweetly susceptible cheek rose out of that.

Where were we going? I couldn't have yet been five. To Sunday School? He'd walk me there, through the avenues of a Chicago I still thought of—because of his guardedness, and my mother's—as intrinsically clement. Did Sunday School begin before I was five? Is my sister Livia born yet? Nothing's as exact as that light, that pours undeniably over each of its creatures.

A neighborhood "doggie" scampers into our path, and I make a move to go pet it; even as I do, he yanks me back by the jacket cuff, and "doggie" leaps, oblivious to our drama, through a porch's crawl-space lathes. He looks down astonished at me. "Albie," he says (as if they'd ever explained it, as if I'd forgotten a lesson) "that was" (I still recall his voice's violent switch in tenor here, as it fills with the ancient loathing) "a rat."

And later I'd find those optical illusions, where a box is facing into the page, then out, or where a chalice becomes two people's faces in profile. Men who stopped their cars and offered you chocolate were evil. The very light exploded one day, in a gallon jar of layered cherries and sugar my father fermented in the sun for *vishnik,* syrupy home-made brandy, and they let me lick that thickness off the wall, a taste like candy and yet prohibitively adult.

In Hebrew Sunday School, the God that they taught us was fatherly; and "fatherly"—for this was 1953 or -4—became a TV sitcom head-of-household, wise and kind and wearing a tobacco-brown cardigan sweater. In a photograph there are seven of us, in a happy scatter of portable chairs, absorbed in cutting HANUKAH GREE ("tings" yet to come) from construction paper. A God a boy could confide in.

But He also smote the enemy host. He was jealous, and said so, and stored up petty grudges in the cupboards of Heaven, and showed His self on Earth as a menacing fire.

Says Eliade: "What is holy attracts man and at the same time frightens him. The gods reveal themselves as at once benevolent and terrible. In India, beside his gracious and kindly form, each god has a 'terrible form' *(krodha murti):* his fierce and frightening aspect. One of the most frequent Vedic prayers is to be 'delivered from Varuna.' And yet the worshipper cries, 'When shall I at last be with Varuna?'"

Jung chronicles the history of "the Christian reformation of the Jewish concept of the Deity: the morally ambiguous Yahweh became an exclusively good God, while everything evil was united in the devil. In the East"—and in my ping-pong, back/forth Sunday School understanding—"the gods (Kali is a case in point) could retain their original paradoxical morality undisturbed."

What *were* we to feel, when Abraham meekly obeyed His orders, lifting the blade above Isaac's yielded chicken-bone breast? Rembrandt has placed the free hand covering Isaac's upthrust face—at once it bares and tautens the throat; it presses down with awful patriarchal history; it obliterates identity completely, like an ether mask, an ether mask in the shape of some spiderly sea creature, already halfway blotting the bound boy into eternity. The stiff, nay-saying angel in its treacley light can't counterweight this horror.

And what did this have to do with that other father?—Irving Goldbarth, harmless man who tweezed the splinter out of my finger, and checked the fluent working of the tiny bellows of breath in my chest a dozen times during the night, who waited up, who balanced the books, who gently steadied the scared tush for the doctor's shot, who helped the volunteers search for miners' corpses but who openly wept when an adamant thirteen-year-old refused—and I remember: unnecessarily snidely refused—to take part in the Passover *seder.*

Later, JFK was assassinated, "by a lone gunman." Later still, a group of gunmen. Nothing is one thing. No one is one face. Most of my years in graduate school were defined by a series of Nixon's lies. I remembered the dog in his "Checkers speech," and one time I began a (very bad) poem: "I smell a rat here."

I was also lied to in graduate school by a woman whose understanding of the *oeuvre* of Fra Angelico left me breathless, and whose lean and needy body in its slipwork of sexual sweat left me—well, out of breath; two very different, if similar, things. I also lied to her, of course. It wasn't meant meanly; but, convinced that she could never care either spiritually or hormonally for me, I created another me, a *doppel*-me, for her (as it turned out, momentary) delight. The things we do to each other. I've found my notes for another poem from those years, and the quickly scribbled title is misspelled with an *e* instead of *a*: "Duel."

When Neely's finished her final spotlit split, I buy her a house drink. She's a pleasant few handfuls of spandex, and knows it, and shrewdly plies that knowledge. And in any case, I love to hear their stories. By drink three, I'm getting a smoky-throated ear-load: when the white-and-black bitch teamup robbed her working clothes in Phoenix; her little sister's hysterectomy; her boyfriend the jazz piano man, the bastard; she knows CPR; she's seven credits away from an accounting degree. Some giggles, many *looks*. A spectral army of Other People's Neelies gathering around us. Her turn eventually comes up again on the rotation board and she leaves the table, slurring over her shoulder (a joke I think, she's so young after all, but you never *know*), "I was a man before. I had The Operation."

That night, I study my face in the bathroom mirror, looking for traces—how much of Irving Goldbarth adheres, after all of these years, to the boneworks? Fannie Goldbarth—where is she in here? *Exotic ancers* the sign had said, the *d* fallen off, but I don't think there's an "ancer" for these after-midnight solipsistic questions of mine in the oleo-yellow fluorescent light of our bathroom.

Skyler's sleeping; I kiss her even so. I love my wife (it's too simple to think three drinks at Tabby Katt's mean anything else) and a fancy of mine, and always made more powerful when we're beside each other in bed, is that we're parallel lines—we're traveling, at two different speeds, toward the vanishing point, whatever it is, wherever it waits for us Out There.

"Oh, Mr. Beer Breath. . . ." When I wake, we're each rolled into our separate sides of the sheet, and I think of an opened Torah: its individual, scrolled-up halves; but also the column of revealed text for the day, that they share in common.

A Beautiful Photograph

In a Guggenheim proposal, describing her photographs' subjects, she said, "I want to gather them like somebody's grandmother putting up preserves because they will have been so beautiful. . . ."

Preserves . . . / It floats in a jar.

Or: *they* float in a jar—back to back, like spat-defeated lovers feigning sleep, the fetuses contour just enough of their occluded formaldehyde light. We can see their fleshy ridge of connection. We can see their swollen, sausage-casing shapes.

They don't really "float," that's how we're trained to see and say it. They have enormous weight, in part because this grainy half-formed humanness is centered by Arbus in otherwise vacant, otherwise featureless, slapdash sideshow tenting. The one on top faces up, into three or four inches of liquid. The other is bearing it, having its own face softly, dreamily smashed to the bottom glass.

And if, instead, they'd lived . . . ? I'm looking now at her famous portrait of the identical twins from Roselle, New Jersey—sisters, maybe six years old. Their matching corduroy dresses are dark; and, standing so symmetrically close that their inner arms overlap, they look as essentially seamed as the fetuses. One is almost pouting. One is almost smiling. Each is almost the other. "Everyone suffers from the limitation of being only one person," she said.

"She would photograph actress Estelle Parsons's twin daughters over and over again; she would photograph elderly twins and twins married to twins. . . ."

And of her brother: "It was as if they had passed through some secret experience together . . . they sat or stood, not looking at each other, but close as twins."

And of her husband: "They had the same mournful, watchful expression in their round, dark eyes. Sharing secrets, forbidden pleasures, little indulgences, they had lived like twins so long; it had been their way of surviving."

And of her daughter: "almost identical haunted moonfaces. A private subliminal knowledge seemed to flow between them . . . each was the other's mirror image—the other's twin."

On that deserted stage, in light so tactile it's almost aqueous, grittily aqueous, Arbus's spine-fused fetuses are, like many of her signature works, ethereal and creepy at once. This even could be a diagram of the Creation, as the *Beréshit rabba,* out of the Jewish *midráshim* tradition, tells it: "Adam and Eve were made back to back, joined at the shoulders; then God divided them with an axe stroke, cutting them in two." Eliade: "By the fact that the human race descends from Adam, spiritual perfection consists precisely in rediscovering within oneself this androgynous nature." Plato claims this also explains our lust: the halves' desire to reunite in the shape of the Primal Being.

"I've never heard anyone talk as frankly about sex as Diane Arbus did. She told me she'd never turned down any man who asked her to bed."

"She told how she had followed a dumpy middle-aged couple to their staid East Side apartment. She had sex with both of them, she said. When she maintained she'd had sex with a dwarf or a couple of nudists, her friends would listen—some in awe that she had the courage to go so totally with her obsessions."

The twins are everywhere; or couples on a ballroom floor, the energy of a twirl having blended their bodies; or couples made similar by the creases of age; or the untested smoothness of youth. "Two girls in matching bathing suits, Coney Island, 1967." "The King and Queen of a Senior Citizens Dance, New York, 1970."

And her gallery of those whose twin is inside themselves, an Other under the surface, rising gracefully or tormentedly up—the drag queens, leather lesbians, and half/half carnival freaks of her darkly

A.M. forays (laden with her clanking lei of cameras) into what she called "the pits of hell." And she said: "But there's some sense in which I always identify with them."

She said: "A whore I once knew showed me a photo album of Instamatic color pictures she'd taken of guys she picked up. I don't mean kissing ones. Just guys sitting on beds in motel rooms. I remember one of a man in a bra. He was just a man, the most ordinary, milktoast [sic] sort of man, and he had just tried on a bra. Like anybody would try on a bra, like anybody would try on what the other person had that he didn't have. It was heartbreaking. It was really a beautiful photograph."

The butch and the fey, the knifed-up and the stripped-down.

"I want to gather them like somebody's grandmother putting up preserves because they will have been so beautiful. I want to save these things, for what is ceremonious and curious and commonplace will be legendary."

Here by Its Absence

The cave art in the Argentines includes—along with those elegant light-footed llama-like beasts of the Ice Age pampas—two hands done in cinnabar on the pale cave wall: one, meatily here by imprinting the color directly from the hand to the rock; the other, having color blown around it through a tube, is here by its absence.

Intermittently, all day, I've seen my father's face. It surfaces in the skins of the faces of strangers, ripples, and vanishes, leaving them jowly or planar or wheaten-cheeked, whatever: like a *déjà vu,* in which a moment is suddenly another moment, as markedly as if steel strutwork shaped it; though—a blink, and it's smoke.

Today nothing is safe from merging into its elseness. Remember the flicker badges they'd sometimes include in cereal boxes?—Batman and his secret identity Bruce Wayne, sissy playboy. From *The Psychology of Everyday Things*: "My office phone rang. I picked up the receiver and bellowed 'come in' at it."

Today my wife is plodding her way through Western Civilization—

some monumentally leaden loaf of a tome—and I'm high over the outer-most ozone, neutron-powered and astral, having found my stash of yel-lowing sci-fi comics from the early fifties: "Lobster Men from Outer Space!," "The Deadly Sirens of Saturn's Rings!" We must be quite the mismatched duo seated on the porch today—her researched facts; my overreaching, supercharged conjectures. It's amazing we don't break off at the hinge and blow away in opposite directions. It's amazing the light, the dense noon light, that strikingly played across Descartes and Margaret Sanger and Hannibal, and also winks off rockets in the void, decides, if "decides" is the word, to hold us, for the moment, in its dis-passionate version of parity.

There's a story by Borges, "The Disk." A traveler, claiming to be a king in exile, opens his fist: but nothing's there. Nonetheless, "You may touch it," he says to the narrator. "I felt something cold, and saw a glit-ter." The strange king says, "It is Odin's disk. It has only one side. In all the world there is nothing else with only one side." By this, we know we're in the land of fable. When my wife and I quietly argue, each of us is one cold, glittering, unswayable side. Yes, but there *are* two of us.

I leave the porch for a short walk. Why do we think of the dead as counselors in our come-and-go confusions? Homer thought so; so does Joe Shmoe. For my purposes today, it's handily misty. Is there a step, a voice? Thousands of people witness Jesus' face in the discolorations of a herring fillet, or Elvis in the gravy stains on a menu. Can't I ask to see my own father for longer than one gray *plink* in the wrist?

There are sensational tales aplenty of parents spookily but confid-ingly appearing out of the ether, in moments of crisis: "and he helped me land the plane." For me, it isn't like that. In "Warlords of the Microverse!" the fumes from a mysterious elixir shrink our hero, past electrons, to a world—it happens to be, of course, a world of high ad-venture—in the invisible dye in the fabric of Things As We Know Them, a plane of existence among the neutrinos and tachyons. I hold out my hand, as if I could feel the mist. I suppose if I lived on the level of mist, then I *could* feel it.

By night, we're side-by-side again in the bed, at peace—Skyler and myself. We're happy more than we're not. She sleeps, and I stroke her hips, I stroke them *hard,* I want to feel the tree of bone inside her body.

We know from physics, though—we're empty air, we're a piffle of elements strung in empty air. She's here and she isn't here.

The tribal plow or deboweler or fish hook: is also "art" on a gallery wall.

A.D. 1250: the women the village calls witches are fallen deeply asleep on the earth floor of a shack, their funky aria of snores is assertable proof of this. They reek of their ritual coating of secret ointment.

They're here; they're flying.

The Division of Reality

A side road gets declared in the history of Western Civilization, around the time of Descartes, that rapidly becomes the main freeway of intellectual travel. As it's used, it takes us out of our old universe completely. (A simplification, yes; but a helpful one.)

The worldview of the Middle Ages—mythic, symbolic, its rootedness in cyclical time and in a cosmos of living matter governed by a heedful God—could not control the plagues. "Every technique of this organization of knowledge was used: prayer, ecstatic mysticism, scapegoating, medicine based on sympathetic magic, and so forth. All failed." Then, "under the pressure of its critical problems, Western Europe developed a new way of organizing reality."

This is the Cartesian, the Renaissance, viewpoint. It separates mind from body; objective worlds from subjective; and the parsable realm of nature from the calipers-bearing experimenter. Science as we know it begins. Time becomes a possessable line of small forged logical links. The plagues are finally kept at bay. Now "sanitation" is a concept. Commerce and industry are around the corner, and Newton is waiting there, polishing an apple on his lapel. You can see the sun of a heliocentric universe shining in that redness, blessing the laws of thermodynamics, asking to be squeezed through a prism and compartmented. Everything's bright, yes?

But "the division of reality into a sphere of matter and a sphere of mind provided a very powerful methodology for the study of one and a very inadequate methodology for the study of the other. Our power to manipulate and control the 'outside' world—matter and energy—advanced greatly, but we made no advances in the understanding of our own behavior and our inner experience."

The residua of an older road fare poorly in the new. Cartesian duality says "a thing cannot both be and not be at the same time." And by 1650, the year of Descartes's death, the witches of Europe are having their nipples singed, or worse. We'll eventually fly to the moon, and thereon plant our flag (and whack a golf ball); oh, but not before we attempt to eradicate those who meet to wield their broomsticks and fly through their own shadowed minds.

When I think of the splitting road, of the nameable handful of splitting roads the species has followed, I also think of a charming diagram in *Time Warps* by John Gribbin. It shows a filmstrip in which a stick-figure man approaches a chair, considers sitting, but then continues on; and extending from this, and so making the shape of a Y, is another, alternative filmstrip where, at the frame of decision-making, our stick-figure fellow indeed sits down. "The argument put forward so vividly in science fiction and now being increasingly discussed by physicists and mathematicians is that whenever such a choice comes up the entire universe splits in two, and *both* choices 'really' take place, with two separate universes developing as a result."

I like it: this posits a "layerverse" of endless contiguous universes; the ones most near us, horribly boringly like us; and the farther we move in any direction (here, direction's defined as "possibility-sequence") the stronger the malleability, until we'd see (if we *could* see), below the clear light of an afternoon sun, the "*me's*" of ourselves we otherwise only encounter in dream and lunacy. This might *explain* dreams, lunacy, or even something like precognition: "vibrations" from layerverse level X.

(It might explain the recognition we feel on viewing Arbus's diverse citizenry.)

But mainly, simply, I'm taken with the integrity this reinvests in each of the nanodecisions of that Grand Guignol gestalt we call our lives, our daily, our only, lives.

Now I can imagine Nate, our mailman, needing to rest in the shade of the Pest-Kill bug, on this sonofabitchin 103-degree day in Wichita, Kansas. I can see him mop the sting from his eyes, below the outspread plaster wings like ironing boards and the French-horn-like proboscis— at the mercy of every yahoo with a postage stamp. And: will he or won't he gratefully accept the chilled, forbidden beer I'll offer him when he's on the porch? Does he or doesn't he slyly delay the bundle of third-class mail for the substitute's shlepping, tomorrow? Out of each of these, the blossoming of two cosmoses, two futures.

In the sci-fi newspaper comic strip *Twin Earths* (which started its rather successful run in 1951) we're introduced to Terra, "a planet identical to our own in size and appearance" but traveling the sky in our orbit, at our speed, on the *opposite* side of the sun—and so forever unknown, or at least unknown until one of its agents contacts Garry Verth of our FBI. Terra is 92 percent female, and most glamorously so, as drawn by artist Al McWilliams. In 1903 (Earth year) the Terran femmes developed flying saucers, and . . . well, many *ands,* much atom-blaster mellerdrama.

I can't say it's *distinguished* writing, but I'll suggest it serves well as an emblem (much of comicdom does) for some of the twofold pleasures and afflictions that define us. So when Wallace Stevens writes of "Bonnie and Josie . . . / Celebrating the marriage / Of flesh and air," he's established his own binary planets. I think of Terra and Earth as the astrological influences over Katherine and Jessica Goddeke— twins, but born in different years, a span of minutes on either side of the first of January 1992.

John Casti claims that if a signal received from outer space "shows that there is a 'second Earth' out there where extraterrestrials worry about the stock market crashes, go on vacations to 'Hawaii,' and play baseball, then the message would probably result in a vast, almost un-believable disappointment." I'm not sure about that.

I *am* sure Neely's bringing her jillion-dollar grin and beating tom-tom derriere into Daddy Zach's, an after-hours jazz club where her boyfriend jams piano in a five-guy group called Protoplasm.

He loves it, up there. He loves it especially when she's in the audi-ence, wearied out from jiggledancing, lost now in a replenishing cloud of his burning playing. The keyboard responds to his fingers like an ani-mal being stroked, the music glimmers off into the stratosphere—and, after a day of Post Office labor, he's all of a sudden phantasmal and pure. "Yeah! Nate, the Piano Potentate!" the emcee says. "Let's hear it!" After a day of dull delivery, the music carries him—*he's* delivered.

Later still, they're asleep together, his hand as black as anthracite on one buttery cheek of her rump.

A Forum

Until she was seven, she was in the care of "Mamselle," a French nanny. Once, they passed a tin-shack bumtown built in the bed of a dried-up reservoir. "This was a potent memory: seeing the other side of the tracks, holding the hand of one's governess." She had asked, even then—but had been refused—to clamber down and investigate. She was unflappable. She itched to touch the face inside a face. "She once confided that she envied a girlfriend who'd been raped. She wanted to have that punishing, degrading experience, too." Where could she find prisoners condemned to die? Streetwalkers? "She never looked away, which took courage and independence." She said, "If you're born one thing, you can dare to be ten thousand other things."

Some days she'd leave at dusk—"she seemed to be more alive in the dark"—and walk all night: the subway corridors, the bus-station uri-nals, anywhere extremity set up camp, or a wayward tenderness flour-ished in rubbish. Blending in. Becoming habitual. Turning the furtive peek into a stakeout. There are contact sheets over years, in which you can follow her gradual progress "from the street to their home to their living room to their bedroom—like a narrative, a process leading up to some strange intimacy."

The razor blades didn't send her away. She'd stand in the steam of a sewer grating like some corner's resident *dybbuk*. And she'd stalk for long past the first weak spasms of dawn, until maybe 7 A.M., in hopes of something transcendent in the day's as-yet-untainted light—"a fat lady in a Santa Claus outfit somersaulting heavily down a grassy hill; a solitary young man, totally nude, raising his arms to the sky."

These, this, she photographed:

The American Nazi Party. Presto the Fire Eater. Russian midget Gregory Ratoucheff. Morales the Mexican dwarf. The eight-foot "Jewish Giant" Eddie Carmel. Child hookers working the piss-scent alleys of Rome. The Human Pincushion. Sealo the Seal Boy (his hands grew out of his shoulders). "A big black lady who wandered around the beach, calling herself God." Charlotte Moorman the stripper cellist. Potato Chip Manzini. "When we were breeding our dogs, Diane took pictures of animals copulating." Congo the Jungle Creep. Fortune-tellers. Mob chauffeurs. In the Hades-like mist of the Monroe Street Ukrainian Baths she secretly shot, as her ladyfriend Cheech said, "wrinkled old crones with hanging boobs." Miss Stormé de Larverie, "male impersonator." Lady Olga the Bearded Wonder. The desk clerk at a transvestite hotel. Bondage parlors (a leather-booted mistress is dripping hot wax on a naked, kneeling penitent). Prince Robert de Rohan Courtney, author of over 9,000 poems in a private doggerel language, who lived in a 6-by-9-foot room he called "the Jade Tower" and claimed being heir "to the throne of the Byzantine Roman Empire." Epidermal artiste Jack Dracula, he of 306 tattoos (28 stars on his face alone, around a fancy pair of trompe l'oeil goggles). The pet crematorium. Many dozens of nudists. Harelips. Gimps. An orgy in a New Jersey motel ("where everybody sat around eating peanut butter on crackers before they fucked," she said). The Important Order of Red Men, shoe-store salesmen and plumbers and druggists who "dressed up in Indian feathers and brandished sequined tomahawks." Slaughterhouses, issuing their unthinkable, tissuey rivers. Vicki Strasberg, a transvestite whore. A lovely, gypsy-bloused albino sword swallower ("her arms are stretched out like Christ on the cross, but her head is thrown back triumphantly"). A New Jersey housewife cradling her pet macaque, in an unintentional faux-pietà scene. A pec-oiled body-builder proudly displaying his three-foot trophy in a shabby backstage room. The weazened. The deformedly luscious. Hunchbacks. Glitz-trip party girls on a wine-damaged mattress the morning after. Moondog, blind, in his Viking helmet decorated with tusks, the only maestro of the "oo" and the "uni"—"percussion instruments of his own design." A group of middle-aged retardates at a home in Vineland, New Jersey—"these people are so angelic," she said, and made her Pentax a recognized fixture amongst them over several visits: the faces are so distorted they nearly seem to blur at their perimeters, as if nature gave up on precision here, heads sifting into a passing laugh or an eerie yelping, planets clouded unfathomably at their poles, and Earth isn't spoken here.

"Such a gallery of the pitiful and grotesque in close-up has never before been seen," somebody said—it was a contemporary of Leonardo da Vinci's, passing judgment on his sketches of the human parade.

She didn't invent these people; she found them, she gave them a forum.

She also recorded a Boy Scout meeting. Tricia Nixon's wedding. Coretta King. A police academy. Ozzie and Harriet. Borges. Gloria Vanderbilt's baby boy. The Metropolitan Opera. The DAR. She wanted a range, she explained, "both posh and sordid"—"all posed," her biographer says, "in the same grave, troubling manner." *This* explains the retracted assignments, the canceled bookings, the spit. We don't want to be reminded.

Anubis's head is sleek, designed entirely of sly energy tapering into a long-jawed angle. Anubis: the Jackal-headed god. He parts the darkness of the tomb itself with that friction-resistant snout.

Horus the Falcon-headed god. And Thoth, the god of scribes, with the head of an Ibis: its elegantly attenuating stylus-like beak. The goddess Sekhmet, Lion-headed. Pasht, Cat-headed (from her, our word *puss*). Hathor, with the generously bulbous head of a Cow. More so, the Hippopotamus head of pregnant Taheret. . . .

The whole zoöcapita pantheon. When I was a child I sometimes toyed with the cartoon notion of lifting them like bottles of oil-and-vinegar dressing, and shaking until the sections were marbled together unseparatably.

This is the fear: that hackles erect, that sex is nested hairily in a crevice, that we carry relict canine teeth, and whatever might seem deific in us comes laced with the touch of the beast.

"Both worlds seemed as one to her."

Trying to put her face on, for a breath's space—could it fit me? Would her foreign nerves link meaningfully to my brambled-up receptors? or dangle like color-coded wires from a broken phone?

Hello? *Hello?*

The Other Side

And Angela of Foligno "was a wealthy, weak, immoral woman"—no details are provided, I'm sorry to say, though they're enjoyable to imagine. And Andrew Corsini: "the most immoral youth in Florence." And Torello da Poppi: "led a diabolical life." And Mary of Egypt: "was, beginning at twelve and for seventeen years thereafter, a prostitute." The list of malefactors who become Saints in the Church is long and strangely persuasive of sudden about-face turnings in the moral course of certain people's lives. For instance, Hubert of Tongres, "a fierce immoral man" who "was converted by a white stag." Having brought it to bay, he listened to it speak ("or to a voice out of the leaves"); it sent him to Bishop St. Lambert of Maestricht for religious instruction.

I'm also fond of a story Evelyn Waugh tells, of a night in 1929 in the Sudanese brothel quarter of Port Said. He and his friends are dragged (he *says* they're "dragged") by "three girls in bedraggled dress" to a house with *Maison Dorée* painted over its door. But neither the women nor the atmosphere is appealing, and Waugh and his party leave, to further wander the district. "On our way back we came upon another gaily illuminated building called *Maison Chabanais*. We went in, and were surprised to encounter Madame and all her young ladies from the *Maison Dorée*. It was, in fact, her back door. Sometimes, she explained, gentlemen went away unsatisfied, determined to find another house, then as often as not they found the way round to the other side, and the less observant ones never discovered their mistake."

I was thinking of this, of all this, as I looked at an Arbus photograph, a landscape of a tree-lined lake. It's spring. The water is shirred by the breeze. There's so much light, the farther trees seem candied in it. Then the hills, and the sky.

But when you look to the bottom, you see the electrical outlet, covered by water and grass. It's a photograph *of* a photograph that's a lobby mural. Nothing is one thing. Simple truths.

I was looking until the season changed, and the trees were cased in a lilac-tinted ice. The snow came up to my ankles. The tired light was winter light, its touch on the frozen water trembled. Wind rose, like a thin voice in the branches. It was winter, and a winter bird dropped down the sky as if it were scratching designs in crystal. A voice in the branches—I kept on walking. It darkened, and I kept on walking, the sky grew deep in stars, the night was close, and it whispered, then quieted. It was winter, and he was calling me.

Calling Up

1. The Light That Hit the World in 1958

Sky King's niece was Penny. There was a copilot (maybe a nephew? a chum?) named Clipper the first season, then he was dropped. We even remember the name of the ranch, The Flying Crown, with all this kitsch corroborated by "Some Fun Facts" in the liner notes to an album jacket I had as a kid, and have just dug up in a junk shop's sloppy half-price boxes: *Saturday Morning KID'S SHOW Tunes!* But no one remembers the plane's name.

'Melia looks up from her book—a study of paranormal experiences reputed to various literary lives. About an hour ago, as we were hammering down the cast of *Lassie,* she recited, from out of whatever achronological level she'd wiffled to, "In my ninth year my father suffered a dream in which Death had appeared to him, as he is commonly painted, and touched him with his Dart. That good man came home, took to his bed and accordingly died" (it's Coleridge speaking). Then she returned to silent reading.

Now she blurts, from her unguessable astral Anywhere, "The *Silver Dart*"—this gives it a kind of oracular authority. But after some noggin-thumping and serious liner-notes research, Captain Midnight turns out to have piloted the *Silver Dart,* to the terror of saboteurs everywhere. Buzz Corry, hero of "Space Patrol," commanded the thirtieth-century rocket *Terra;* with Miss Tonga and Cadet Happy, he defeated the Wild Men of Procyon, Captain Dagger, Mr. Proteus, Mazna the Invisible, and the evilmost Prince Baccarratti. Even the sound of their shoestring-budget blastoff is clear: the whine of antique dental machinery.

Sky King's plane's name, though, remains below the dust of thirty years. Our friends go home. I'm jittery; Skyler yawns. We leave the last half-inches of beer in their steins for the night. Some formulaic kissing. Then sleep.

For her; not me. It isn't the plane's name really, keeping me staring all night out the living-room window, trying to read lost words in the stars. I couldn't say *what* it is.

The light that hit the world in 1958 is . . . where? Is out there, somewhere. Light doesn't die. The me who's ten is traveling the galaxies smoother than the best-attended engines of the Space Patrol. In telescopes with which the wild Procyon scientists scan the farmost skies, my father's still alive. . . .

I'm looking, cargo-cult-of-one, for that plane. Its freight is simply everything that's happened. If the universe curves, and light in the universe curves, that plane is going to land one day, and my father step out and say, "Albie, it's late. Stop thinking your crazy thoughts. Now go to sleep."

2. Alberts

On the Wichita State University campus, there's a red brick building you see on your right as soon as you take the main drive—squat, and almost perfectly foursquare, not unlike a lovingly-upkept bunker from World War II. Sometimes I've watched it from farther away—a bouillon cube, ox-red and weakly charged with beef.

This is the original Pizza Hut. Yes, the first one, built on some 600 borrowed bucks and offered successfully, nineteen years after that, to PepsiCo for $300,000. "That was a steal." Maybe. Now it's a stela, of sorts. No chip of pepperoni has been inside this fussily janitored block for years. Its plaque reads:

PIZZA HUT NUMBER ONE
FIRST OPENED AT BLUFF AND KELLOGG STREETS
JUNE 15, 1958

The building was moved to this site to serve as a symbol and reminder to our students how young individuals through hard work and initiative can still rise from modest beginnings to positions of leadership and success.

We laugh at it, of course. "I'm trying to write about it," I say to Skyler. "Do you think I could say it's architecturally . . . you know, a bungalow?" She says, "It's a low bungle."—That kind of thing.

On the second of August, 1939, a letter was sent to President Roosevelt from Old Grove Road on Nassau Point, Long Island: "This new phenomenon would also lead to the construction of bombs . . . powerful bombs of a new type," Einstein said, suggesting funds to "speed up work being done within the budgets of the University laboratories." So there's another plaque I've seen—you know, the squash court, West Stands, Stagg Field, University of Chicago:

ON DECEMBER 2, 1942
MAN ACHIEVED HERE
THE FIRST SELF-SUSTAINING CHAIN REACTION
AND THEREBY INITIATED THE
CONTROLLED RELEASE OF NUCLEAR ENERGY

though laughing at that's less easy.

We commemorate. *Homo historical marker*, that's us. Off Highway 71 near Audubon, Iowa, a sizeable chunk of sky is covered by Albert, "The World's Largest Bull," concrete and steel measuring thirty feet tall by fifteen wide "at the horns," all painted credibly enough in buff and umber. He weighs in at forty-five tons. His balls hang down like a punching bag of the gods. He's not forgettable; but, just in case, there are postcards.

We commemorate, we love to, I suppose we need to—evidently too much hubbub-ballyhooed accomplishment occurs to trust the brain unaided. If we don't find plaques, we don't find the concept of history altogether. "Where there was so little difference between past and present" (Daniel Boorstin is writing of ancient India) "the quest for history seemed futile. In a society that did not know change, what was there for historians to write about?"

You stumble over fire in a world that's never known it, say a lightning-gutted oak: that place is sacred, is recorded in scratched antler bone as sacred. But enormous successions of hunter-gatherer generations must have passed without such singularity. Time was a life, your own life; everything else was a cycle. Monuments have no place in a cycle. Myth is round; nostalgia exists on a line.

And yes: if too much too-eventful stuff has intervened, why, I can look up Albert on one of his postcards.

Yes, or this one—reproducing a painting by Zeljko Premerl. Einstein in the desert. A turtle is cupped in his hand, a turtle *that* small. Its neck's exposed, an inch of nuzzle against the soft round of the physicist's palm: it trusts him. Its shell is glowing, as if from within; the lines between the burls give it the look of a Tiffany lamp the size of a doorknob.

Einstein sits on a throne fit together from bones—or, more exactly, it's the skeleton of a giant Galapagos tortoise. All around is sand, then mountains in the background, and a missile: red-tipped, itchy to launch. Essentially, the scientist is mediating between the small life and the monstrous devastation. He isn't happy for this: his face pulls at the corners of his eyes. His whole face, weighted with his knowledge.

The painting's dated 1976—it's thirty-seven years since his letter. He hasn't forgotten, though, or left his post. It's why he's here: he's a sign. He won't let us forget, either.

3. Part One, with Ratchets

In early March I visited 'Melia's hospital room. The clot lodged in a lung this time. For someone only thirty-five who'd stared at death through the width of a strand of fibrinogen or less, she was incredibly much her bellicose gutsy self—by this time, surgery was decided against, and she was "simply" waiting for the thinners to unclog her chest, and working at not wondering where the clot would declare itself next time, and when.

As always, her courage astounded me—humbled me, more accurately. We made some standard chatter. I did unnecessarily nasty imitations of my colleagues. 'Melia was equally wicked with medical horror stories: a surgeon who'd accidentally sparked a patient's bowel gas and was blown across the room. And: "Did anyone ever remember the plane's name?"

"Not yet." Catching glimpses of the lei of internal bleeding across her breast. "Say, what were you working on?"

"Before this?"

"Yeah. Before this."

'Melia's . . . interesting. "Before this" she was doing a series of former lovers in clay. "It got more serious, but first I was going to have them with their pants around their ankles. From a Coleridge line I picked up in that book. 'As if this earth in fast thick pants were breathing.'" (Laughs) "That's what I was going to title the series: *Fast Thick Pants.*"

A TV's set in the wall. One channel is totally oldies, and when Pizza Hut's done flaunting a medium "sausage supreme" with the weight of a lead gong, eerily familiar music mists into the room . . . *The Time Tunnel.*

Each week Doug and Tony, blatantly handsome Hollywood-version scientist he-men, entered their spiral-hypnotic Tunnel (part of Project Tic-Toc) and exited into some past or future Earth. The Vikings. Space invaders. You-name-it. Now 'Melia and I stare fixedly, as if through invisible surveyor's tripods or rifle sites, down twenty years of time-gone-by. "Reruns," she says to me, "reruns. They're like ratchets dragging you backwards."

This one, Doug and Tony need to find a certain common yard bird in the past and relocate it in the future. Something like that. The bird's become the focus of "a shift in cosmic vectors," a kind of fluffy foundation stone for the building of all of sequential time, and the fate of the planet (*ho hum*—once again, for Doug and Tony) hangs in the balance. It's a two-part story. Part one done, an oldies rock show hoarsely do-ron-rons from the speaker.

"I'd better get ronning myself. Skyler sends this:" (A kiss to her cheek).

An oldie, "Cherish," shoo-bops in my mind the full way out of the hospital warren, getting lost, redoubling, opening up wrong doors, the song containing entire people inside it, things that happened, intact, and then a room of jars with organs pickled in alcohol floating whole that same way. Brains. A heart.

4. Scattered Bodies

For weeks I was jealous of 'Melia's clay figures. I *also* wanted an empty-ing out of the vacuum cleaner bag of love, to sort with picky relish through its gleanings, maybe golemize those bits somewhat, and by spirit and sputum refashion a mannequin Ellen, Morgan, Claudia, who would crackle with the living static of yesterday. I'd think of 'Melia over her unformed lumps of it as a sorceress able to call up, even if sem-blanced only, the dead.

But I can't work clay, and no litany I tried—their charms, their bro-kenness, their various smiles and storm warnings—worked much better. I could "call up" my old lovers, yes, by phone: if they had phones, and were listed, and kept their same names, if the decades are wired under-ground for long distance. But that was the only call-up conjuring I felt capable of, a tepid one at that, and resisting its urges wasn't difficult.

I *can't* deny, though, the sooty woo of a junk shop. Pages wearing their foxing as lush as stoles, paint-scaled lawn jockeys grouped like a leper colony's Christmas carolers, Persian lamb and Spanish fly, tin condom cases, a homemade lute with a varnish so flypaper-rich you'd swear its maker's face was gummed in its surface retrievably all these years. . . . I'll dive into such detritus with the fervor Schliemann, Leakey, Dr. Frankenstein, Vesalius, and Don Juan brought to their bod-ies of work.

A gimp, one-runnered rocking chair. An advent calendar—tiny doors flung wide like the raincoats of flashers. Strands of pearls. A fish-bowl of matchbooks, of pop-bottle caps, of rubber sardines. I'm hooked, I'm looking. Somebody—many somebodies—forgot these things, these once-dear things, and I'm excavating the cluttered underside of their amnesia.

Limpid confirmation tresses, in their vellum binder. Here: a ratty raspberry-velveteen-covered wedding register of guests' best wishes in fading tea-stain ink. This basin of sturdy eggnog glazeware, missing its pitcher. These crystal knobs. Fletched Pawnee ceremonial headgear on its side like a roadkill. Three original 1936 Mickey Mouse alphabet blocks that can't spell anything, in any combination, except for the nonsense gutturals damage always utters. This is one port in solidity's diaspora.

John Donne, that man whose mind was filled by numinous beings in strict theological order, says that one day we will all be resurrected, wired entire again, each tooth a bar fight batted out, each ovary snipped from its system: back, and functioning, and humming in well-oiled pleasure. He tells the angels, "Blow your trumpets," and "Arise from death, you numberless infinities of souls, and to your scattered bodies go." It may seem, waiting in his grave for close to four centuries now, that only an eyelash-flicker of chronology has passed. It may. I have my doubts. But John Donne has his faith. Right now, his eyelashes may be soaking in the nutrient-troughs of some deific escrow, held there incorruptible, waiting for the signal to follow their chromosomal maps of the cosmos back home.

Those confirmation tresses: will they, that day, tremble in the seizure of being sparked in their cells? I have my doubts. But, still . . . that half-bald wedding book, where half of backlands Kansas seems to have scribbled its wishes one moth-brown day in 1886, *Ma Saw and Brother Snitched/So now the two of you is Hitched.* . . . Do objects people loved return to life when those who loved them do? Donne's mum on this. The physics of it is unknown.

What Boschian miracle-scene will it be like, caught on Rapture Day in rows of junk-shop rupture, when the fiddle necks and two-penny nails and wristwatch straps and anchor chains are called to completion, stir, then whisk the air with their sudden ascension? Every Russian

53

Easter egg and whorehouse-parlor piano slamming its long-dispersed constituent slivers to Oneness seamlessly, and rising. . . . The physics of this is wholly unknown in a universe where the condition of anything being itself is: we're flying apart.

Every minute we're entropy's playthings. Boards warp. Hair thins. Rust spreads like a living map of Alexander's advance in a movie. I'm going to walk the unkempt junktique rows, and call up every love that's brushed against these objects in the days of their utility, call up into light against the grain of time. Plate silver. A pair of jade gods. Fiestaware. A much-smudged Captain Midnight mug. The thumbling netsukes. A spare but sinuous-silhouetted Shaker chair. These toucan salt-and-pepper shakers. A fifteenth-century copper filigree Turkish inkstand. Some old admiral's scrimshaw pipe, with stand. Ceramic mermaids. Cranberryware. A taxidermied otter. Valentines. Chamber pots. Butter churns. Tea balls. Humidors. Hair nets. "Press-Rite" collar stays. This deck of cards with tiger-pattern-negligee'd demoness showgirls saying 1958 will never come again. . . .

Each time we save one, we apply a brake to the bone-shaking speed at which our latticework dismantles.

This is breathy rhetoric, yes. Look, let's get dirty in a corner box, specific. In this carton here, in January 1988, I persevered until I turned up *Saturday Morning KID'S SHOW Tunes!* and it was 1958 I hummed out into.

5. At Night in a Room by Simonides

I implied that Einstein wrote a letter to Roosevelt, encouraging funding of atomic research.

Einstein typed that letter and signed it; the text was Leo Szilard's.

Less well-known than the hero who squared MC for the world, still it was Szilard, Hungarian émigré in London, who—supposedly at a red light, waiting green—"realized that if you hit an atom with one neutron, and it happens to break up and release two, then you would have a chain reaction." He filed a patent containing the phrase in 1934.

Well, that's how memory works for most of us. From everything, from *reverie*-thing, from all of this colliding—I'm ten. It's 1958, I'm in a hospital bed.

The pain's not major. The frightening apparatus, though—so reminiscent of dungeon torture devices the vile scientists of Procyon contrapted with hooks and blades—has had my muscles almost epileptically stampeding at times. The room smells *too* clean, *stinks* of "clean"— they're covering something up. Long animal screams with human names or God's attached eke through the walls. The day before, an eighty-year-old woman, Mrs. Kreitzer, her intestine hanging out her rectum, maundered down the hall. Three decades later, and her name is as clear as the *Bic* on the pen I'm writing this with: Kreitzer, Mrs. Kreitzer.

Thirty years, and I can see each line of helplessness ordealed in my parents' faces. Some I helped engrave myself—as if *they* were responsible for the invisible machinations of germs. In 1958 we lived next door to Vito's Pizza; Vito couldn't "speeka Eengle" but his gooily voluptuous goods communicated panculturally in straight talk to the tongue, and these I craved, and they were all I needed as weekly reward for good conduct.

So the more the Chief Nurse said that any "outside food" was outlawed, the greater I whined, the more I intuitively knew to ply the idea my "favorite," my "special," food was what I needed, what my parents surely understood in a mystic familial way that I needed, to speed and even seal as completed, my recovery. They were miserable, I was heartless. The Nurse's lizard-eyed Procyon minions kept stern watch.

Finally, in fact, my parents argued. I'd heard this before in minor ways. "Let's heat it up." "You're nuts, it's always better cold the next day." "Why spend money on that?" "On *that*? Well, if you really want to know a thing or two. . . ." But never in front of me, like this, with a slap. I can hear it right now. After all, it's my fault.

She ran wild from the room, and it was my fault. He offered one weak smile of "it's alright" that rode his face like light on what you knew was miles of murky water, and it was my fault and he walked out crisply—spoke to me some last consoling father-stuff, then walked out with the pieces of the day in his hands—and it was my fault. As if the shots, the ether mask, and the IV needle weren't enough.

Now I could tell you in detail every object in that room. The terrible energy in not sleeping will devote itself to the round of a glass, to the infinitesimal nuances of dark or daybreak, with equally terrible clarity. I was awake and suffering: no individual dot in the ceiling's sound-proofing panels escaped my notice.

The classical "architectural technique" for improving the memory, as devised by Quintilian and basing it on Simonides of Ceos, was "to think of a building; and study its rooms; and deposit in each an image that will concretize the idea you wish to remember." This was *the* pre-Gutenbergian wisdom. Students of rhetoric would find a deserted building and methodically attend to the minutiae of each corner and sill, attempting to warehouse their consciousness.

The glass is three-fourths filled. My lips are sticky from my system's bout with crisis, and they've left two imprints, gray slugs, on the rim. The water's gray, too, in that last of the sun, and eventually the final flex of sunset gilds the surface of the water—when disturbed, this gold compacts itself to a wavery crown in the center—but soon the whole room's dark and the water transparent. Even so, a night-light gives the sides of the glass a powdery definition. . . .

Every object. And my father's voice, its useless consolation remaining. "Albie, it's late. Stop thinking your crazy thoughts. Now go to sleep."

6. Brains. A Heart.

I don't want this melodramatic. My parents found each other. Originally, sure: that full moon shirred by clouds, and when they'd reached the center of Humboldt Park Lagoon he threw both oars overboard and asked would she marry him. That's a family legend. The moon! The stars! But now I mean only this: their mutual radar was working, and at Pete's Eats—a cafeteria not one block away from the frenzied hospital main entrance—they met, conferring into reconciliation.

I don't want this impossibly mystical either. They found each other, why not? Bonds form in over a score of years of intimate knowing; maybe some bonds preexist us; and we hear our names called out, through an invisible rail our ear is against, and we hearken. If it happens in a minor key—my near hand opens up and Skyler, deep asleep still, curls her hand inside it as assuredly as if her hand could see— some major moments are on record.

This is what 'Melia's been reading, in writers' lives.

Was it with anger, tears, or her rehearsed flirtatious sliding of a ribbon back and forth across her nipples that he loved to watch so much, that Anne implored him to stay? I simplify it. All three, likely, and sturdy attempts at reason. She was pregnant, and unduly weak. France never seemed so far. But he was in casual debt to Sir Robert; the journey, as proposed, was but two months; he tied the ribbon near her nape, in that intricate Chinese skein she always requested his nimble fingers crisscross up her hair. . . . "Within a few days after this resolve, the Ambassador, Sir Robert, and Mr. Donne, left London; and were the twelfth day got all safe to Paris."

This is from Izaak Walton (surely I can't improve on his version):

> Two days after their arrival there, Mr. Donne was left alone in that room in which Sir Robert, he, and some other friends had dined together. To this place Sir Robert returned within half an hour; and as he left, so he found, Mr. Donne alone; but in such an ecstasy, and so altered as to his looks, as amazed Sir Robert to behold him; insomuch that he earnestly desired Mr. Donne to declare what had befallen him in the short time of his absence. To which Mr. Donne did at last say, "I have seen a dreadful vision since I saw you: I have seen my dear wife pass twice by me through this room, with her hair hanging about her shoulders, and a dead child in her arms: this I have seen since I saw you."

To which Sir Robert replied, "Sure, sir, you have slept since I saw you; and this is the result of some melancholy dream, which I desire you to forget, for you are now awake." To which Mr. Donne's reply was: "I cannot be surer that I now live than that I have not slept since I saw you: and am as sure that at her second appearing she stopped and looked me in the face, and vanished."

It is truly said that desire and doubt have no rest; and it proved so with Sir Robert, for he immediately sent a servant to Drewry House, with a charge to hasten back and bring him word. The twelfth day the messenger returned with this account:—That he found and left Mrs. Donne very sad and sick in her bed; and that, after a long and dangerous labor, she had been delivered of a dead child. And, upon examination, this circumstance proved to be the same day, and about the very hour, that Mr. Donne affirmed he saw her pass by in his chamber.

Pages later, Shelley's dead.

The sea salt lines his lungs; you could crack them over your knees. According to Trelawny, the corpse is stained "a ghastly indigo." Then: "more wine was poured over Shelley's body than he had consumed during life. This with the oil and salt made the yellow flames glisten and quiver." Sea wind feeding the fire. Gulls above like paid mourners.

Byron, even, needs to look away. "The frontal bone of the skull fell off; and, as the back of the head rested on the red-hot bottom bars of the furnace, the brains literally seethed, bubbled, and boiled as if in a cauldron."

"The heart remained entire." Trelawney snatches it out of the cracklings. "I collected the ashes. . . . Byron and Hunt retraced their steps to their home. . . ."

There's a tale: Mary Shelley would unlock the heart from its vanity table case. It looked japanned now. In her grief she would hold it and concentrate. There is no physics to measure grief. There is no proper history to the shortwave radio set. In her grief, in the swaddled-up night. "There is an account she would call him; or *recall* him, this is what it would have been. Betimes, he would answer. She would witness him writing, or stomping in a writer's frustration again about the room." In her grief, at her bedside. "She would feel the touch of his palm at her breast, as truly as if they leaned against a column of the villa and the moon on her bone buttons was a calendar of moons he was, by one at a time, undoing."

7. Part Two, with Presents

Nor did melodrama play a part in 'Melia's recovery. Overnight the clot became the wisp of a clot, and though her blood now was nearly as thin as water, she was ready for home.

I visited her room a few hours prior to checkout. I'm the troglodytish type that doesn't own a TV—but I wanted to see how Doug and Tony were managing their travails. First, an oldies "Horror Review" devoted to 1950s Japanese monsters: Mothra, Rodan, Godzilla (the *rex* of them all), and the various lesser-known clones, was each in turn destroying downtown Tokyo. Fires broke out. Ninety-story buildings crumbled like dry cake. Dorms full of coeds were caught with nothing but bath towels betokening modesty.

"Y'know, there's something less than full credibility here."

"You're crazy—that's a twelve-yard stretch of saliva in those jaws, and you don't *believe* it?"

"Do I look scared?"

"You've just got rid of an Unidentified Flying Clot in your body—of course *you're* not scared. You're not a fit audience."

"Sure but—"

"Ssh."

It's night and they're crawling through savage landscape, sneaking toward a camp of clearly evil human beings, or maybe not even human beings; ape-faced protomen, perhaps, or extraterrestrials. In any case, the campfire dances maniacally over blunt features. Why would our scientist buddies care to risk their moussed-down suavity, tangling with this foul crew? Easy: on a flat rock in front of the chief of this Hun-like consortium, there's a super-duper far-future cage, and in it: something fluttering, warbling.

All of time, down to the first amoeboid cytoplasm-sex, and up to who-knows-what ecstatic court-and-spark on farflung planets, is at stake. There's tussling, running, brief soliloquies on being brave, the piling-up of adversity, shouts, the cage itself and its avian occupant thrown in the long high arc of a football play. . . . I don't remember it all and, anyway, before the final scene, an orderly interrupted: the office was ready for checkout.

Doug to Tony, a long high stadium-rousing epochs-hopeful pass—or Tony to Doug . . . the rest, I can imagine. . .

. . . as I've had to imagine patches into the fabric of that other hospital scene. Our memories never are perfect. This is what I see:

They make a gala entrance into my room that following morning. They're holding hands. They've brought presents—even presents (gimmicked-up memo pads) for the nurses, even the Chief Nurse, she of the vigilant scowl. "How ya doin', Professor!" (Ten years old, and he called me Professor.) It's no question, but an assertion of vim. Whatever nightlong patchwork they've done to *their* emotional fabric, its thread is bright gold in this otherwise-lusterless setting.

All their bluster beamed, sublingually, "Everything's okay now," with its subspeech subtext, "Everything was never *not* okay—right?" (This is my earliest understanding of the endless assault revisionist history aims at personal memory.) A lot was at stake in that hearty "right?" Would I be sweetly conned? (This is one of my earliest understandings of power.) For minutes there, in antiseptic no-space, *they* were the children, simpering, scheming, naked in intention, and my word would hurt or heal.

So I bought their line; we all hugged. One of my presents was a tin windup turtle ("Turtley," I dubbed him: I had no knack at names), his spring was durable enough so that his waddling progress took him the length of the wheeled bedside stand. The second present was strange, an album jacket, *Saturday Morning KID'S SHOW Tunes!*—there was no record player in the room.

But then, there was no record in the jacket.

My father kept watch at the door, his arms crossed. "Good morning," I'd hear him repeat. And I pulled out a small but exemplary wheel of Vito's mushroom-and-double-cheese.

"It's always better cold the next day," my father said over his shoulder.

"Your father's a nut case," she told me, laughing.

8. Photo-Graph

Light doesn't die. Its source might—not the light. We know now, *any* star we see, we see at the end of a beam of light that's Time-Tunneling space. And if we see a star that's dead, by its continuously residual light ... well, here's the picture my mother snapped at the hospital exit: I'm waving good-bye and he's holding me, his exuberant package, with clumsy affection while both of us squint in the sun.

Light doesn't die; we *can* call up. It's the commonest scientific wisdom of twentieth-century poems, repeated in hyperimaginative contexts like this one until it accumulates spiritual force: the past can be grabbed by its photoelectron lapels and dragged into immediacy. "The North American Hopis see time in terms of events rather than of units. Their language avoids our confusion with past and future, by putting everything in an elaborate and subtle multiplication of the present."

It's one big calling-up world out there. Throughout the early 1940s Stefan Ossowiecki, an elderly Pole, "a chemical engineer with no conscious interest in prehistoric archaeology," was subject of a number of impressive tests at the University of Warsaw. Listen: for twenty minutes, he's been clasping a small and seemingly insignificant stone, and now he speaks: *I see very well, it is part of a spear . . . I see round houses, wooden, covered with gray clay, over walls of animal hide. . . . People with black hair, enormous feet, large hands, eyes deeply set. . . .* "He went on for an hour, giving a detailed view of the daily life, dress, appearance and behavior of a Paleolithic people," although Ossowiecki himself had no idea to which specific period scientists already dated the stone.

Until his death in 1944, he was tested with thirty-two objects out of the Warsaw Museum—Acheulian, Mousterian, Aurignacian, Neanderthal, up to the present day. "[Although] these accounts were stimulated by objects that only experts could be sure to recognize . . . his descriptions are not only consistent with what was then known about the cultures in question, but sometimes included information that has only come to light as a result of discoveries made since he died."

The same proof-after-the-fact validates truck driver George McMullen, "who has no formal education and never reads anthropological literature." Discovered by Professor of Archaeology Norman Emerson, McMullen has been repeatedly asked to bring his expertise to field expeditions, pacing the area, stiffening, hackled, describing the people who lived there—age, dress, rituals, buildings. "He once walked over a patch of bare ground, pacing out the perimeter of what he claimed was an Iroquois long-house, while Emerson followed behind him placing survey pegs in the earth. Six weeks later, the entire structure was excavated exactly where McMullen said it would be."

Eyes closed, holding the stone—the same as (though the opposite from) a gypsy over her crystal ball with the future therein. Eyes closed, and seeing. Calling up.

Tierake! Teirake! (Arise! Arise!)—the by-now-ethnographically-famous South Pacific porpoise callers: specifically, "of the High Chiefs of Butaritari and Makin-Meang." They claim their spirits dream-travel under the western waters and, there, invite the porpoise-folk into the world of people. Arthur Grimble witnessed the leading caller of Kuma rush from his hut after several hours of silence, fall facedown to the sands, then amazingly leap up "clawing at the air and whining." The porpoises had arrived.

"They were moving towards us in extended order with spaces of two or three yards between them, as far as my eye could reach. So slowly they came, they seemed to be hung in a trance. Their leader drifted in hard by the dreamer's legs. He turned without a word to walk beside it."

The sun along each of those elegant silver-blue backs. The villagers stooping to ease them over the ridges, crooning. More each minute. Responding. Called up.

And the family dogs that appear at the door after 500 trotted miles of foreign terrain. The spectral visit of lover to lover, mother to daughter, sometimes cities distant, sometimes over an ocean, in crisis-excitement. Gossip-fodder oddities on their own, somehow persuasive in mass, these stories exist indeed in mass, and shelving them under "Paranormal" won't belie the weight of their compelling, crackpot evidence.

Or gospel: *Operator, Operator, Get me Jesus on the line.* We need to call up. A ghostly child the size of a thimble can stand at the ears of the men and women of my generation and plaintively yell to the deeps of their half-sleep haze, *Oh Laaasie, LAAASIE*—the collie never fails to come, from wherever she's been in the brain's back brambles, her theme music faintly trailing. Junk shops are memorabilia emporia, outpouring this century's souvenir postcards, autograph books, memento pins and badges, keepsake lockets, Kodak albums. . . .

Here, my father's alive, I'm waving good-bye to the camera. The sun of a single day of 1958 is something elusive, fixative, intimate, impenetrable, alien, is particles, is waves. My mother's included here, too— her blur of thumb.

In English, it means "light-image," of course. In Hopi, I'm also waving hello.

9. Mushrooms

And this is a photograph, too: On the steps of the Sumitomo Bank, the heat and light of the atomic bomb imprinted a man's crumpled shadow. "The steps have been left as a reminder—after a nuclear blast, only the shadow of a man remains, a shadow in the stone."

And this is the final stitch of Leo Szilard's threading through my thoughts: "When in 1945 the European war had been won, and Szilard realized that the bomb was now about to be used on the Japanese, he marshalled protest everywhere he could. . . . He wanted the bomb to be tested openly so that the Japanese should know its power and could surrender before people died. As you know, Szilard failed."

And this is the testimony of humankind's failure; these are recollections, thirty years later, of hibakusha, explosion-effected-ones, "Hiroshima's survivors":

"I was horrified at the sight of a man standing in the rain with his eyeball in his palm. There was nothing I could do for him."

"A woman with her jaw missing and her tongue hanging out of her mouth was wandering around the area of Shinsho-machi in the heavy, black rain."

"I was too shocked to feel loneliness for my husband. It was like hell. A living horse was burning."

"A woman under a concrete block, 'Please help me.' Four or five of us tried, but we couldn't move the block off her. What to do? We said 'Forgive us' and walked away. . . . Another lady, the blood was oozing from the corners of her eyes. My mother, the skin of her hands was hanging loose, as if it were rubber gloves. My father, disappeared. We never even found his body."

"Then I heard a girl's voice from behind a tree. 'Help me, please.' Her back was completely burned and the skin peeled off and was hanging down from her hips."

"There was a charred body of a woman standing frozen in a running posture with one leg lifted, and clutching her charred baby in her arms."

"The girl was alive and maggots crawled in and out of her body, but she was too weak to trouble with that. They tried applying oil and seaweed, but later she died."

"The sky was red. The sky was burning. Above the city was the mushroom cloud."

And this is how the world reacts, and how the world's always reacted:

"When Simonides offered to teach the Athenian statesman Themistocles the art of Memory, Cicero reports that he refused. 'Teach me not the art of remembering,' he said, 'but the art of forgetting, for I remember things I do not wish to remember, but I cannot forget things I wish to forget.'"

And these are the children of hibakusha:

"Our generation does not like to talk about our fears. We consider them taboo. It is better to talk about ordinary things."—*He talks continually about mah-jongg, which he loves to play all night.*

"I never think about what happened here. When I am finished with work, I bowl, go to bars and the movies. I want to have a good time."

"Everyone in Hiroshima faces this problem—how much to remember, how much to forget."

And this is how we remember:

At the Peace Museum, objects themselves—metal, rock, stones, tile, glass—are as eloquent as the human survivors. More so, even; they never halt their story. "These objects were gathered right from the burning ruins by a geologist."

"He even collected shadows."

In the year before the *Enola Gay* dropped its monstrous atomic payload, Stefan Ossowiecki was murdered, one of millions, by the Gestapo. Where's *his* shadow? Now who's going to rummage the cornermost cartons and find his skull, and tune it in like a receiving device, as he did? Who's going to be the mouth for that bone jaw, and testify?

And why are these ghosts upwelling over the slightest of arbitrarily reminiscent cues in my portrait?—Einstein sorrowfully cupping his turtle . . . Albert winding his tin one up . . . *Albert with Mushrooms in Hospital* (medium: *memory*; dated: 1958).

On the way out, 'Melia tells me, "All of those clomping Japanese movie monsters, those iguana-things about the size of Rhode Island—they were created by radiation, an atomic explosion or leak or whatever. They keep on returning. They won't let the country go. They won't let those people forget it."

10. Chain Reaction and—Sssh!

For months I woke with nightmares.

To whichever one of them fumbled from bed with the comforting word and shoulders-stroke, I'm sure I'd describe—part shamed for

having been its recipient, part in fascination with its credible grotes-
queries—some jumbled tale of tentacled Procyon-beings chasing me,
roping me down. I'm just as sure now they were doctors and nurses,
stored in whatever battery a ten-year-old has, for the necessary repres-
sions by which we get through; stored, and transformed; and released,
in the brain's own willy-nilly time, as jolts of fang-creature evil.

Days were otherwise. Whatever peril awaited me in the sunlight, it
was sized to an understandable world: an older kid could pick on you, a
dumb remark of your parents in public could cause the deepest stain of
humiliation. But mostly I see those days of my childhood as nurturing
and calm—my life is lucky this way—and when I stepped into the courtyard with my khaki-color plastic soldiers, or with that hollow high-
bounce ball my peer group called a "pinky," the Chicago sun would fold
around me (even in winter, even bundled cumbrously against snow)
with that relaxing and utterly *there*-sense of a warm, fresh-laundered,
flannel-something snuggled up to my cheek.

And at night, in bed, in the minutes before they'd come to flick the
light switch off, I'd survey my room with intuitive grasp of those same
architectural-based mnemonics Simonides formulated. To the grain of
the headboard (now a jungle) I'd assign Flash Gordon. Tarzan, ready
to leap to my aid, perched ever-wary on a dresser knob. Aquaman, the
water-breathing warrior of the briny deep, on my desk. Gene Autry.
Rin-Tin-Tin. I had dozens of cardinal points, and equal dozens of chosen protectors. Whatever these figures meant to my friends then,
they're the trivia stuffs of our nostalgia now, the once-upon-a-time by
which an adult generation comes to recognize its hidden members.

Last year, when Skyler came home from her week in the hospital—
home, from her spine and its nerves having reached an uneasy accord—I saw her grown-up's version of those aftereffects. She was
afraid, the way we all are after being depersonalized and pained while
tied. Some nights, that whole week fit in dark minutes. I needed to
hold her. Sex wasn't the point. She needed to feel being herself again,
in a known and controllable space.

Holding this woman I love, I was them, I was me when they heard my first panicky calling and flung on the cheap terry bathrobe and brisked to my room. "Albie . . ." (piqued a little) "sssh . . ." (pure comfort, that; it came with a long back-stroking glissando) ". . . sssh."

I'd seen them do it for each other, too. "Oh, Irv," she'd say, in a sigh that floated the centuries' caring ethereally, through time, through her, and into the kitchen. Or: "Faygeleh," he'd say over and over, rubbing her shoulder as if it might shine. That was the nickname he'd use for those long moments. "Faygeleh," he'd say, "*little bird*." . . . . /

/ . . . "Doug!" A high one, arcing, arcing . . . "Yo, Tony!" Catching it, cage whole, crazy flapping inside it, and running toward the Tunnel mouth, into it, out of it, breathless, undoing the cage door and holding that rapid chickpea-of-a-heart a second, here at the proper coordinates, petting it, letting it go, the world saved (*ho hum*—once again, for Doug and Tony), the theme music swelling, the title roll, watching the bird grow small against the word TIME and then vanish. . . . /

/ . . . It was a miniature key; sprites might have forged it. But then, the case itself wasn't even as large as a family Bible. She unlocked it, she'd noticed, especially on nights like this: she'd spent the day alone, and now the moon through some atmospheric effect or another had layered her room in nacre. There: his heart. She lifted it out of its silks. It was dried by now to the size of a child's fist.

She knew what they said: that she imagined she commanded him to appear from Beyond, and the like. But they were damnable fools, possessed of little more than chickens' wits.

She closes her eyes. And when she opens them, *his* eyes are closed, in thought, above a blotted page, the way she best likes to envision him, working, thoroughly absorbed and, so, blind even to her close scrutiny, crossing another word into oblivion, muttering, humming now like a struck tuning fork. His hair is as wild as weeds. He might be writing *To a Skylark . . . . /*

/ . . . The *Songbird.*"

It's been so confusingly long since the question, not one of us recognizes its answer. We're just a bunch of sloshy old friends sitting over some beers at 'Melia's.

"The *Songbird,*" she says. She's sure this time. Yes. "Sky King's plane was the *Songbird.*"

On a Sunday, campus is close to completely empty. In straight sun, the Pizza Hut's ruddy brick glistens. From far off, it catches the light like a polished mahogany shoe. Up close, if you touch it, the building seems to generate animal heat of its own.

When I was a child I'd sometimes go to the closed-in back court sidewalks and, if nobody else was around, I'd stretch out belly-down, my cheek against the concrete. All morning, the sidewalks were storing up sun. That sweetish warmth washed into me, a kind of presexual pleasure that melted my groin, and from there let a tree of warmth branch through me. Finally it curled my toes. It filled me everywhere. I lay there like a pupa of light.

Even at evening's start, the warmth stayed stored there in the concrete. The Earth remembered the sun. When I was a child, the Earth would whisper those memories, whisper its deepest secrets, confidingly into my body.

The Lake

"Poetry in Porkopolis"—so says the review in a Philly paper.

So far, four slim issues have appeared. *She* thinks they're harbingers, presentiments—of what, she isn't certain, but she knows they sputter raw, unheralded thought waves through the chill Chicago air, that they're transmitters, that they're *of* the times.

The angels of this later age are radio beams, exuberant twentieth-century angels, long as light is long; they'll sing in a box on the sitting-room mantel, and they'll streak their way past the Twins and the Swan. The angels of this later age are dirigibles and biplanes. Angels like these require new high priests and priestesses, new seeing.

It's February 1913. Harriet Monroe is in the offices of *Poetry,* exalted *cum* depressed in a kind of emotional tossed slaw, as she investigates the morning's mail: laurels and brickbats, warbles of adulation and derisively rich Bronx cheers.

"So. Alice . . ." (this is Alice Corbin, her associate) "do we stride ahead through the end of the year, or refund our guarantors' charity?"

Alice says nothing; Alice continues to look from the Cass Street office window into one of those bleak Chicago winter skies the color of yesterday's alewife scales. The answer is obvious to Alice: this is Harriet Monroe, a quiet reed of a lady who's going to rub those dowdy Philadelphia noses into the living poetry meat of Porkopolis until its tang is appreciated.

Harriet Monroe: the Gertrude Steinian'd, Albert Einsteinian'd, *wunderkind,* cube-kissed, Modernist spirit is on her; the rah-rah Dada hoodoo-lips of 1913 are readying to juicily play a rootie-toot-toot on the quiet reed in the head of this quiet reed of an editor-lady.

New winds are blowing.

In 1913, Igor Stravinsky's *Rite of Spring* premiered at the Théâtre des Champs Élysées. "It marked the beginning of modern music." We know that now. "By mid-century it had become part of the standard symphony repertoire."

Yes. But that night, audience member Gertrude Stein, amidst the booing, witnessed one of the apoplectic gentlemen near her smash his cane into the top hat of an agitated neighbor. A woman elegantly cascaded in diamonds slapped the hissing man beside her. Cards were exchanged, for duels. A rain of catcalls fell to the stage, and choreographer Nijinsky stood on a chair in the wings, hands megaphoned at his lips, to scream the rhythm so his dancers could remain in sync with music that they couldn't—for the great affront and ruckus—even hear.

And does Stravinsky look so *very* revolutionary, seated with his hands in a casual clasp, in the drawing Picasso did?—a bookish-looking dandy of a man (Picasso, delightedly effervesced by the composer's mustard-yellow trousers and yellow shoes), his thinning hair and saucery glasses lenses. In his head, though, was the whomp-and-thump: it's not, after all, as if Harriet Monroe sat for her portraits breathing visible fire. (She had it, though.)

Everything then, it seems, was revolutionary. Of Igor Stravinsky: "He radiated that he was one of the men of the future." Stuck in the present, border guards at the Italian frontier at Chiasso checked his luggage in a routine search and confiscated that carefully rolled-up portrait Picasso had made a gift. They saw it as a military map.

And Picasso . . . ? In 1913 he and Braque are inventing new eyes—bee-eyes, omnifaceted eyes—for the world. His *Bottle of Vieux Marc, Glass, and Newspaper* (actual newspaper, pasted and pinned) is 1913, ditto *Student with a Newspaper,* ditto *Glass and Bottle* by Braque, as well as Braque's *Woman with a Guitar* and *Guitar and Program.*

1913: Joyce is working on *Dubliners,* Eliot on "The Waste Land."

1913: Lawrence publishes *Sons and Lovers.* Frost, *A Boy's Will.* Willa

Cather, *O Pioneers*, and Joseph Conrad, *Chance*. *The Tempers* (William Carlos Williams). Whomp-and-thump. Marcel Proust: *Swann's Way*.

Everything caught in the toppledown, reorganizing wind.

Stravinsky wriggling like an inchworm through a window at the rear of the Théâtre, on the lam from his own mêlée.

When we think about the past, we need a pattern. Need to survey those millennia of unprecedented invention, and call it the Neolithic. Take its tongue-curl fear and its blood-on-fire glories, and find in them a system: they mean such-and-so. My years in the clergy, we say. The months that were strung like beads on the thread *divorce*, we say. The Dark Ages. The Renaissance.

Because of my own homegrown predispositions, I see dots of 1913 constellated into meaningful shapes we tend to call "High Art."

On other days, the funky, junky hellizaboomin' cellar-end of the scale may be as rife with ripe events. In 1913 ingenue Krazy Kat and nemesis/sweetiepie Ignatz Mouse are given (after longtime second-banana status as filler for *The Dingbats*) their own comic strip. "It continued to be published through World War I, the Roaring Twenties, the Great Depression, and World War II—a run of thirty-one years. Among comic strips it is a certifiable masterpiece. In the world of art and literature it is an innovation." (Picasso was wild about it.)

1913: Edgar Rice Burroughs is high on the fan mail pouring into the offices of the crock-o'-schlock *All-Story*: in that middle-level pulp 'zine, he's just published his brainchild, *Tarzan of the Apes*, and now he's awaiting his editor's first words on its sequel. *Under the Moons of Mars* is also in *All-Story*; but should he pursue this ability full-time? (It's a question that torments him as did that of filial retribution for Hamlet.)

Or it might be the sciences, either applied or theoretical. 1913: Danish physicist Niels Bohr successfully maps the atom's vasty nothingness and rings of orbit whizzery; of Bohr's model that year of the hydrogen atom, Einstein later wrote that it "appeared to me like a miracle."

1913: Sigmund Freud is the author of *Totem and Taboo*.

1913: William M. Burton receives a patent for a process in which oil is converted to gasoline. In Highland Park, Michigan, Henry Ford predicts that his new idea, a "moving assembly line," 250 feet in length, will fully quadruple his current production of Model T's.

The future is seeded. The century is zooming. We need to see it this way.

Or it simply might be the Omaha tornado of 1913, which created a canyon five miles long through the center of the city on that year's Easter Sunday. *To My Dear Sis*, says the slanted hand on the back of a locally printed photograph postcard, *oh sis you can never imagine what it was like. By By Dollie.*

Patterns: for the rest of his life, he'll see his days in terms of funnels, in terms of sun and then fulminous dark. There won't be a week that he doesn't wake from a dream of his wife's hand looking like a shrub growing out of the rubble.

On February 17, 1913, at the armory of the Sixty-ninth New York Regiment on Lexington at Twenty-fifth, an International Exhibition of Modern Art took place—the famous "Armory Show" that liberated American tastes from what had been over a century of complacency.

Matisse, Duchamp, Cézanne, van Gogh, John Marin, Kandinsky, Francis Picabia, Odilon Redon, Braque, Brancusi, Gauguin—they entered American consciousness here, for the first time, having something like the effect of a "Composition for Whoopee Cushion and Pinwheel Fireworks" suddenly bursting forth from a chamber quartet. (Also among the catalogue's 1,270 listed items were those by a "Paul" Picasso.)

The slogan of the show: "The New Spirit." "I went to it and gasped along with the rest," said William Carlos Williams. Ninety thousand attended over the month of the Show and were given the whammy, the quick-kick-to-the-pineal-gland, by Futurism, Expressionism, and Cubism, out of nowhere it seemed, and at once. Martin Green calls their varied aesthetics a "repudiation of recognizableness."

When Mabel Dodge, who ably primed both energy and money for the Show, wrote Gertrude Stein three weeks before its doors were opened to the public, she called it the "most important event that has ever come off since the signing of the Declaration of Independence, and it is of the same nature." As she put it later: "I was going to dynamite New York and nothing would stop me." (Store this image: eventually we'll return to it.)

On closing night, when the last of the dazzled spectators had been led away from *Nude Descending a Staircase*—hooting or razzing or nearly devotionally silent, each according to his or her accommodation—the doors were locked from within, and the Sixty-ninth Regiment fife and drum corps played, as a larger regiment of at-attention magnums of champagne were wheeled into the center room.

Somebody costumed-up in a knee-length beard and a Lincoln stovepipe hat weaved through the crowd with an exaggerated palsy claiming to be the representative of the National Academy of Design. They took turns whirling him in a turkey trot. Then everyone—janitors, ticket sellers, artists, impresarios, wan intelligentsia, guards, and guides alike—grabbed hips and "followed the painter Daniel Putnam Brinley in a snake dance through the rooms."

This is the same tune being hammered away on brainplates simultaneously from hither to half-past-yon. In Chicago, Harriet Monroe is one more 1913 note in a music clamoring—now whispering—now wockawocka hoochiecooing the planets out of their courses—under the capable, inescapable maestroleadership of Professor Zeitgeist, consummate conductor.

("*Sight kites*, dollink?" Krazy inquires of Ignatz, staring up at her newsprint sky.)

But there are lulls in this music; in that quietus, indecision wells.

The editorship of *Poetry* is no full-time job—as yet. As art reviewer for the *Chicago Tribune,* Harriet Monroe is just returned from viewing the Armory Show and, half against her will, is sore dismayed.

Matisse is "fundamentally insincere" and an "unmitigated bore," and his work consists of "the most hideous monstrosities ever perpetrated in the name of long suffering art." Cézanne is "the shabby French vagabond," van Gogh "the half-insane Flemish recluse and suicide," Gauguin, of course, "disreputable." The Show is good—for a laugh. She says on February 23, "If these groups of theorists have any other significance than to increase the gayety of nations your correspondent confessed herself unaware of it."

And yet . . . she stares at her desk. Those canvases, so patched with jagged shards of color. . . . They stick in her mind. That's what shards do, she says, what shards are supposed to do. Art shrapnel.

Very uneasy, this reed of a lady. Color straight from the tube, great gouts of color pouring out of the faucet. . . .

She stares at her desk as if its sea-green blotter might, with concentration, turn transparent, letting bits of wisdom bobble up to the top. She toys with a recent gift to the office, a Pegasus molded in rich lead crystal.

"Alice? I think I'll go for a brief perambulation down at the lake." She points to her pile of letters and poems, and gives her wrist a shrug that says the arbitration of such as *these* would be beyond even the veriest Solomonic of wisdoms. "You know how the lake air sweeps my thinkum clean again."

Alice says nothing, but kindly so. Harriet buttons her lamb's wool coat to the chin. "I'll return in the hour."

Alice knows that we're as tumbleweeds in the winds of the times, and that whithersoever they blowest, we rollest. Harriet leaves, a gray coat in a brisk gray gust of February.

Think about the pioneering Norwegian polar explorer Fridtjof Nansen—how he made his three-year-long, three-thousand-mile circuit of formerly untraveled Arctic waters by intentionally freezing his ship into drift ice, letting it bear this fleck.

That's how I see the zeitgeist working—carrying us, the many flecks, though some don't know they're in motion, and some are farther behind, and some in advance.

The year the call came saying the cancer had spread from my mother's lungs to her shoulder and back, I saw the world in terms of cancer: that was my template. Everything radiated death. A friend gave birth to a healthily yawling girl, a thing of immense pink beaming: even that, somehow, I managed to see in the shadow of bereavement. When a cream-puff-hairdo'd news anchor coughed—a quick dry nothing— that was just a symbol of my mother's cough, that tearing up of the wet cells of her lining.

When you're in the Mob, then the world is the Mob, and the rest of the world is not-Mob: that's the code. When you're a Hassid Jew, the least impossible cheese mite of Creation is proof of your universe, and your every stale or scented breath, your fuck-breath and your boredom-breath, these all are the breaths of a Hassid Jew.

Every day, we prescribe ourselves lenses.

When the President flickered onto the screen and said that call-in radio shows were spreading hate through the nation like a cancer—I wept all day.

So cold, on the ice. So cold—and the wind in its single direction.

This is what I learned: that courage, and charity, comfort, and concern—are only the little c's.

In 1913, *Arts and Decoration* gave its March appearance over to the Armory Show. Included were both an essay by Gertrude Stein called "Portrait of Mabel Dodge at the Villa Curonia" and, as a complement, Mabel Dodge's essay on Gertrude Stein—who was, said Dodge, "prodigious. Pounds and pounds and pounds piled up on her skeleton—not the billowing kind but massive, heavy fat . . . her body seemed to be the large machine that her large nature required to carry it." Her laugh was "like a beefsteak."

She'd be laughing it more, and more openly, now. She was finally her complete self. This was the year that her brother Leo moved out of their house on the rue de Fleurus, leaving Paris for Settignano. February: he sold his Picassos, gingerly packed sixteen Renoirs and two Cézannes, and then was gone—his own enormous width of physical presence, in its absence, seeming to open up extra rooms.

Not that he'd subjugated his steamroller sister, who could? Still, in the days when they were inseparable, it was Leo who always expatiated, Leo who made the polysyllabic point to the mesmerized acolyte. Now, the future begins: it's Gertrude now, and Alice B. Toklas, sitting iconographically in the gaslight on salon nights, sometimes waking with each other in the bed beneath Picasso's *Hommage à Gertrude*. (Was he thinking of the apartment's few bronze Buddhas? Surely he's painted her as pounds and pounds and pounds of Buddha.) "I was alone at this time in understanding [Picasso]," she wrote later, "perhaps because I was expressing the same thing in literature."

"The Stein salon was, among other things, a kind of echo chamber in which certain enthusiasms and art theories and reputations were enhanced, intertwined, and further mystified at the expense of the intellectually insecure. It was also an anteroom where would-be disciples waited in hope of meeting the painters themselves, in hope of entering their world. The painters were the source of all truth and the focus of all glamour."

Now the beefsteak laugh is frequent, and seasoned with what she calls—she wanted it always, and now at last she has it—*la gloire*.

For some, the arrival of glory is more recalcitrant. In February 1913 Edgar Rice Burroughs sits in his office at the Chicago branch of the magazine *System* (Wabash and Madison Avenues), surveying his future. *Dismal* is the word, at least if the present and past are an index.

System calls itself "the magazine of business." For an annual fee of fifty dollars, a businessman can write to *System*'s Service Bureau as often as he likes, for detailed counsel on any dilemmas. Burroughs's job is to write this counsel—and yet "I knew little or nothing," he'd say in his *Autobiography*, "about business, had failed in every enterprise I had ever attempted and could not have given valuable advice to a peanut vendor."

This is history, not modesty. It officially begins in 1895 with his stint as bill collector for the Knickerbocker Ice Company (returning one day to where he's tied his horse, he discovers it's eaten the leaves completely off the trees of Lieutenant Bondfield of the Chicago Police Department). That fall, he's appointed Professor of Geology at the Michigan Military Academy ("needed a Professor of Geology and I was it . . . the fact that I had never studied geology seemed to make no difference whatsoever").

In 1897 his patient father is helping him receive his early discharge from the cavalry. A stationery store in Pocatello, Idaho, fails (the Good Lord "never intended me for a retail merchant!"). Cattle herding. Treasurer of his father's American Battery Company. Dredging gold at Stanley Creek in the Sawtooth Mountains. Railroad cop for the Oregon Short Line Railroad in Salt Lake City ("Can't say I am stuck on the job"). Crawling steel girders for a seventeen-story warehouse under construction. Peddler, door-to-door, of "Stoddard's Collected Lectures." Selling candy ("Flops"). Lightbulbs ("Flops"). He's recently pawned his watch. He hawks Alcola, a patent-medicine "cure for alcoholism." Corsets ("Flops"). Pencil sharpeners ("Flops"). Some diary entries: *Head aches for years—No lunches—Great poverty—Am just about ready to give up.*

Now with two accepted stories but even more rejections sliding about confusedly in his noggin; and bambino number three on the way; and the news this morning, February 15, 1913, that George Tyler Burroughs, his father, who's seen him patiently through all of this two-bit uselessness, is dead at age seventy-nine . . .

. . . the creator of Tarzan lets the cold waft into his propped-up *System* window. He moans at his memo-strewn desk like an animal struck in the road as the 1913 bandwagon nattily speeds along . . .

. . . a croak of a note, another out-of-sync espousal of self-doubt in the otherwise snappily confident, to-the-moon-and-back tune of the times.

The future is always being created. (So is the past.) Why does it seem—somehow—this year—the future is being created *more*?

In 1913 the U.S. income tax law goes into effect.

The *New York World* introduces the "crossword puzzle."

Grand Central Station opens; so does the Panama Canal.

A man named Cecil B. DeMille, in search of a spot to shoot his first "movie," a Western, nixes his original location—Flagstaff, Arizona—and chooses instead a sleepy, unpretentious California town called Hollywood.

President Wilson delivers the first in-person State of the Union address in 112 years.

1913: it's a blueprint of "tomorrow"; it's a great dividing cell.

Yes, but when Edgar Rice Burroughs walks off the job at the seventeen-story warehouse under construction, somebody else is tapped to fill his place, and this man stinks of fear of heights for ten-hour days for the rest of his life—*he'll* tell you what it takes to bring a blueprint to completion.

And as for "dividing cell," not the metaphor, no, but the real uterine thing that you'd see on a lab smear, that you'd smell on a middle finger . . . aren't there wadded-up cotton balls in a Paris brothel that are actually—in a line of direct causation—the engine that powers some of Picasso's savviest canvases?

I'm trying to say that the gleaming, lightsome dreams of any era require somebody's heavily cranking up the dream-gears in the basement dankness.

1913: Gandhi is arrested. Russian revolutionary Josef Dzhugashvili signs his name for the first time as *Stalin* ("man of steel"). *Union organizer* and *anarchist* enter popular usage. Some refuse to forget that when Edgar Rice Burroughs quits his job as a railroad dick, another man is tapped to fill his place, who breaks his lantern over the head of a bum in the mouseshit dirt of a boxcar; every day this happens somewhere in the bottommost dark of 1913. Everywhere, rabble is ready for rousing.

The political spirit isn't unlike what one might find in the lab of Niels Bohr: a ferocious excitement, a newness—yes, but first, existing models need to be dismantled.

Here's an atom of social upheaval: on June 4, 1913—Derby Day— a suffragist named Emily Davidson brazenly sprinted onto the track at Epsom Downs directly in the path of the King's prize horse, attempting to seize its reins. She was trampled to death: a martyr to her cause.

The month before, 10,000 had marched in New York on behalf of women's voting rights. Guerrilla suffragists cut major telephone lines (the London–Glasgow cable went in February of 1913), mutilated designated national treasures, set the homes of politicos afire; one diehard threatened Winston Churchill with a whip. When jailed, they hunger-struck—they were bound and forcibly fed with metal funnels like geese.

In Chicago, Charles Moyer, outspoken president of the Miners Union, was shot in the back and dragged through the streets. I have the reproduction of a photograph from 1913: freshly painted, a one-horse advertising wagon poses at a curb, the SOCIALIST CARAVAN, traveling COAST TO COAST in the hope of stirring up 2,000,000 VOTES IN 1916 FOR THE SOCIALIST PARTY. 1913: February 5, a seventeen-year-old garment worker, Ida Braeman, was shot (to death) in the chest while demonstrating peaceably with a group of strikers in front of a Rochester tailor shop. Their demands were for an eight-hour day and overtime pay. She had planned to announce her wedding engagement that evening.

Ida Braeman—a Jew. The new winds carried *shtetl* smells and the goods-hawking squawk of a peddler oratorio. March 31 of 1913 proved itself a record immigration day at Ellis Island: 6,745 impatient embodiments of alien need and alien energy entered under the sign of Liberty's come-on torch; by May, the previous nine-month total was 900,000.

Coarser voices enter the chorus, ghettospeak patois (*"Pat oys,"* says Krazy Kat, and heavy on the *oy*). Professor Zeitgeist striking up a ragtag carny band of banjo and washboard, blues and klezmer—striking up a martial air, a blat of the brass with the force of fists inside it.

1913: Robert Hayden is born. Ralph Ellison a year later. Darker streams of the American current. Harlem nights and demeaning niggertown days.

In 1913 George McManus's comic strip *Maggie and Jiggs*—that daffy, broguey love song to the upward-rising Irish—appears. (Jiggs's appetite introduces mainstream American tastes to corned-beef-and-cabbage.)

1913: Delmore Schwartz is born, who will carry his Jewishness commando-style into the halls of academe; and Karl Shapiro, author of *Poems of a Jew* (and who, in fact, will become the editor of *Poetry* in 1950).

New winds—and they bear the Old World garlic scent of my father in the kitchen at midnight, one night seventy years in the future, piling together an Irving Goldbarth special, the imprimatur of which is a redolent *greps* (a belch) and a very soulfully appreciative sound he always called, on making it, a "shmecka-da-lips." (I can hear it now.)

I'm there, too, in that future. I'm thirty-eight and my father is going to die.

When Judy determined she'd leave for a year in Japan, I (sadly) equally determined I'd support her in this, in whatever small symbolic ways I could. That was the summer of bricks of green tea stacked a foot high in the kitchen; a potted bonsai—just about the size of the heart's small bramble of arteries—at the front door; a kimono on the doorknob at the bathroom, all of its misty mountain peaks and whiskery orange fish while Judy showered her trim American jogger's body behind the fogging curtain and I sat in bed imagining the apartment empty of all of this, and of her.

Now that was Austin, Texas—gift shops filled with armadillos welded out of pop tops. Finding even *kitschy* Japaneseiana wasn't easy. But I did it. I was thirty-eight and fresh from the muck of divorce, and Judy's sly and saucy twenty-two was fuse enough in the craziness for sudden love to blast me out of reality. I'd have chopped my left leg off and fashioned a hillock of sushi from it, if she'd wanted.

But she *didn't* really want anything, not from me, except a noncommittal, background kind of "being there." Her yearnings by then were all Far East, and the summer was merely a block of months to wait through. I already missed her: I *pre*-missed her. With her ringleted head on my chest and the oozes of sex still slick around our thighs, I already mourned her absence. I would stroke her so fierce I could feel the shape of the bones—the precious ivory smuggled into my life that I'd have to pay back. So this became the screen through which I saw each minute: Japan and bereavement. Zen and stir-fry and haiku and loss.

It's what we always, *always* do, it's what our brains are wired to do from even before our natal push down the chute: take welter, and force enabling order into its details. How from all of the numbers, *every* number, every *combination* . . . we will blow for luck on our hands, and bet a specific six or eleven, or whatever, is going to absolutely declare itself on the rolled bones. Into tumult, we structure these rungs through a day. (In excess, this becomes the skewed obsessing of conspiracy theorists: *Kennedy* has seven letters, so does *Lincoln,* etc.)

On the morning I drove Judy to the bus, I knew her "year" in Japan exempted her from my ongoing life forever. "Moshimosh," I said, and kissed her a last time, in my drear confusion using the phrase she'd taught me for their telephone "Hello." And then began the months of aimlessness and hungers.

When the phone call came from Chicago saying my father had died—the leukemia won that race ahead of his unreliable heart—of course, I flew in the following morning. I cried, I held my mother as *she* cried, and my sister, and I flung the ritual handful of dirt down the graveshaft. But the truth is (though I'd loved him) that my grief was partially *labored* into existence, yes, and never fit my insides square and true: I'd been experiencing the world in a certain preestablished pattern, and his dying didn't fit.

I watched my mother as I clumsily recited the Jewish "mourner's prayer": she wasn't really here, *she* was transported by his death to somewhere untouched by anything cognitive. One night before I left their house, as I wandered it in the darkness while my mother and sister fitfully slept, I thought I saw—this lasted a second only—a ghost-him stand in the kitchen, layering up a deftly done ghost-sandwich. *It's okay,* he winked. He'd always forgiven me everything.

When the news arrived for Picasso, "he was in such emotional turmoil that he could not work." Eva wrote to Gertrude Stein, "I hope that Pablo will make himself start working again, because only this will help him forget his pain a little." And he did, and the world in its omnidirectional energies went onward from that moment when it had stopped—it always stops at the death of a parent, in this case Don Ruiz Blasco. It was May 3, 1913.

But the universe doesn't have a "theme," a "plot." Interpretation is a sliver in its slipstream.

1913: as the nations whet their blood-blades for the first of their World Wars, the news in Arvada, Colorado, on December 12 is snowbanks eight feet tall. Or another photo postcard sent that year: "127 Rattlesnakes Killed in One Day. Near Dupree South Dakota." (They're draped on a handheld pole so laden, it needs a second pole to be angled under it as a cross-support.)

1913: Chaplin makes his film debut (as a villain). The Kaiser bans the tango. Mount McKinley is scaled ("the highest point on the North American continent"). A statistician working for Prudential Life "declares cancer a national menace." In New Mexico a grasshopper cloud is reported, five miles by eighteen miles: for anyone caught in its Biblical thunder, the revving gun-planes of Germany must have been planets and planets away.

Small things. In 1913 the Noesting Pin Ticket Company, then of Mount Vernon, New York, was founded. Henry Lankenau's patent for "the Gothic clip" was assigned to that farsighted business concern; today, it claims to have made "the world's largest selection of paper clips for over 75 years." Its catalogue includes the Gem, the Frictioned Gem, the Perfect Gem (you'd *think* one needn't proceed from that), the Marcel Gem, the Universal Clip (again, you think . . . but, ah!), the Nifty Clip, the Peerless Clip, the Ring Clip, and the Glide-on Clip.

Elsewhere, the perfected design called "Hookless No. 2" was unveiled. Quoting Henry Petroski: "U.S. Patent No. 1,060,378, issued in 1913, is now often taken as the milestone marking the introduction of the zipper." Looking—as well it should, in its ancestralness—like a trilobite risen from stone.

Small things. In 1913 D. H. Lawrence is wintering at Gargnano, Lago di Garda: "There is a great host of lemons overhead, half visible, a swarm of ruddy oranges by the path, and here and there a fat citron. It is almost like being under the sea."

The Armory Show was over in the middle of March. June 7, under the leadership of the International Workers of the World, the striking silk mill shleps of New York and New Jersey—many of them Polish and German Jews with ties to socialist traditions, and Italians who honored a history of fiery activism—produced what's come to be called the Paterson Strike Pageant. Twenty-five hundred marched up

Christopher Street and Fifth Avenue, singing the "Marseillaise" and the "Internationale," as led by an eighteen-year-old worker, Hannah Silverman.

What were they asking for really? Decent lives. And what was the answer? Local and state militias, and the clubs of the police. An old, old story: its statistics are repeatedly on record through the centuries.

But this, as a response, was new. You could feel the waves of calories break out of that unstoppable parade. It led to Madison Square Garden, rented for that one night. "In 1913 it was a magnificent Renaissance building, in cream-colored brick and terra-cotta trim and with arcades copied from Italy on both the street level and the roof garden. On top of the tower stood a sculpture of Diana by Saint-Gaudens. . . ." (Martin Green). The Pageant organizers had spelled IWW in red lights placed around all four sides of the tower, keeping this secret until the last moment, until it was too late for authorities to find and unthrow the switch. It burned, a declarative torch, for all of Manhattan to see.

Twelve hundred workers had parts onstage, for an eager audience of over fifteen thousand (nearly a thousand needed to stand). "The air was electric." There were six scenes, all enacted in front of the same two-hundred-foot backdrop of a dismal Paterson silk mill, prison-gray and prison-weighty; the stumbling narrative goes from zombie workers lumbering in for another day's demands, through various stages of increasing self-awareness and rebellion. By the end of the Pageant, the audience joined the performers in singing strike songs and in cheering Wobbly heroes, and in hissing and booing the mellerdrama police. The whole building: a raw red throat of festive indignation.

And who were the forces behind this historic event? Bill Haywood, Elizabeth Gurley Flynn, John Reed, and Carlo Tresca—all of them, mixer-uppers at the Mabel Dodge salon. As the merits of Cubism flew through that room and were denounced or exalted, there was the dapper Tresca, for instance, someone who'd been "arrested 37 times for blasphemy, sedition, criminal obscenity, conspiracy, and murder; and was shot at, bombed, kidnapped by fascists and had his throat cut" (hence the waggish beard?).

In the Mabel Dodge apartment at 23 Fifth Avenue, corner of Ninth, the Armory Show and the Pageant were equally welcome, equally promulgated soundings of the times—they were a double-headed trumpet announcing one full-steam-ahead thing.

Around the bearskin rug in front of the white marble fireplace, below the Venetian chandelier—here, dissidents Emma Goldman and Margaret Sanger held forth (Dodge helped finance Sanger's incipient journal *Woman Rebel*); and painters John Marin and Picabia, and photographer Stieglitz, might be found enjoying the passed-around bottles of kümmel shaped like Russian bears. In 1913 Dodge presented Pageant dynamo (and enamorato) John Reed to Picasso and Gertrude Stein.

"Far apart as the Show and the Pageant stood, they spoke the same metamessage to the same people. For at that moment in history, art and politics came together, and so people's hopes and fears came together also. . . ."

Wedded in that wind! Professor Zeitgeist, with a fistful of batons. Strike up a marriage song!

". . . Since then, people have looked back to that moment in envy."

They were wedded that way in the minds of both supporters and detractors. They were whomp and thump and boomalayboom, of a piece. Green speaks of "a climate of strong hopes for . . . change for the better in all things. If by now [the Show and the Paterson Pageant] seem disparate and disconnected events, that is because we have lost touch with those hopes."

Yoking the two in condemnation, the *New York Times* said of the Armory Show, "It should be borne in mind that this movement is surely a part of the general movement to disrupt, degrade, if not destroy, not only art but literature and society too. . . . The Cubists and the Futurists are cousins to anarchists in politics." (One can hear the spat-out *ptooey*.) *Art and Progress* typified Modernism: "the chatter of anarchistic monkeys." Enthusers used the same lingo, only giving it their own dervish, doctrinaire spin; and Hutchins Hapgood said of the Armory Show that he viewed it "as I would a great fire, an earthquake, or a political revolution; as a series of shattering events—shattering for the purpose of re-creation."

Hapgood again (on January 1 7, 1 9 1 3): "There seems a vague but real relationship between all the real workers of our day. Whether in literature, plastic art, or the labor movement . . . we find an instinct to blow up the old forms and traditions, to dynamite the baked and hardened earth so that fresh flowers can grow." The image then was common (you'll remember I asked you to "store" away Dodge's saying, of her helping birth the Armory Show, "I was going to dynamite New York"). Or that famous supercilious newspaperese, of *Nude Descending a Staircase*: *(ptooey)* "an explosion in a shingle factory."

Duck, boys—here comes some art!

In Coconino County, on a blustery cartoon afternoon, those sharp art splinters streak through the sky, then slow, and float there coaxingly in the winds of the times, beseechingly, as if they would lead us upward, out of our blindness.

"Sight kites, " Krazy says. Seeing-eye creatures filling the air. If only we'd grab their tails.

With its farther shore invisible, and its water and air connected in intricate moodiness, Lake Michigan is nearly oceanic.

Today it was gray, the kind of February lake gray that will bluster out on the water and be unrelievable dullness at the shore rocks, somehow managing to even out of these two far states a monochromatic unity.

Harriet sat on a rock, and stared at the distant bluster. She was alone out here—you'd need to be wacky to sit at the lake today—and what she really was doing, she knew, was staring into herself. For what?

"Some kind of reconciling," she said out loud, to no one.

"Pardon, ma'am?"

She was almost airborne at that.

"I didn't mean to frighten you, ma'am. Must be you didn't see me." Well *of course* she didn't, mister; he was hunkered-up on the rocks in a flat-gray overcoat (somewhat frayed, but also serviceable in a middle-class way: she noticed things like that), he could have been out here to *impersonate* a rock.

She must have studied him suspiciously, disdainfully suspiciously. "Well, no offense intended, ma'am," (he'd sized her up: her own ty-coonish dove-gray coat, and her bearing) "but you don't own the lake."

And she very well might have angered at that, or simply walked away—but, to her credit, she laughed, and then both of them laughed, and then they sat in their separate silences, waiting to see if there would be more. He had a heavy, *lumpen* jaw, she saw, but childlike sweet features floated above it. And although she desired her solitude, she also owed him a pleasantry; and so: "Tell me. Do you visit here often?"

"No ma'am, I don't. But I have," now doing something of a gesture that lassoed the overhead cloudiness, "thinking to do." Then, truly as if a child were suddenly to admit in a histrionic whisper *I have the Scabies* or *I have a frog named Hepzibah:* "I have Creditors." (And a father dead, he could have added.) "Creditors, and their collector bullies," he said, as if to himself—an almost singsong children's counting rhyme.

"Yes, money men can be *very* pusillanimous." Now with this summation, she thought their talk completed.

"*That's* a good word!" and a paper and pencil appeared in his hand from out of the coat—from out of a rock—as if he were a magician. He butt-sidled nearer to her, showed her he'd inscribed her accidental gift. By way of explanation he said, "I'm a *Writer.*"

"Not a poet or a journalist, I trust. My head is populated enough by them."

"No ma'am. "I'm"—what? What *was* he, if he was *anything* deserving of the category at all? "I'm a teller of tales."

"Tall ones?"

"Very tall ones. One goes clear up to Mars."

"And are they persuasive, these escalatory tales?"

"You *do* use the words! Well, yes ma'am, two are published, with checks in the bank. But the question is. . . ."

. . . and then he was confiding in her, copiously, a piping confessional gush not even Emma ever heard—after all, Harriet was an editor, and radiated discernment—starting, where?, oh gosh, back in Idaho punching cows, "I peacock-strutted about in Mexican spurs with inlaid ivory and silver-dollar-sized rowels"—and horseshit duty ("No offense, ma'am: I meant it literally") in the cavalry—and serially onward—every failed bottom-grubbing workload whether clerkly or spit-&-sweat—the whole balloon armada of high hopes bursting one by one—but not just failure, no, he admitted, it also bespoke a wanderlust, a need to take the nowness of his life into the next thing—into newness—she was listening keenly now—she was a reed of a lady angled into the force of this prolixity—and it was this newness, it was the flow, that nourished him—but now with baby numero three (and a father dead, he could have added)—now with this writing thing—he talked of *ape*-men and *green* men—crackpot-silly, he knew—he loved it—half ashamed—it paid the bills—for a moment it did, but—

"May I ask your name?"

"I'm sorry, ma'am. It's Edgar. Ed."

"How old are you, Ed?"

A pause: because he knew he'd been sounding like some poor mooncalf. "Thirty-eight."

"It's time you settled down, I believe. It's time you stuck to one thing."

"Yes, yes, of course. But *is it the writing thing*?"

She looked inside him then, with that invasive critical eye of hers, she looked the way she'd hoped to look inside herself, at her own interior bluster. He held still, as if for an oil portrait. A minute went by— that's a very long time, on a naked rock in late February lake wind.

"Yes. Do the writing, Ed. Do the writing."

This was said in such finality, it came with an oracular ring, and it clearly sealed the end of their conversation. He was glad, for he took kindly to this woman, but felt embarrassed now at his self-exposure. And she—? desired her solitude.

To be polite he asked, "Can *I* help *you* in your cogitating, ma'am?"

She made a little wry lasso-twirl with her hand, and mimicked bringing in some of the far-out lake air closer.

"Thank you, Ed, but we have done all we can for each other."

And so they nodded understandingly, and he retreated a small ways up the shore. She continued to stare out into the distance. . . .

Chicago poet Paul Carroll:

> . . . the lake,
> Green and gray as the color of some ghosts,
> Kept cracking against the rocks on the beach at Fullerton
> Like a practice of swords among the Caliph's Guard.

—*that's* my Lake Michigan! If you stare like a gypsy wisdom-woman into its crystal heart, its there and not-there heart, its always-been and never-was centrality . . . you can see the forge, the wellspring cuntlife genesis where Earth and Ether cohabit, and where the living and the dead are veins of the same ineffable state, and mingle, there in the Great Salon that never sleeps and is beyond what we call time.

A flicker: she saw he was ready to leave.

"Ed!"

"Yes?"

"There's only one s at the start of *pusillanimous.*"

"Thank you, ma'am. I'll get better."

1913: Ezra Pound introduces Yeats to Japanese No drama.

1913: Ezra Pound is married.

1913: Yeats composes and publishes "September 1913 "in the *Irish Times.*

1913: Norway gives women the vote (the United States required seven years more: three more than Soviet Russia).

1913: Arthur Eddington, at Cambridge, assumes the Plumian Chair of Astronomy (he will soon describe the sun's internal structure, the actual *how* and *why* of its lightworks, for the first time).

1913: *Bicycle Wheel* by Marcel Duchamp ("the first piece of modern art employing motion").

1913: "As a last resort, a Michigan surgeon implants a dog's brain in a man's skull."

1913: Richard Nixon is born; jazzman Lionel Hampton; brewer Adolphus Busch; Albert Camus.

1913: Author Edgar Rice Burroughs zippily finishes writing eight novels: *The Return of Tarzan, At the Earth's Core, The Monster Men, The Cave Girl, The Warlord of Mars, The Mucker, The Mad King,* and *The Eternal Lover.* (The Ballantine editions of Burroughs in the 1990s are claiming, "It is conservative to say . . . that of the translations into 32 known languages, including Braille, the number [of his books] must run into the hundreds of millions.")

1913: The nexus of the Armory Show is exhibited at the Art Institute of Chicago in March and April, where the ridicule exceeds New York's (the Institute's director quietly slips out of town beforehand). There are a few lonely advocates. One of them writes in the *Sunday Tribune* of April 6: "A number of protests against the present international exhibit have been printed in the newspapers. . . . The present critic, being one of those who, after seeing the exhibition in New York, strongly advised its being shown in Chicago, believes these protests to be ill-advised."

It's Harriet Monroe, Champion of Revitalizing Winds. And she'll write in *Poetry*: "The old prosody is a medieval left-over, as completely out of relation with the modern scientific spirit as astrology would be if solemnly enunciated from the summit of Mount Wilson. All the old terms should be scrapped."

In the Cass Street office, she lifts that Pegasus paperweight: *so* heavy! Such an impossible chunk of gravity! And yet somehow, it's flying.

If time is linear, art is linear: narrative, perspective and horizons. Knowledge is linear: lines of books. / If time is cyclical, art is circular. / If witches are possible, witches are actual: best set white-hot embers at their soles! / A culture's understanding of "gravity" is manifest in its scientific texts and in its architects' imaginations, equally—in its angels and its warships. / When a model exists, experience fits that model. / Who we love, we love because of what we love already (or what we don't). / The battle every day is versus Randomness, and this we face with the same assurance by which we fashion gods and sexpots, saints and serpents, out of the infinite chaos of the stars.

In Carl Barks's justly famous saga *Lost in the Andes,* Donald Duck (the Museum of Natural Science's "fourth assistant janitor") uncovers a long-forgotten stash of square eggs ("Think of how easily they could be packaged and stored," a magnate says at Interglobal Eggs, "they would stack like bricks!"). Soon Donald, accompanied by triad nephews Huey, Dewey, and Louie, is off to Peru in search of the "region of the mist," and there they find the home of the eggs, Plain Awful, a lost-to-civilization hidden empire of (yes) cubic-bodied men and women, and cubic-bodied hens. The buildings are cubes. The loincloths: tablet-looking squares. The eggs, if they go bad, will cause a discomforting "ailment in which the gastric ducts tie themselves into square knots." Food is a cube on a square plate. Hats are little boxes. *Mais oui,* circles are taboo, and the gum-chewing nephews in their innocence blow three very sacrilegious bubbles, leading to many a plot conundrum, until the happy finale (everybody friends again, the ducks instruct the pleased Plain Awfulians in square dance).

Show me a year, and I'll show you a human need to systematize its contents. Show me eternity, and I'll show you a human need for "years."

1995: I drive the fourteen hours to Chicago. I'm me: before I stop at my mother's house (and really, it's on the way) I pass the offices of *Poetry,* on Walton Street now, and I nod in acknowledgment: it's been ceaselessly singing for eighty-three years, for over three generations' shaped breath.

And then I take the Outer Drive to Foster and, for three or four minutes, I idle at the lake. The air is clear today, as if squeegeed clean, and even so, the distant x I stare at has a viscousness about it. What tomorrow-sky is in the sky, is chipping away for release with its one-atom egg-tooth? Clear, the air. But weighted, and active, and involuted: a lung.

You see? "Breath," "lung." My mother is coughing herself away in respiratory units. And I'll sleep in the basement under that sound, and I'll visit her chemotherapist on Wednesday, and I'll wake from my sleep with my heart like a fist at my sternum, and I'll smile reassuringly for her as the burn of pain takes over another inch she abdicates, and I'll utter the usual pieties, and I'll see the year this way, this only way, and I'll form everything into that seeing.

One night, I step outside for a quick fresh breeze. I start to hum: a wail of a hum, a tiny, sad, and tuneless tune-to-sift-the-dirt-by.

I'm a mouth harp, that's what I am. Professor Z. is bent to me, is playing an intimate music.

Snapping pennants! Vendors waving sugar-wafers and wursts!

At Griffith Field in Los Angeles, Georgia "Tiny" Thompson Broadwicke makes her final inspection of every last buckle and strap.

The year is 1913. She's about to become the first woman ever to parachute from an airplane.

The excitement tongues her skin.

Her name is going to live forever.

# Fuller

1.

She worked with burnt hands. Burnt, in a way, from the inside out. The tips were fine-cracked like old paintings. And she'd been working today, again, from even before the first blood-colored light of dawn rode along the hosed slops of the market gutters. Now, hours later, the air in the shed, gassy from the cauldrons, swelled the delicate skin inside the nose, was furry on her shoulders like a stole. And so she lay her face on the pinewood table, resting in its inevitable coating of coal dust and iron grit. . . .

The dream was the same, although—well, *thinner* this time, since she wasn't fully asleep. But it was the meteor all right. It flared across the darkness in her head, a lovely thing of tons, that was giving itself away by turning to light, until only a thimbleful remained.

That last irreducible splat of metal landed somewhere out of seeing. Some people—a few, and she was one—began a desperate search, devoting themselves completely to its finding: a flurried dream-montage of shovels, steam-powered digging contraptions, fever-dampened brows.

But at the same time as she was concentrating wholly on the earthbound search, her dream-self saw that the light stayed on, a bright thing with a clear form, in the otherwise flat black sky. It was a giant flame, a kind of Bunsen-burner flame with its recognizable spearhead shape, but then that seemed to break, reform, and take on a nimbus: more like the flame at an altar, in front of the niche where a totem spirit looked down. . . .

It billowed—the nimbus, undoing itself like radiant veils fanned out from a dancer's hips. The flame was a lily. It blossomed, fragile, gold-white. . . . It was butterfly wings. It was butterfly wings. *Flame and lily and butterfly wings. . . .*

And then, as always, Marie Sklodowska Curie woke, reaching for the condenser plates, syringes, and electrometer.

The shed they called their lab was just that—an abandoned shed in the yard of the School of Physics and Chemistry, 42 rue Lhomond. Its glass roof couldn't completely keep the rain out, and its feeble row of windows did little toward freshening the gases from their chemical vats in the yard, that would enter the shed itself and build up in a yellow block over their benches. The German chemist Wilhelm Ostwald: "It was a cross between a stable and a potato cellar." It was her province—Pierre's was assimilating this labor—and here, ill-funded and virtually ignored by her scientific peers, she worked her huge piles of dark earth into something that glowed (in December of 1898 Pierre would name it: *radium*). "This miserable shed," she once allowed it to break through her reticence. Her days there could be over twelve hours long, and one winter the temperature sank to and stayed at six degrees above freezing.

But she'd been used to this from her days, not that far past, at the Sorbonne. Her student garret was six flights up, and she climbed them daily like a lab rat in an experiment, for science. In winter she carried the coals up for science, and when the ration of them gave out, she piled her coats on her blankets and shivered blue for science. The water in the washbasin froze overnight and she'd thaw it over her lamp-sized alcohol stove to boil the morning's egg.

And so she was prepared for this. The tons of pitchblende residues arrived from Bohemian mines, dumped into hillocks in the yard like a countryside landscape imported by some eccentric into the heart of Paris. From thousands of gallons of pitchblende liquor she'd distill—and this was her triumph—one lovely thimbleful, literally a thimbleful, of radium. Each batch was "ground, dissolved, filtered, precipitated, collected, redissolved, crystallized, recrystallized. . . ." Then more than once in that grimed-up clutter, the small row of porcelain crystallizing bowls would be knocked over, and the whole procedure started anew. You could look around the latch and see her over the fuming cauldrons, transferring products from one to another with an iron bar about as large as she was. "I would be broken with fatigue at the day's end," she once wrote.

And she wrote these were the "best and happiest years of our life." For science. When the heavy sacks from the Joachimstal factory first arrived, she rushed outside and slit the top one open in her eagerness with a little callus-grooming knife from the shop, and thrust her hands in like a child starting a castle at the beach, then running her fingers through the rich brown dust and pine needles, combing it, holding it up to her cheek. "The untroubled quietness of this atmosphere of research and the excitement of actual progress . . . I shall never be able to express the joy."

For this work, this demanding search for a final light, she dressed as she always had in black, or in the near-black "plain dark dress" that she was married in, and which could be worn to the laboratory "and not show dirt." She honeymooned in a black and practical pants-skirt that allowed her bicycling ease, and the black straw hat of those early years remained her single concession to headwear. Almost any diarist's memory of their first being introduced is "somber" . . . "quiet" . . . "composure" . . . "black." The three small linen-covered notebooks of 1897 were black (near a century later, these are still considered *dangerous to handle,* from the first contamination they received at her irradiated fingers). She called the family cat and it slunk to its post at the table leg: a stark little thing of uncompromising black and white.

Because of such garb and a lab routine so strict as to be ritual, it's easy to see her, schematized across the intervening years of popular legend and genre scene, as radium's nun. The Sister of Pure Experiment. Still, descriptions normally satisfy themselves with "plain"—you hear it about her, written in this city of fashionability, over and over—but never "severe." So, there was something. I think she hummed, applying a flame to a beaker's residue. She may have hummed a black song, something all the way back to the soil of Poland and down to the black of the bedrock, but I do think she hummed, at least sometimes, in the chill air, serving science.

A thimbleful.

At dinner one night, with a few guests making chitchat in the growing dark, Pierre reached into his waistcoat pocket and brought forth a tube of radium salt.

He held it by the glass lip. The air in the room was the deepening indigo-black of dusk, and the tube gave out its cool blue glow through that with eerie assurance. It highlighted random patches of cuff, of silver tongs, of veal, like a fox fire. Nobody's eyes could leave it. The maid was frozen midpour. He turned to her.

"This is the light . . . of the future!"

"Oh, Pierre," Marie Curie said drolly.

There are photographs, the two of them in their black clothes posing formally in that turn-of-the-century angular stance, or simply being captured side-by-side in concentration over a problem of electrical coiling, of adamant formulae not feeding into an answer . . . and their black clothes blend. They make a single body. There is no shadow, no fold, of division. She has many black buttons, a long row down her bosom, that aren't your business or mine.

On some nights they would return to the workshed, standing in the center of its cold, hard, bituminous floor, and be a single dark shape in the dark of the world, and hold their hands, and breaths. The containers were glowing. The bottles of liquid and capsules of crystals shone: faint luminous silhouettes. This she called "enchantment," though she was a woman of empirical method and measurement. Enchantment. All the world was cast in blackness, and here atomic hearts in their bowls shone out.

The everyday life went on. She shopped for a bicycle tire, she oversaw the roast, she signed for an order of sulfur.

She recorded. 5f. 50c. for a pair of woolen cycling stockings. 4f. 50c. for laundry. 50c. for omnibus travel.

She bathed the baby ("Irène is showing her seventh tooth down on the left"), she paid the nursemaid, she brought back an overripe cheese.

The price of three cups of coffee. A booklet of postage stamps. Some lids for the jam.

She purchased a roll of strainer-cloth. She filed the beakers away by size. She mended. She minded.

She answered her mail.

2.

Loie Fuller was writing a letter.

Loie Fuller, the dancer, "living poetry," "hands like the tips of birds' wings," "an enchantress." Her typical evening's bill: "the dance of pearls, in which she entwines herself in strings of pearls taken from the coffin of Heroditas; the snake dance, which she performs in the midst of a wild incantation; the dance of steel, the dance of silver, and dance of fright, which causes her to flee, panic-stricken, from the sight of John's decapitated head persistently following her with martyred eyes."

She began professional dance in burlesque, and in Buffalo Bill's Wild West Show. But her autobiography just refers to this as a period spent "out West." Now she danced at the Folies Bergère, and for countesses' parties. She danced in skirts 100 silken yards in circumference, manipulated by sticks. She commanded a brisk, select platoon of electricians. Bankers wired her from overseas. Her name appeared on ladies' silk kerchiefs—surely one of the century's earliest star-referent marketing ploys. She danced forty-five minutes straight—fatigued so afterward that the management supplied assistants to carry her home. This was the routine for years.

> *The Dance of the Meteor.*
> *The Dance of the Flame.*
> *The Dance of the Lily.*
> *The Dance of the Butterfly Wings.*

Her *Fifteen Years of a Dancer's Life* is filled with the breathy exclamation of long-protracted girlhood (people and objects are often "exquisite," two or three to a page) and with a charmingly histrionic feel for reportage:

"I am astounded when I see the relations that form and color assume. The scientific admixture of chemically composed colors, heretofore unknown, fills me with admiration, and I stand before them like a miner who has discovered a vein of gold, and who completely forgets himself as he contemplates the wealth of the world before him.

"But to return to my troubles."

And she does.

"All that evening I never stopped emitting little groans like those of a wounded animal . . . I was cut to the very quick."

"I cannot describe my despair. I was incapable of words, of gestures. I was dumb and paralysed."

"I trembled all over. Cold perspiration appeared on my temples. I shut my eyes."

"I hated them wildly, and I fell into convulsive tremblings, which shook me from head to foot."

Often, so adventure-crammed is her calendar, this dramatic reaction seems earned, as in "Cologne, where I had to dance in a circus between an educated donkey and an elephant that played the organ. My humiliation was complete." At other times it's the humdrum that's inexplicably fraught with excitement: at an agent's office "I said in a whisper to my mother: 'I am going to knock on the door.' She turned pale, but I had no choice in the matter. My head was in a whirl." She actually did knock, too. "Even if I ran the risk of heart failure."

Ah, but all Loie suffers, she suffers for her Art. She's still very young when she studies herself in the first translucent silk gown, the sun highlighting her body. "This was a moment of intense emotion. Unconsciously I realized that I was in the presence of a great discovery, one which was destined to open the path which I have since followed. Gently, almost religiously, I set the silk in motion, and I saw that I had obtained undulations of a character heretofore unknown." What were they like? Ordinary folk will never know. "You have to see it and feel it. It is too complicated for realization in words."

"I wanted to go to a city where, as I had been told, educated people would like my dancing and would accord it a place in the realm of art." Educated people did. With an awesome intensity, educated people did.

"When I came on the stage each spectator threw a bunch of violets at me. It took five minutes to gather up the flowers. When I was ready to leave the theatre, the students took my horses out of the shafts and drew my carriage themselves, shouting 'Vive l'art! Vive La Loie!'"

"Some days later I was engaged for a performance that was to take place at the hotel in honor of a Russian grand duke, two kings and an empress."

"Just at this time there was presented to me a viscount, who laid claim to my heart and hand."

"On returning to the Hotel Sands, the most beautiful hotel in the city, I found there the municipal orchestra come to serenade me."

Or a party at which "Caruso sang. The courtyard of the hotel had been transformed into a lake, and the host and his guests dined in gondolas."

Most tender and comic both, I think, is the secret, ardent admirer who declares himself by revealing his all: his butterfly collection. "There were 18,000 of them. He pointed out four in particular, and told us he had bought the whole lot for the sake of those, because they looked like me."

In another room are "sixty-two Turners. . . . Finally he came near to me and then, embracing the hall with one big sweep of the hand, said: 'These are your colors. Turner certainly foresaw you when he created them.'"

Art, you see. Art.

Loie first arrived in Paris in 1892. Marie Sklodowska, 1891; she'd struggled her country girl's luggage onto a platform at the Gare du Nord and the steam from the train, as thick as bunting, was still in her hair a day later as she walked the hill above the Sorbonne. She was like a bag packed full of Poland. She couldn't follow spoken French. But here were the laboratory benches and library shelves of her waking dreams. "A new world opened to me, the world of science." She made no friends. "If sometimes I felt lonely, my usual state of mind was one of calm and great moral satisfaction." That year, it was calculus and physics; the next, elasticity and mechanics. The notes are exact and must have been exacting. In 1893, when she finished her kinematics and electrostatics studies and went on to her final examination, to take first place as *licenciée en physique,* Loie Fuller was also transplanting her chosen learning to Gallic soil. The sun through Notre Dame's famous windows "enchanted me more than anything else . . . I quite forgot where I was. I took my handkerchief from my pocket, a white handkerchief, and I waved it in the beams of colored light, just as in the evening I waved my silken materials in the rays of my reflectors." This fervent rapture, however, displeases a watchful cathedral attendant, who leads the young danseuse back out: "To be brief he dropped me on to the pavement." The world is rich in schools and lessons.

Of Loie's learning, of Loie's theory of historical verisimilitude. . . . She's asked about her claim to recreate the ancient dances of the Hindus and Egyptians. "There are very few documents treating of the subject, but it seems to me that it should be easy," she answers in a snap, "if one put oneself in the state of mind that prompted the dances in times past, to reproduce them today with similar action and movement. If the custom still existed of dancing at funerals, a little reflection will show that the dances would have to suggest and express sadness, despair, grief, agony, resignation and hope." I see a board of French archaeologists shudder at these assumptions—it passes down the line of them one at a time, like the shimmy of second-string Folies chorines in a sensual-comic glissando. . . . Or would they applaud and shower their novice scholar with nosegays? Likability was an aura about her. Admit it: you're coming to like her. The most extraordinary assemblage liked her.

There was, it seems, this empathy. At sixteen she inveigles her way to a closed performance of Sarah Bernhardt's. From somewhere in the audience: "I believe I understood her soul, her life, her greatness. She shared her personality with me." Later, though still a stranger to the language, she meets Alexandre Dumas. "Instead of taking one of his hands I grasped both emphatically. From this time on a great friendship, a great sympathy, subsisted between us, although we were unable to understand each other."

One night (by now she's conversant in French) the astronomer Flammarion, cartographer of Mars and founding father of *L'Astronomie,* is among the crowd in her dressing room. Dumas is also present:

" 'Is it possible that the two most distinguished personalities in Paris are not acquainted with each other?'

" 'It is not so remarkable,' replied Dumas, 'for, you see, Flammarion dwells in space, and I am just a cucumber of the earth.'

"'Yes,' said Flammarion, 'but a little star come out of the West has brought us together.'"

Rodin tours Loie through his "temple of art." The Princess of Romania feels a sympathetic bond before her guest has spoken three sentences: "'Do you think that a princess should always be cold and ceremonious when she receives a stranger? Well, so far as I am concerned, you are not a stranger at all. After having seen you in your beautiful dances it seems to me that I am well acquainted, and I am very glad indeed that you have come to see me.'"

She came to see them, or they came to see her. The one would almost inevitably ensure the other. This was Paris, 1904, and bountiful with human stars in a way Flammarion's nighttime skies could never really match. They dazzled. Want it or not, the lines of constellations would be established between them. Rumor. Handbills. The more sensational press. Loie Fuller was writing a letter.

Everybody was talking about it, "radium" this and "radium" that. Perhaps it could be used to light a costume from a blackened stage? She would need enough for—oh, ten yards to start. . . . The table's candle flame was prismed to a dozen dancing harem girls, crystal and gold in her inkwell. They would be flattered. She would be flattered. They would picnic together and talk in one exuberant voice about Art. Monsieur and Madame Curie, she began. . . .

"Refused, she experimented with a phosphorescent pigment which blew part of her hair off and caused her landlord to evict her."

But exchange of letters continued. Should you care to meet. . . . Yes, very much so. . . . They met. There was this empathy.

3.

I go to bed thinking two expatriate women walking a Paris street . . . there's an organ-grinder, just like in that grainy, ebullient photograph by Atget . . . and the door to an absinthe bar, with luscious female seraphs framing the fanlight. . . . A drizzle has left the air sweet. One woman uses her hands, as if molding her very American French in front of her, tucking it here, adorning it there. . . . The other's hands are clasped behind her—the way her hair is in a bun has become a model for her body—and every now and then there's just an understanding *oui,* and a brief smile like a secret dossier eked open for a peek. . . .

Then I drift into sleep with them, true to my wife already asleep beside me, but sleeping with them, too, nonetheless. They're speaking Spanish now. They're walking the streets of Paris, rues A through Z, and speaking Spanish. One's a man. It's crazy. Sleep does that. Now I'm on the deck of a ship. We're watching the dolphins. One of us is the man, and one the lady, but which is which? "They make a dotted line of the sea," she says or he says or I say—in Spanish, although the high-school Spanish I really know is relegated strictly to saying I had fried eggs for breakfast. "That must be the contract God signs every day." It's a good rejoinder. And then we go visit a castle together, the organ-grinder's whiny tootle fading in and out and in again. . . .

Sleep does that. I remember when I was in seventh grade Joel Rosenblatt showed me his father's ham radio. All of those voices, all of those strangers, all night long in so many languages, thousands of miles apart yet overlapping on the frequency band . . . all that, and one man plugged into reception.

Conchita Jurado was a penniless, gray-haired, bespectacled school-teacher, who during her sixty-seven years led a fabulous double-life that kept Mexico's high society spinning. Masquerading as the elegant Don Carlos Balmori, the wealthiest living Spaniard, famed duelist, big-game hunter, owner of railways and castles in Spain, Conchita began her career by disguising herself as a young suitor and appearing before her own father to ask for her hand. As Don Carlos, she was the center of a *mysterious and exclusive society known as Las Balmori, whose members were those who had been duped by Don Carlos. The club membership fostered the Don Carlos reputation by passing out $100 and $1000 checks. Each year now the memory of Don Carlos is revived (in December) with a pilgrimage to Conchita's grave.*

—*Terry's Guide to Mexico,* 1926

Halfway through the night I wake. My wife is speaking gibberish. Again, in her sleep, the neurons discharging through language, as they must do for the zealously mystic who "speak in tongues." I've seen films of them, flopping like fish on the floor, the gods taking over their speech.

And I've read studies—how, panculturally, the gibberish has a pattern, of chemical storage and release. If you plug into that deepest frequency, if primal jack and primal outlet meet in the world of molecular structures and fit, perhaps the language opens up into something shimmering and accessible. Perhaps two women, who shouldn't by any of this world's rules have any ground in common, walk a Paris street in intimate conversation we'd find impossible, opaque.

On a level of chemicals or gods, my wife is surely saying something of vast importance—her voice is plaintive, her forehead is trying to make a fist. I think in that world her sister is dying again—thirty-four years old, my age. I think she dies again every night, and will for a while. I think if I knew the secrets of infant grammar shared worldwide despite the parents' language, if I could crack the code of schizophrenic babble in locked wards going back to the first dark raving we made in the caves. . . . But I don't know Spanish, even.

And how many nights did Conchita Jurado wake midsyllable, not sure, in the surrounding confusion of insectwhirr and starclutter, which of her selves she was, and who'd begun that sentence?

Now I realize why the Spanish *r* and *tilde* colored the chatter of my Francophilic dreamstreets—I'd been going over that snippet in *Terry's Guide,* a note for a possible poem to follow my Curie prose piece, and it stuck in the gym-sole bottom of my brain. Sleep does that. It's crazy. I think if. . . .

"The clock in the radio." Now it's come to words I know, and soon (this much of the pattern I understand) she'll quiet speechlessly back to true sleep. For these few moments, though, it's the clock in the radio, over and over, whatever that is, wherever, and she wants it desperately much. The clock. In the radio.

Something to do about Time. About the reception of Voices.

On any day at Niagara Falls, the crowd shows a wild variety. I was there on one of those rare unexpected springlike days in December, and the wall of spray at the Rainbow Falls admitted a perfect arc of the spectrum, each of its colors in strident declaration. The couples kept coming: in turbans, in leather jackets, in tuxes and low-cut gauze concoctions, one pair was a business suit and a kimono. . . .

But on the Canadian side you can tour the tunnels cut into the very rock, and for this you need to buy a ticket, take the elevator down and, in a long and smelly locker room especially designed for nothing but metamorphosis, suit up in clumsy rubber.

They're solid yellow or solid black, and all alike from hood to boots. Remember grammar-school street-crossing guards, out in the rain? The suit is enormous—it's like a small room about you, a room in the shape of a fireplug. The cuff of its sleeve is guaranteed to hit exactly the middle of your palm, and you're a child again, in second grade, in a shirt too large, as if everything wasn't anyway in those days made to diminish you. . . .

Your fingers show, and a strip of eyes—it's all that's left of your earlier self. Then you walk out into the world of your duplicates. . . . This was more amazing a sight for me than the water, though that's amazing enough, the endless tons of lace, the pummel of lace that could kill you.

The tunnels are dim and always vibrating in the roar of rock being violently worn. The air there is water, the water there is the air, it's that simple. By this time you're one of a hundred comic-book sperm up their designate tubule—each alike and each carrying, deep inside, an individuation.

You look. Now anyone could be someone else.

I think that's true, or partly true, for all of us, and what we call "friendship" or saying "we felt like sisters" or "it's as if I could read his mind" is the everyday version of more extreme occasion. But first it requires this facelessness stage, these tunnels, a swim inside the primary origin-goop.

I think Conchita Jurado would know this. I think she's been there, often, and back. I think there's an atom of this Niagara Falls between a man and a woman in any real marriage, beyond the honeymoon suite and the tacky photo of both of you loonily waving from inside a fake barrel going over fake water's long plunge . . . one white, commingling osmosis-atom of this Niagara Falls.

She wakes in the Mexican morning and knows intuitively who she'll be today—some regal Blue, or a passionate Red deep-shading into Scarlet, or a domestic Yellow. . . . She knows, and dances with great elation into a room where grapefruit halves are scrubbing the air with their scent. She's spent the night, again, in a place where colors blend back to the first White Light, and now she knows enough to start to know how it breaks, into faces.

Although she's not anyone yet, for me—I place her note in a pile, under the clipping in which the poet H.D. is on deck watching dolphins, I have more immediate needs. I've been writing awhile already—writing Fuller, writing her letters—and when I pass the bedroom door on the way to my study, I see that Morgan's awake. The hair close in at her temples is damp from a tough night.

"You were talking again. 'The radio in the clock.'"

"Oh, Albear," she says, just that, and rubs it all out of her eyes, and is fully returned.

That's her name for me: Albear.

Her sister's dead of cystic fibrosis at thirty-four, my age, my calendrical might-have-been, my other. Death makes a kind of sensitivity in the living, and you think that way for a while. For Morgan it's more extreme, the love having been extreme. She has her own, genetic, might-have-been she has to learn to live with.

The others are everywhere. How many angels can dance in the head of a man? The others are everywhere, the way we're always walking through thousands of radio voices though rarely picking much up. It doesn't require death. It might be just a husband kissing a wife and there isn't a clear-cut border. Simply, two women might walk down a Paris street. It's a springlike day in December. They're happy, though only one is obviously carefree; the other is like a tune in a music box painted pure black and her friend is figuring how the crank works. She points, with a whoop, to where it streaks cleanly out of a cloud.

"In English we call this *Rain. Bow.*"

4.

"In Polish, *tęcza.*"

She started naming things in Polish as they caught her eye, the cart of mannequins wheeling toward a boutique, the flavored ices in the vendor's wagon by color, an organ-grinder in his crumpled amoeba-shaped cap, she gave each name and then a pause that pushed up against the name like a mark of punctuation, so it was as if she were reading out figures on a chart. But Loie started to give the English as a counterpoint, and made it into a singsong, and in a moment they were skipping down the twisting byway hand-in-hand, singing bilingual duets, a book stall, a bicycle, a string of beads, a puddle, a splash, an oops, for this we say "oops."

They sat on a park bench letting their hems dry. Loie knew some of Poland's famed, exiled women. She'd met the actress Modjeska, the Countess Wolska. . . . It was in her student days, they seemed so lost to her now, that Marie Curie cut herself off from even the meaningful walks with other Warsaw students, rambling the Latin Quarter with

Poland's gilded saints and feisty sausages filling their talk. . . . It returned to her now, and for a little while she couldn't do more but sit
with its sweet weight pressing down. They watched a corner hustler
switch his pea confusingly under three silver cups, and a group of
tourists guessing. But the two of them were quiet, Loie seeming to understand this rush of reverie.

When they walked on, there were other topics: light, how light ex-
ulted a woman working it through her silks; how there would sometimes be a phial of light in the shed at night like a single finger caught
pointing the way to an Answer of Answers. . . . Loie felt lifted a mile, to
be taken as an equal by someone like this, to talk of—she'd write it this
way in her diary—"deep things." Marie Curie felt opened an inch.
She'd even let her visitor pin a flower to her blouse. For what they
meant, they were equal—that mile, that inch—and the two walked
back to the Curies'.

Loie wouldn't be welcomed into the laboratory; it wasn't a mixing
like that. But she was served a decent wine in the parlor at 108 Boule-
vard Kellermann, Pierre uncorking the neck with all of the naïve flair
of a child magician's first try at the rabbit and the hat. Then there were
little soulful cheeses and one plate apiece of sardines.

Loie told her adventures until the sun set: when she was stranded,
without a penny or crust of bread, at the Russian border ("I walked up
and down in the darkness like a caged beast"). When, on a lark, she
locked a testy French reporter in her stateroom, effectively kidnapping
him to America ("At first he protested, not without vehemence, but he
soon cooled off and gaily assumed his part in the rather strenuous
farce into which we had precipitated him"). When she arranged the
escape of the lovely actress Hanako, from a low-life Antwerp dive
("where she had to sing and dance for the amusement of sailors").
When "a magnificent negro, six feet high, who looked like some prince
from the Thousand and One Nights" showed her the Senegalese sunset prayer—and, as the sun *was* setting then, the Curies' parlor saw a
demonstration of those sinuous prostrations. Such things! Who could
imagine?

For their turn, after much prodding, Pierre read a paper. "This is special, Loie, for us. Pierre inscribed a copy of this very study and made it a present to me, the first present, after we met. Pierre?" He stood and cleared his throat. "On symmetry in physical phenomena: symmetry in an electric field and in a magnetic field," he began. Loie was in heaven.

It was late enough then, time to send Irène to sleep and for Loie to meet her carriage.

"Irène, dis bonne nuit à Mademoiselle Loie."

"Bonne nuit, Mamselle."

"Bonne nuit."

That April, having returned from a tour of Vienna, she took them to visit Rodin.

The short, bull-muscled man extended his hand and Loie introduced the three to one another, the names, and then a trading of everyday *bonjour,* and then a hush, as if the gate to a tunnel of silence. The sculptor motioned, a cock of his overlarge and overbearded head, and they followed up the hill to his studios, the "temple."

These were the rooms in which Rodin had naked models wander freely, to catch each tense, each blued-over bruise's rise and relax, each nipple's stiffen or sleep, in absolute candor. He'd said, "People say I think too much about women. Yet after all, what is there more important to think about?" He'd said, "No good sculptor can model a human figure without dwelling on the mystery of life." He'd said, "The mouth, the luxurious protruding lips sensuously eloquent—here the perfumed breath comes and goes like bees darting in and out of a hive." One of his Balzacs held a kingly hard-on in its hand.

And here he was, silently pointing to this small bronze of a dancer, to that wax study of Eve, to the life-size couple in such an erotic clasp, the veins in the marble surely held blood . . . and running his hands across the stone, the dimples in stone, the swelling hips of stone, until they were flesh, until he wasn't polishing but kneading. . . .

Was she shocked, this quiet daughter of Warsaw? *Yes.* Was she quickened, was something in her raised and made raw by these figures pushing at life as if *it* were the stone? *Yes.* Did she walk the halls with Loie hand-in-hand, like sisters? *Yes.* But Loie still, and only, called her "Madame Curie," isn't that so? *Yes.* Were they two studies of one woman? *Yes, in different media, by different artists, under different stars.*

"In the two hours we passed in the temple hardly ten words were spoken."

"Missyoor, M'dahm Cur*eeey.*"

They both ran from the kitchen to the parlor. She was on the sofa, sitting in the posture of *The Thinker,* eyes enormously crossed.

That night she insisted on dancing for them, a private show for two, "since your labors will not permit the theater." She would do three numbers "providing Madame will assist me in wardrobe preparations between the acts, yes?" (1) A medley of her most famous creations. (2) *The Harlequinade,* a comic number still in preparation ("If smiles bud *here,* my friends, at the Folies they will blossom."). (3) *The Dance of Science-Light,* in special tribute to her hosts. "There will be no orchestra, nor my intricate light arrangements. But you will allow me to place the lamps like so . . . ? Our spirits will know the music."

His wife returned in a few minutes, sitting next to him. (The warm quip from their friends at the School of Physics: that they sat like the halves of a balanced equation.) A minute more, and Loie appeared.

The space of the lucent parabolas she defined was disproportionate to the space of the parlor; every kick and swivel she performed had been invented for different dimensions. Even so, an eerie beauty entered the room with her; and in her floating sashes and sleeves, as they circled the sofa as if with wings or whipped at her ankles like egg whisks, air and oil light were wed phantasmagorically. At times the light in the colored silks took on the solid shapeliness of Rodin's hand-sized bronze dancers, like attendant putti about her in a cloud.

She was a meteor, then a flame, then a lily, then butterfly wings. . . . A dream came back to Marie Curie, not whole cloth, but a tatter of dream. Something . . . "A premonition of tonight," she thought. And then rethought it, in more appropriate metaphor, "A rehearsal of tonight's performance." Pierre let go her hand and she went to help with the alien underpinnings.

"*The Harlequinade.* The clown imagines herself a regent, and struts to her own discomforture." Yes, they did smile. She was a tatterdemalion pixie-toes in pratfalls now, was bundles of motley thrown in arabesques. The first performance had left them unsure of proper response, but when Pierre let go her hand this time they both clapped like children at carnival doings. He heard his wife laugh all the way out of the parlor and into the changing room, it might have been Irène with a playmate.

Again, Pierre was alone. The final number now, *The Dance*—what was it?—*of Science-Light.* A high kick out of the doorway, and the hands upraised to make a single timeless, faceless incense-smoke of the body, a gray gauze crazily spinning and seeming to rise—faster, fervent, almost clumsy in fervency, very clumsy and very fervent, throwing energy off in radiant chunks, the face a faintish glow in mist and then the arms dropping heavily down and she curtsied in front of him, still by himself, and breathless from her effort. "Marie."

5.

But by then Pierre couldn't applaud without pain. As early as 1898 the aches had started, the lethargy and the reddened, tender fingertips. He was put on a special diet for "his rheumatism." She had gone in for a lung examination and sputum analyses.

Lifting a test tube was painful. Dressing himself was very painful, at times. Nobody knew. They were the first. On June 19, 1903, Pierre had addressed the Royal Institution in London, summarizing their radium experiments, and adding to this with tricks from a tube: its light, its altering a wrapped photographic plate. A week later, he wrote to thank the Institution—his fingers could hardly grip the pen. Fifty years later, the presence of the radium could still be detected in parts of the Institution, which needed decontamination.

Her weaknesses came and went and reappeared. His legs trembled. A colleague in radium, Friedreich Giesel, discovered his breath alone touched off an electroscope. The violet marks of burn continued appearing. A touch could do it. These were occupational hazards, little purplish medals won in the quest toward explicating the atom. Pierre had a permanent scar, he spent long bouts of spasm in bed. It was his rheumatism; it happened "because of the damp in our shed."

They were the first. And so nobody knew: about the clocks of cancer it set ticking in the marrow, about the shredding of the fibers of the lungs. Expectant mothers today, if they work in the radium industry, are cautioned not to expose their bodies to greater than .03 rem per week. But she must have been absorbing one full rem per week, a lady in a black dress pouring from flask to flask. The gamma-radiation tests were in the future, the radon tests were in the future, far in the future, and nobody knew. On December 11, 1903: "My husband has been to London to receive the Davy Medal which has been given to us. I did not go with him for fear of fatigue." They were going to have their second child. From flask to flask. In August that year, on a bicycling trip, in a cheap room in a seaside hotel, she broke into early labor. It was dead—a girl—in an hour. "There is no direct evidence for the cause."

In November that year, they won the Nobel prize. The 70,000 francs would support new radium research. The rector of the Academy of Paris was in touch: Pierre was to have his own lab, with a small support staff, and his wife "would receive a salary for the first time in her career." But for the banquets and the autograph hounds and the agents who wrote of lecture tours and the melodramatic headlines in the press, they had no time. They were weak, they were busy; they needed to seek, in strictest purity, the submost script on the blueprints of creation. Marchand, the French Minister in Stockholm, received the prize on their behalf. "One would like to dig into the ground somewhere to find a little peace."

They dug in, they worked. She became pregnant again and bore Eve, who was healthy. "The children are growing well," she writes her brother in 1905, and goes on: how they'd cry, and how she'd rock them quiet. Robert Reid, her biographer, adds: "But they were not the center-point of her life." For feminist causes she had no patience. They both refused to reap a penny of personal gain from their labor. There were bits below the bits below the pulses circling in an atom, and they dug in, and they worked, at what she called, in the early days, "our legitimate scientific dream."

They dreamed, they dug in, they worked. He studied effects of radioactive emanations on mice and guinea pigs—the pulmonary congestions, the weakening leukocytes. That his body was also a guinea pig's for science, his papers never hinted. Nobody knew. What might have happened, given time, to this upright man with his life on fire, nobody will ever know. There wasn't time. On April 19, 1906, while crossing Rue Dauphine in an afternoon rain, he slipped in the path of a horse cart. The driver, a Louis Manin, was weeping as the gendarmerie arrived. His left rear wheel had smashed Pierre Curie's head into fifteen or sixteen pieces.

"The fragile brain," he once called it. Now it was on view in a run of gutter water and blood. She took the news and later identified the body with that reserve the world had come to expect. There were no tears for the journalists from her, nor did her own hurt hands torment themselves in public.

But alone in the upstairs room, she started a diary, really the first love letters she'd ever attempted. She wrote to the dead man. "What a terrible shock your poor head has felt, that I have so often caressed in my two hands. I kissed your eyelids which you used to close so that I could kiss them. . . ." She led her sister Bronia into the bedroom. There was a packet wrapped in waterproof paper and in it, the bloodstained clothes. Dried flesh was stuck to the garments. She started kissing these little discolored remains of her husband, tenderly, repeatedly, until Bronia grabbed them and threw them into the fire. . . . And now, she allowed herself tears.

"Within two weeks of the death she was dealing with correspondence concerning the future of her laboratory, and within a month her laboratory notebook starts again . . . precipitating, purifying, observing emanations, and always measuring—hour after hour."

This is the work for which she was awarded a second Nobel prize—the first person ever so double-awarded. The simple initial picture of the atom's innards was being filled in. The International Radium Standard was being methodically formulated. Radium and polonium were established in the periodic table of elements. These were the years of her giving definitive shape to the start of the nuclear age, and the eyes of these years would see her as the autocratic, unyielding prima donna in black—"not a very nice person," as a British physicist put it.

Her own eyes would fail—cataracts, four precarious operations and at their end a thick pair of pebble glasses. The ureter infection. The open sores. A worker in her labs in the old days, Demenitroux, dead at forty-four of pernicious anemia. Theodore Blum, a New York dentist, recognized the cancerous jaws of woman after woman: years of licking the tips of brushes dipped in radium paint, for watches with luminous hands. He named it "radium jaw." The bad news wouldn't stop, or her fears, or her conscience.

Irène was a woman now, her own doctoral thesis presented successfully at the Sorbonne. These were, in a way, the years of fulfillment. At the 1911 Solvay Conference, two solemn rows of civilization's most eminent living physicists are posed for the camera—twenty-nine men and a woman. She and Einstein stand (four faces away from each other) in the back. Jacob Bronowski: "Here the great age opens. Physics becomes in those years the greatest collective work of art of the twentieth century." And here, at the fifth of the Conferences, in 1927, one year before the death of Loie Fuller, she and Einstein have moved to the first, the seated, row. There are twenty-eight men and a woman. The International Radium Standard Unit was, and is, the *curie*.

"35f.25c. for the black (lace) dress in which to go to meet the President of the United States. . . ."

But there are moments when something else is required, something other.

Loie had written: breast cancer. All of the surgeons wanted to cut it off, but one, who said that radium needles would surely cure it. What, please, what did Madame recommend?

—Nothing helpful, nothing lucid, only the name of her own physician, Régaud, and her love, and her wishes. The thank you was "tremblingly scrawled" to her: "Dear, dear friend. Once again in your debt."

She remembered . . . walking, the halls at Rodin's, Pierre on one side of her, Loie the other. Wasn't there something . . . *a pea*, beneath three silver cups, a seed, from one to the other. . . .

It was a warm night under a peach moon even her filmed-over eyes couldn't dim. It was an empathetic night. She felt so hopeless, and out in the garden she made her hands into a basket shape, for carrying such a burden. She bowed her shoulders low, and then bent to the ground with her lips in the cared-for grasses and sobbed and said his name to him in a soundless calling that tasted of dirt and early April green, and then she was up again, and facing the moon and whatever impossible powers peopled its darker side, and here was a fist for the moon, and here were two arms open to anything shining, anything bright that the sky had to offer her, even if it burned, the light could take her now, she dared it to, the light that was only a milk in her eyes but a coal in her gut could lift her if it wanted to, she was ready now. . . .

Irène looked out of the mullioned glass. It was something she had never seen before (although it had happened, once, before). Her mother was dancing.

> . . . *It seems to me that it should be easy, if one put oneself in the state of mind that prompted the dances in the past, to reproduce them today with similar action and movement. If the custom still existed of dancing at funerals, a little reflection will show that the dances would have to suggest and express sadness, despair, grief, agony, resignation and hope.*

6.

*Peter Van Eck was a more mysterious affair. She first met him in 1920
on the trip to Greece. At one point she called it "a conventional meeting
or voyage-out romance," but she never seemed very sure whether he really
appeared, or she dreamt him altogether or partially, or if he was a supernatural visitation. Moreover, he appeared to have had a double, whom
she called "the Man on the boat," who resembled Van Eck, but not closely
enough for certainty. The most interesting encounter occurs when, after
a nap in the afternoon, she goes out on deck, where she meets Van Eck.
Her uncertainty about him is described as ambiguously as possible, even
to the quality of light: "He is older—no, he must be younger. But it is
near-evening, it is this strange light. But the light is not strange," and so
on. Then they watch some dolphins together, swimming in "a curiously
unconvincing pattern."*

—Kenneth Fields, on the poet H.D.

"They make a dotted line of the sea," H. D. says.

"That must be the contract God signs every day," Van Eck says, if
he's there, or if he isn't there, or his double says or doesn't say. Anyway,
it's a good rejoinder.

They both lean on the rail awhile, fading in and out of the evening
light—as if being stitched through the light. Perhaps on the light's
other side, the effect is the same: they're there, then gone, and here for
a moment.

"Do you understand?" says Van Eck.

"*¿Quién sabe?*" she says back, in the voice of Conchita Jurado.
Although I only know Spanish enough to ask for two fried . . .

"Eggs?" It's the stewardess, waking me up.

Breakfast.

I'm in a plane

going home, from Vermont, where I've been for four strange days to give a reading of my work. I think I read well, the response was sweet, and afterward we ate Chinese in delicious, imperial portions. The weather was lovely enough to keep me delaying departure—the way the sky is a blue cream floating on top of those hills. But I knew it was time to go because I woke with my wife's face softly pressed against mine although I was alone in the bed, had been alone four nights a thousand miles away from her. You know what I mean. We all know, in ways and at times. I felt that gentle sleeping breathing of hers, and felt the wrinkle she gives behind it every few minutes. And so I knew, and I picked up my check and packed.

I do believe in a sloppily mystical way that people can share a face; or a face can travel beyond its body; or there is a single Face, of which *our* faces are pieces. Such stuff aside, there are Siamese twins. There are binary stars. Personae. There is a dancer in a role, and it doesn't end at her pores; we wouldn't want it any other way.

I think if all of these faces at 7:00 A.M. around me slurping coffee could be overlapped, we'd make white light—but first we'd need that closeness. There's a stepping-up of value through diminishment, as in: the amount of gold or gourmet truffle on the market; anything "cute"; or a plane as the distance around it increases. We taxi and lift, another clumsy tube of human cargo circling out of the Burlington Airport, and start to shrink by the 20,000 foot level, so compacted by endless space around us we must become the heaviest thing in the universe—only the eye of a deity could hold such weight, and even the eye of a deity couldn't keep our faces from blending. Smaller, and more transparent, and smaller—a single, sunny floater in the peripheral vision of God.

But there's another way to say it:

It was a warm night under a peach moon. It was an empathetic night. Loie signaled (a foot tap) and the first notes of *The Harlequinade* rose perkily from her flautist, then the piano came in. The crowd was large and very receptive, and after two dramatic acts they normally loved this wackier number. "The clown imagines herself a regent. . . ." She took a breath, leapt onstage

and felt all of the weight of age and lack of option on her shoulders. Now she knew she should be twirling—she saw the conductor, he started the twirling bit—but here she was, shaping her hands in a basket, for carrying such a burden. She bowed her shoulders low, and then bent to the stage with her lips in imagined grasses and sobbed and called a far-off name—the orchestra was puzzled now, but trying to pace her, slowing itself and deepening—and then she was up, and facing the moon and whatever impossible powers peopled its darker side, and here was a fist for the moon, the audience stunned by the energy, some of the women openly weeping and then a few of the men, and here were two arms open to anything shining, anything bright that the sky had to offer, her orchestra silent completely now and the audience starting to give voice to its feeling in a communal moaning, even if it burned, the light could take her now, she dared it to, then cheering although the dance wasn't done yet, on its feet like a single huge animal cheering, the light could lift her if it wanted to, yes, she was ready now . . .

and falling spent to her greatest applause, where we'll leave her

in notes for a poem I'm doing, 20,000 feet up. I file her brusquely away in a pile of scraps that keep slipping over my "tray-table"— documentation.

The Indian (also New Guinean and Philippine) fireflies flash in simultaneity—a dense swarm in a tree will go off as if comprising a single brain being charged by a single great thought; the lag from one to another is, at the most, 20 milliseconds. / Or how about fish? Of about 20,000 species, over 10,000 school. I've seen a school of 10 like shiny dimes, that moved as whole as a dollar bill. / There is communication we don't understand yet, bird to bird down a V, though our mouths go *oh*!, our cells go *oh*!, in its presence. In one experiment Russian scientists took a momma rabbit far offshore and deep, in a submarine. Colleagues slit the throats of her babies, one by one. Invariably, she set her electrodes registering like crazy at the proper second. / It can't be surprising a sleeping mother wakes in response to a cry from the crib and finds the first few beads of lactation have started already—Kathy tells me, Mimi, Janis, Joelle. / The novelist John Cowper Powys told Theodore Dreiser, on leaving his home, "I'll appear before you, right here, later this evening. You'll see me." Dreiser did, quite clearly, hours later—and right then phoned up Powys's house in the country, a leisurely train ride off. Powys answered. It can't be surprising. There is communication. / There is a traveling out of the body reported through time in a legacy library-large. August Strindberg believed the astral body of his third wife, Harriet Bosse, would arrive in his room at night and masturbate him. Other cases are less suspicious than this, or contain an intraverification; the monk Alphonsus Liguori, in 1774, reported sleeping and sending an astral projection four hours away, to Rome, where he said the pope had just died. The pope *had* just died, it turned out. And those who attended his final minutes "had seen and talked to Liguori, who led the prayers for the Pontiff." / It crosses death. Conan Doyle—whose Holmes is an exemplum of the rational, empirical process, skepticism, and model objectivity—received, through his wife Jean, letters from his dead son Kingsley "in childish scrawl." Yeats's wife Georgie did similarly—as if her pencil came from the wood of an ancient threshold between two worlds. Rosemary Brown transcribed new compositions by Liszt, Beethoven, Chopin, Brahms, Schubert, did a program for the BBC, and made a record: "Mrs. Brown is not a skilled musician; she does not even have a gramophone in her house" and yet "her" compositions "could be considered practically first quality by the particular composer." One frowns, one shakes one's head and continues to measure the den for linoleum tiles. But toward the end of his life, that consummate man of measurement, Monsieur Pierre Curie, researched spiritualism. X rays, radium, ectoplasmic appearances . . . they were one world then, for him, for others. On tour in Britain, Conan Doyle spoke to 150,000. *Of course* they half-believed. They dreamed. Some took the wafer on Sunday. Every one of them had turned around once, sure he was being watched, and he was, and you have, too, admit it. You would have bought a ticket. / It doesn't have to be so mystical, so much the rapping table or the clank in the night. I mean any kid alone in the playground talking to his invisible friends. I *know* they aren't there. You tell *him*. I had a dalmatian named PeeWee who could change his size a dozenfold at will. / The dwarf spy Richebourg, who could pass as a baby, and so smuggled messages out of the tumultuous France of 1789; arrived in a friendly house, he'd whip the dispatch out from his baby-blue quilt, politely burp, and light up a cigar. How many people was he, how many can anyone be? / The study *Sybil* "describes a total of 17 personalities" living in one crowded, fractured mind—there are about 100 cases of so-called "split personality" in psychiatric literature, from Mary Reynolds (1817) to now. / What inspired rapport does it take for an archaeologist, turning some lumpish inscrutable object of unknown use, to suddenly see it with Neolithic eyes and scream *lamp*! or *sickle sharpener*! / Everyone travels. A shaman lives "in his actual tribal world and in the sacred world of Primordial Beings" and writhes with it and says he flies, but everyone travels— you're here with me right now and we've come a long way, haven't we?

20,000 feet up.

There is this empathy.

Alhough I'd rather just say it this way: I'm a man coming home and I'd rather say just these two simple things:

I've checked out of a hotel, which is a stable state for an endless flux of bodies.

And I've had Chinese food. Those fortune cookies: little curled-up sleepers holding their common bits of tomorrow. They could be anyone.

Then Morgan's picking me up at the airport. Back home, I file the notes away. I'll start it tomorrow (I don't have a title yet) if an opening scene, some line from Curie, comes. But for now, I need to catch up with the last four days of my own life, which kept running here like a lamp left on, while I had another life, four days complete, in Vermont.

Phone messages, letters from friends . . . I'm hours at writing back to them.

"So. What was Vermont like? Poetry groupies?"

"Morgel. . . ."

That's what I call her: The Morgel.

After our holding each other, she drops off to sleep (she's worked a full day, then gone with me through luggage-grief at the American Airlines complaint desk). In a while I see her REMs—like eyes that are reading by Braille. She gets letters from people I'll never know, letters she'll never remember.

Then later, from out of her sleep: "Good night, Albear."

Bonne nuit. "Now,"

the poet Jon Anderson says,

> "In the middle of my life,
> A woman of delicate bearing gives me

Her hand, & friends
Are so enclosed within my reasoning
I am occasionally them."

I wake up. It's dark. I can't even see you beside me. I can't see me. I lie in this darkness awhile, and feel something thin and nearly weightless, a kind of film, on my face, and shaped to my face's arrangement of muscle perfectly. It must be I grow used to it after a while, or maybe it simply sinks in. Wasn't I going to turn to you and ask for the pen and paper, to take down jottings for my prose poem? It must be through my skin and in my blood by now, though just a few minutes have passed. I feel my lips make their first stretchy part of the night's accretion of sealants, and then it's my voice: "I'll need the condenser plates, syringes, and electrometer."

Farder to Reache

Kepler was born in 1571. He knew about as much of the night sky and its mysteries as anyone alive in his time. We might say his skull contained the sky of the sixteenth and early-seventeenth centuries, held it in place like a planetarium dome. Today we still haven't improved on his famous three Laws of Planetary Motion.

And yet the notion that the universe might be infinite—that there wasn't an outermost sphere of stars that bound it all in—terrified him, filled him with what he termed "secret, hidden horror. . . . One finds oneself wandering in this immensity in which are denied limits and center."

This is, of course, the dread of free verse, that one might fall into Whitman and free-float directionlessly forever. Whitman called himself "a Kosmos," and in "Song of Myself" the vision is of a creation whose parts are "limitless" and "numberless"—these words and their kin are used with manic glee and with a great intentionality. This is poetry's announcement of the given of twentieth-century astronomy: the universe is, so far as we know, unbounded.

But it isn't easy to walk through a day of fists and kisses, paychecks, diaper stains, tire jacks, and our building-block aspirations, with the mind fixed on infinity. Every year in beginning poetry classes hands startle up in protest of free verse: "it isn't poetry," which is metered and rhymed, and so is a kind of map of Kepler's universe.

John Donne's poems, for instance—he was born one year after Kepler. And he praises his lover by placing her at the center of an onion-ring sky: "so many spheres, but one heaven make," and "they are all concentric unto thee."

And yet as early as 1577—Kepler was only six years old—the British astronomer Thomas Digges undid the outer sphere, and published a vision of stars in endlessness: "Of which lights celestiall, it is to bee thoughte that we onely behoulde sutch as are in the inferioure partes. . . . even tyll our sighte being not able farder to reache or conceyve, the greatest part rest by reason of their wonderfull distance invisible unto us."

Perhaps infinity isn't discovered along a time line of gathering progress, but by certain sensibility, no matter when it lives.

In that land of simultaneous sensibility, I think that I could knock on Kepler's door and invite him out for some beers with Whitman. Really, he's flinging his cloak on now.

It's a foggy night as we sit around the veranda overlooking the lake. The sky is cloudy, and so are my two friends' faces—they don't know each other, are guarded, and rely on me to ease the conversation.

I do, though; or maybe it's the beer. It turns out we can shoot the shit all night, stein after stein, anecdote on anecdote, until the first light swarms over the water like thistledown on fire. Then the fog disappears—which is, of course, the day clearing its throat for clear speech.

The Space

1.

This is from when Eric still played with The Rhythm Rangers.

One night, in the lees of the night, when the show was over and everyone needed a little boozeola retanking, they drove out south to Snappy's Roadhouse. In the graveled lot, not caring to keep it secret at all, a man was beating a woman. She was no lithe doe of a creature, but he was huge and had the bloodlust. Eric uses the word "Neanderthal." They could hear each blow land distinctly, like a live fish being whipped against brick.

Now Eric is big but mild. "I'm not brave, so I must have been drunk," he says. "I stepped on out of the group—we'd been gawking there dumbfounded really—and cleared my throat and said, 'You shouldn't do that.' He turned around—well, there I was, standing in my vanilla-white stage Stetson, and my bandanna, and fringe, and all—and he snarled, 'Who the *hell* are you?' And I snapped back—I don't know where it came from—'I'm Death! I've dealt out death a hundred times and I'm prepared to deal death a hundred more!'"

At that, the stunned lunk falls to his knees and, in some drunk pathetic display of last-stand anger that already had the soft edge of defeat about it, starts flinging handfuls of gravel and dirt at Eric.

Ever since being told this anecdote, I've carried him—*Neanderthalensis denim*—as a cartoon totem of what I've witnessed dozens of similar times, and seen unsurely peeking out of the pupils in eyes of women and men who are my friends, as out of cave mouths: waiting for night to escape by, waiting for some excuse. I've felt him rise in me and lope across the 60,000 years in seconds, pressing *his* face against the meatside of *my* face, forcing raw chunks of air through my mouth, a perfect fit. And although he's never stepped out of me fully, or out of most of those people I love, I've seen such adrenaline-red contort us sometimes, seen us start to work such bullying over each other. I know he's always asleep back there with one ear cocked—asleep with one hand on his club.

For isn't that the truth of ontogeny's repeating the germinant bullets of fur and eelskin we once were, that are lodged in the psyche, born into us with us? *There,* in the bud—in the gleam of the bud, where gender was undifferentiated—the coward and the aggressor were Siamese pulses, and our hungers were slaked by drinking straight and deep from a runnel of blood. And it's still *here,* a midden buried in the cortex, with its own slithering shadowy life. On nights when we sleep after fighting, I wake and turn to Skyler's turned back. I can feel an anger released through her skin so palpable and steady that I understand it's the radiant half-life of something decaying in us that was whole long before we were fetal.

Meanwhile, Eric's musician friends had alerted Snappy of the bruising taking place in his parking lot. "Boys," said Snappy, "go get him," and out of nowhere two of the house goons filled the night. These guys were Brahman bulls, down to the hump and the dewlap. And they had guns. They needed only to take two token steps in his direction and Neanderthal man, all slobbery now in after-madness, stumbled on back to his van.

You never know, while it's ongoing, what enormous space exists between your perception of action Out There and the action's own needs. I've witnessed this dozens of times in various versions, either sex on either side of it. That rescued woman, saved from maybe a broken jaw, maybe from worse? "You get the fuck out of here, you fucks!" she was shrieking. "You leave my man alone!"

Much later, I told Eric's little tale to a lady I know, a poet. "Wow," she responded. "I think I could *really* make use of that in a poem."

2.

This one is turmeric-red: a soldier, in close-up, in 'Nam, in pain we can't imagine except for the size of the scream pushing out of his mouth. This one is a tree line in winter: each pine under its tipi of snow. This one is "avant-garde" collage: bits of headlines, peekaboo snippets of nudie snapshots, torn Old Masters. This one is a tree line in summer: overnight, the catalpas have blossomed in clutches that look like popcorn. This one. . . .

—Covers of books of poetry, on sale at the Associated Writing Program's annual convention. Everybody's here this year, *everybody*. The poet whose first three collections all take place negotiating the scarps of the Rockies, "clambering juts / until we reach the level / sweep of plateau foliage," is here in the penthouse bar negotiating contractual terms for a fourth book. In the panels room, the poet whose "life is dedicated to bringing Women's Struggle to Third World consciousness" is answering questions on how to apply for a reading circuit of Midwest junior colleges: "And will they make me visit composition classes?"

I can't say "something is wrong here." First, I'm here as well. I'm even enjoying myself, an extra-bourbon-over-the-line's-worth. And second, some few of these people are truly doing writing that tallies the double-entry ledger columns of auricle and ventricle exaltingly. Their published work has flowered great rashes of furor or sudden-struck understanding over my ho-hum innards. If this congregation of spiel and shtick with the welcoming marquee in front is part of some field, the ground from which such necessary labor arises, so be it.

But just a bourbon ago it was easy to feel a load less chummy. I *know* these people, and know *of* these people: their days are devoted to teaching poetry, reading poetry, editing poetry journals, mailing out poems of their own to poetry journals, keeping track of poetry grants and contests like inveterate race buffs scanning their sheets for track tips, gossiping poetry, networking poetry, carrying poetry and self-promotional flyers in their attaché cases, playing poetry tennis, organizing poetry lobbying and poetry-for-social-change and a range of poetry therapies, reviewing poetry, scoring poetry points for reviewing poetry, sleeping poetry, and often enough—it will happen in this hotel this evening—sleeping with another poet who's busily sleeping poetry.

Properly or not, by frightening lightninglike blasts or by continuous scratchings of ordinary matches in convention lobbies, poetry conflagrates their lives.

This never appears in the poems themselves. In one, a deep-sienna photograph—now bleached by decades of sun to a marmalade color—shows the poet's grandparents serving a party of gubernatorial hangers-on, and so implicitly asks what small integrities they may have kept for themselves as secret signals traded across the opulent room, while they tended to White Man's business. In another the poet considers cosmology theory while studying the vibrant spirals painted on vases for sale in a Guatemalan village square. In this one, the poet gives voice to the "dead tongues" lolling out of shoes in a Goodwill thrift shop, "those who hobbled, those who sprinted," whose mysterious spirit now sings to us as the night grows permissive, sings "as one scuffed choir."

Would we want it any other way?—a poem about a poet's peddling poems, then peddling more poems. I think not.

But I also wonder what it means, this space between a life's most constant activity and its public expression?

That night in the hotel room, I look through *my* poems; archaeological ruins being whistled indifferently through, by the wind; and ideas of how much circumstance love may bear, without crumbling, are set against this backdrop of broken-crowned, houndstoothed columns.

The light of a hotel bathroom is surgically stark. Inside my face, another man is stumblingly checking *his* face. I think now he's a third-year welder at Casey J's Assembly Shop, and he's good at his job, and honest with the customers, and he sweats his ass off overtime, sometimes, just to help her pay for the orthodontia work for the seven-year-old kid who isn't even *his*, although he likes the kid and takes him to the ball games that the church group sponsors on Saturdays. All he knows is he tries hard and then some; *damn* hard. Why did they have to humiliate him that way in the parking lot? Okay, so he was drunk and got a little riled—she'll do that to you, she *likes* to do that to you. But he didn't deserve the way those assholes treated him in front of her—hell, no one deserves being treated like that.

"The cavemen," Jim tells me, "are standing around as if they're at the bus stop, they're that real. They're carrying hunks of rock that might as well be thermoses." In preparation for doing his new novel, where the ancient powers speak through tribal masks and reconstructed skeletal figures in museum display halls, Jim's been flying from Austin to New York to talk with diorama masters.

"Think of it, Albert: in just a few inches of space, they need to indicate dozens of miles of distance," he says with his hand waving "miles-of-distance-sign" above his plate of hot *cabrito,* and I *do* conjure up some hackneyed sfumato Neanderthal skyline, ruggedly featured and cave-pocked in receding detail.

"All of the mannequins need to be arranged without shadows, or grouped so their shadows don't botch the illusion. That's the art—like *our* art," and he winks. "No matter how shallow *really,* the good ones sustain an illusion of depth."

3.

We could tell it wouldn't work. We were "in love," but knew it wouldn't work. For one thing, Noona was—had been, for three or four years, and only after intense and willful attempts to reconstruct herself in exactly this way—a lesbian. So it was nuts that summer she cheated on her she-spouse with me, giddy with infatuation, sick with guilt, betraying her recent gay-sexual allegiance (that in turn betrayed her earlier heterosexual identity), confused, ecstatic, keeping both Meg and my-self on *hold* in the thick June air while she queried the sky with a hun-dred of the Grand Old Human Questions, testing her gender prefer-ence, running from it, enchanted by me, committed to Meg, alive past the brim of each neuron, too high-minded for this low sneaking-around, disgusted, delighted, sleepless, and split at the pit of herself like a room freeze-framed a second after the bomb goes off.

She taught me about containment—she could hold herself-like-a-genie all day inside of herself-like-a-lamp. And a genie has undeniable power. I was teaching her things, too, I think, little kinds of zaniness she must have seen as carrying childishness with bravery into an adult life. Our time together, filched and scant, was magic, but we knew it wouldn't work.

When I look back now, what I see are uncountable mornings waiting at 5:00 A.M. in the lot for hospital staff. She walks to her car—the look of pleasure and worn-down hopelessness at seeing me there is so strong it could tumble off her face and crack on the macadam. Then she leans her forehead against the dawn cool of the car, with a weary delibera-tion, as if the inertness of metal itself might transfer over, and bring her a moment's peace. I have my hands in my pockets, then rest them around her, then back in their pockets . . . there's nothing to say, or do. This lasts about a zillion years, and when I look back now, it's all that happened that summer. By August I'd packed up for Wichita, Kansas.

I don't wish to reveal lots more about it, but this is pertinent: Noona was the daughter of an alcoholic father. So much has been written about the syndromes—like a family of representative stick-figure people: The Syndromes! What I want to see now is that six-year-old girl in her frayed plaid skirt, at hopscotch under the el-train thunder one afternoon in the sticky air of the end of the school year, listening to her friends de-scribe *their* summer plans, and inventing, in her turn, like crazy: they were going to drive to England to visit Walt Disney and the Pope.

Already learning to play the nothing-is-wrong-at-home game. Feeling the plaster rigidify over her face—the cast she wore while wait-ing for the healing—then *becoming* the face. Already learning to love it.

So, later, she dated the guy who beat her, needing to explain away the delicate Chinese plums of bruise she'd wear to work. She lived with the guy who cheated on her, in front of her, explaining away his "sister's" unexpected overnight visit and then his "cousin's." They needed her, just like the father, and she needed *that*. So Meg was perfect, whose angers and terrors required tender holding. At Meg's insistence, this wasn't any casually revealed lesbian romance. They were "roommates," if the world inquired. No one could be invited over. Noona's parents "would die" if they "knew"; Meg's ditto. Now Noona was able to turn her back on a planet of victimizing men, yet still lead the life of Deep Secret. Safe in the fortress, peering for enemies out of the slot in its door.

And me?—what hidden history did *I* shlep to our few doomed months? I'm not going to say, but I'll tell you this: it was mightily there. In each of us, from a central mulch where the oxygen gets chemically fired onto the red-cell lozenges: it's there. Richard Leakey, in *People of the Lake*: "Beyond thirty-five thousand years ago, there is no more recent sign of the Neanderthal race. They vanished. However, they may not have suffered complete biological oblivion: they may instead have interbred with the mainstream. The genes of Neanderthalers may be surviving in us all today."

The space is the length of light from our skin to the sun. The space is the span of a hand. It can't be calibrated in the usual ruled units. Listen: Noona was a nurse, as her mother had been. "You see it, in front of your nose, but then you snap it closed inside a locket somewhere a solar system away, in your medulla oblongata, or you can't go on." The first time she carried a raw arm "like a baby" from the operating table, and dropped it. . . . Listen: that sound.

The camera dollying up to her face, then zooming through the irises: asteroids, intergalactic emptiness, universe dust, and then a tiny white moon with a splatter of fresh blood. Noona isn't her real name—not for an instant—but the arm is real and keeps on falling, the size of a splinter you'd get in your eye, forever.

"Go know," my mother always says, then lobs it to her listener with that decades-practiced fatalistic shrug. It means: just *try* to make sense of a world defined by what's obscure and ephemeral. Fight City Hall. Count angels on a pinhead.

. . . now he's picking up the kid with his mouthful of hardware from the Jew orthodontist's, *whoopsie,* twirling him up in the air with that goony metal-plated smile he gets, and then they're off with a thermos of some orangeade pee, to watch their team the Saints beat the holy crap out of the Pillars of Fire, and something—*something,* a petal of but-teriness, you might say loving kindness—opens up in his gut when the kid is around, so he wants to kiss the gimp pop vendor, tell him here's a twenty, keep the change. . . .

On one page, Leakey evokes "the Neanderthal race, a stocky, beetle-browed people." In the life-size diorama Jim saw, "They're staring out of some muttering, conspiratorial huddle, you know, with that trucu-lent jaw-set of neighborhood thugs." As he chews this mouthful, he's cubing his face, in imitation. Slobbers. But Leakey says also, of ritual burial: "Ironically, one of the first and last equivocal instances of this moving behavior is at a Neanderthal site in the Zagros Mountains. There, in the Shanidor Cave, a man was laid to rest on a bed of flowers more than sixty thousand years ago."

Hear the whistle of the wind through that number.

Go know.

4.

There's something plainspoken and forthright to the idea of nudism—wearing only yourself for the world, no intervening arrangements. If you're bruised, that sickly mustard carnation shows. If the wind flicks your nipples, they're fissured. It would seem that here, at least, we're undone layers closer to an openness.

But notice, I said "the *idea* of nudism." Look at those well-known photographs by Diane Arbus, taken at Jersey and Pennsylvania nudist camps over a five-year period starting in 1962: the couple in the

woods, who have achieved some station halfway between a medieval
oil of Adam and Eve, and a peeper's candid snapshot; or the fat, the
simply *fat,* family whose picnic looks like a beaching of sea cows; yes, or
the platinum housewife in her swan sunglasses. "They run the whole
social gamut," Arbus said, "from people in tents to people in mansions
almost."

And she said that after a while she "began to wonder about nudist
camps. . . . There'd be an empty pop bottle or rusty bobby pin—the
lake bottom oozes in a particularly nasty way and the outhouse smells,
the woods look mangy." Now this is strangely finicky perturbation from
someone who reveled in her cast of 42nd Street subjects shuffling their
way at 3:00 A.M. through the alleycat shit and used needles: gaudy
ostrich-plumed dwarf pimps, their stables of rouged-up blow-job peddlers, lip-picking mumblers, gutter scavengers, self-proclaimed princes
in exile, addict pickpockets, guys who'll pay you to kick them, *hard.* . . .
It doesn't exactly make a "rusty bobby pin" look outrageous.

But she'd *expect* the 42nd Street grunge. What I suspect Arbus was
registering is a disappointment in how the average nudist colony falls
off from a preconceived ideal. It's this space between the absolute and
the actual, growing increasingly moldy and dreck-bestrewn, that has
her upset. This space can't be computed by any objectively rendered
scale, but my grandparents traveled it one afternoon as the ferry
rounded Liberty, her torch held toward the heavens, then started
choppily closing in on the din and muck of ghetto New York at the
turn of the century. Such babel-array of pidginspeaks. Such streetcar-
clanging hell nights.

And such possibility. Here, through this space, a charge builds up—
the multicultural *salsa-&-gefilte* power of immigrants—that begins dirt-
poor and ends a generation later with manicured lawns, that huddles
around a trash-barrel fire in winter, sleeps, and suffers, then wakes with
the grandson replacing a furnace filter and clomping back up to the
TV den. Between, a lot of love gets smuggled from one sad time to another. And maybe some brains get bashed in—go know. This isn't
space that exists in topography. Astronomy's "red shift" calculations

can't chart such direction and speed. I'll say this: we share 99.9 percent of our genes with Neanderthal man and woman. When we wake up as ourselves, it's with one-tenth of one percent of genetic difference turning our engines over, blinking in the new day's sunlight, marveling at the purr. Go measure. Angels on a pinhead.

When my grandfather woke with his arm around Nettie, his other arm was crushed by one of the fourteen lowlife huckster Jews they shared their first week's lodgings with. Their world was filth and raw energy, the alley song of the scissors-grinder man, the glow of Sabbath candles doubled by a rat's eyes, scams and shameless flimflam, prayer shawls and finger-sized streetfight knives, the militant suffragette picketers on their feet and the whores on their asses, steaming horse dung on the winter street and a baby found frozen to the light pole so its belly tore off when they moved it, slitting chickens open, slitting holes for buttons, and the irrepressible beauty of a full moon whether or not the bars of the fire escape presented her in prisoner's stripes. He woke, it was night, with fourteen other people around; but he kissed her.

I think Arbus would have snapped it all with relish. Someone did, on occasion. Just like that black poet ransacking family-attic albums for material—I have photographs, or retrospective half-imagined photographs, glazed over by a long marinade of tough going.

I wake, I see Skyler's awake. Whatever we were angry about the day before, I see that sleep has milled it down to the lightest-weight flyaway chaff. Somewhere in the cave-back of our dreams, survival was being fought out: a matter of clubs. We're *here* now, though, just live skins needing stroking.

We pass our hands over each other like metal detectors, looking to heal each other, maybe partially *of* each other, searching to ease the last scraplet of shrapnel out.

There's a standard magazine gag we've all seen: on a shoreline, a middle-aged male nudist passes a nubile young nudist woman. And in the thought balloon over his head, risen like a cloud from his secret-most fantasy deeps, he pictures her: *clothed.*

And so we see that no situation, no matter how all-revealing, obviates our having some life concealed. If there's anything that saves these two from being so cartoony they'd blow off the page at a breath—if anything carries them one-tenth of one percent toward being human at all—it's the rise of that private vision.

5.

In *A Little Book on the Human Shadow,* Robert Bly writes, "I think one could say that most Puritans did not distinguish darkness from Satan," and that, to this day, "our culture teaches us from early infancy to split and polarize dark and light. . . . Behind us we have an invisible bag, and the part of us our parents don't like, we, to keep our parents' love, put in the bag." We do the same for teachers, peer groups, lovers, and careers. Sexuality, spontaneity, anger, jealousy, men their feminine selves, and women their male beings, "a desire to kill animals and smear their blood on our faces, a desire to get away from all profane life and live religiously"—these are the kinds of energies "preserved from our mammal inheritance" and "our 5,000 years of tribal life" that we stuff, early on, in the bag: "And we spend the rest of our lives trying to get them out again."

Bly is eager to emphasize that this interior darkness is not evil: "The shadow energies seem to be a part of the human psyche, and . . . become destructive only when they are ignored." He draws the metaphor of Dr. Jekyll's Hyde-self, i.e., hidden self, that "feels rage from centuries of suppression," running fatally amok. What he suggests (and he sketchily starts to get prescriptive in this) is "honoring the shadow": "If we don't live our animal side or our sexual side, that means we don't *honor* those parts. If we have anger and do not make proper clothing for it . . . that means we are failing to honor our anger."

Two hundred years earlier, Blake wrote, "He who desires but acts not, breeds pestilence." And, "The lust of the goat is the bounty of God.

The wrath of the lion is the wisdom of God. The nakedness of woman is the work of God."

The space in us where shadow theater stages its productions can't be walked in a day or dreamed in a night—"near as a grosbeak, far as Orion," says the poet Antler.

We're the audience. We're the featured stars.

Sometimes, researching the records, we could think that every American town in the decades clustered around 1900 had its pair of "spinster librarians" living in a frame house at the town edge, liked by everyone although pitied as well. Two figures admitted completely and even warmly into community life although rarely invited into people's drawing rooms, they were "so sweet," "yet reclusive," and "uncommonly sisterly toward one another in those small gestures of deference which betoken a large understanding": "Though it was many the June-struck couple who drifted apart, these two gray ladies, as dependable as the cycling of seasons, lasted with whatever their contentment was, through the winter of life." What extra pleasure attached to their sacrosanctdom? what unbearable isolation?

And across town, when his wife attended the charity meet, then didn't Mr. Whistler the banker stroke her petticoats, languidly stroking himself, and living in some enormously silky heaven that folded for propriety's sake to fit in his brain's electrical wiring? Yes. And at the edge of town, the spinster Hawkins is waiting up for the spinster Shea, who rode to church to organize the charity meet, and she'll return with wicked gossip on everyone, and share it as the bun unpins and her tresses fall like a silver fox stole to her shoulders. . . .

Noona, there was always the space a leaf falls through, between us. I don't think that Meg's the answer for you, but some lady ought to be, some day. Maybe you'll read this. Then you'll understand it's a long-delayed letter, written to wish *good luck,* the words I had on my tongue that last afternoon, but its light was too fierce and they crawled back down to curl up in a dark nest of organs.

There are spaces; and under them, spaces. So the poet raised by two professor-parents is revising a poem on feral children supposedly raised by wolves. And who am I to say an equal gap doesn't exist between this plane of very visible, reportable activity, and some level of cellular urgency?—a gap across which charge accrues, and a solitary howling is heard. A leaf falls, hitting ground; and over time, over units of worm and of rain, falls through the ground. These are the lessons of physics. Spaces are composed of more spaces. Spaces composed of similar spaces can love and hurt each other, as if they were solid.

"In *santeria* religion," Jim says, "they séance regularly with the dead. I was invited: all these chicken bones still glistening, and a perfectly credible voice, I guess we'd say 'emanating,' from out of the woman in charge." It's for his novel. "What I want is that same Ancestral Voice conducted up the bodies in the planet, like through circuitry, and sounding out of cowrie-shell ritual masks in the museum corners. And something in your own marrow wants to talk back. Neat, huh?"

Go know.

And the Wild Boy of Aveyron, and Wild Peter of Hanover, and the Lithuanian Bear-Boy. Kamala, eight, and Amala, one-and-a-half, were reportedly found on all fours "among wolf cubs in a giant abandoned anthill on the outskirts of a village in India" seventy years ago. For food, they killed small chickens, eating them raw. "Amala died within a year, but Kamala, who lived to be eighteen, learned to walk, wear clothing, and speak a few words." What a cosmos she traveled every day just to reach the near wall of the courtyard!

One night Sarah, Eric, Skyler, and I quick-hit a neighborhood carnival, the gypsy kind that sets up in a mall lot and is gone next week. It was late. I know the ride operators looked surly and bored. Whatever the reason, those thousand hours we jolted around the Tilt-A-Whirl were *most* unpleasant. We spent the rest of the night on our backs, recuperating, calming our semicircular canals' upheaving fluids. I remember repeating, over and over, the phrase that Eric had first used on the seedy little midway, to persuade me as we promenaded past the thing: "a really *classic* carnival ride."

What made it worse was, we'd eaten at Snappy's. Snappy himself was there, as always, wearing his yoke-front cowboy shirt and el cheapo linoleum-looking toupee. As always, he was receiving or handing over to someone a pile of folded money about as thick as a Victorian novel. And yes, as always, the grease-scummed food was just one-nth of a floury dollop away from being completely indigestible.

But everyone knows that Snappy's restaurant, if "restaurant" isn't overglorification, exists up front to launder the big-time cash flow generated in the compound out back, in a huge L-shaped and windowless building. Gambling. Black-market cameras and watches. "Once I walked into the annex and a sixteen-year-old girl was cavorting buck-nekkid on the tables," Eric says. "I got me some looks said I wasn't invited."

Snappy gets driven around in his own stretch limo, the one with longhorns mounted for the hood ornament. Snappy clicks his fingers and gun-toting hooligans beam out of the floor. Snappy stars in hundreds of photographs covering not only the walls but the *ceiling*: shaking the councilman's hand, wearing his fraternal organization cowl and corsage-like medals, visiting the orphans' home with a sackload of goodies, fishing with the missus. Other photographs are warmly inscribed: ventriloquists, magicians, local politicians, old-time country fiddler groups, a number of tassel-tittied strippers, rodeo cowboys, civic leagues.

I wouldn't want to start counting the precariously balanced team of Snappies inside this man.

But I would like, one time, to tour the back compound; to casually walk up to the eight-foot plaster horseshoe framing its single entrance; to cover the distance as he does daily, dozens of times, in just a few steps, to walk from the whirr of the world's common traffic, the litter a breeze skitters under my feet, then my hand on the doorknob in shadow.

There are many books I've brought back from the convention. Poetry poetry poetry.

Here, the cover of this one is the Earth itself in geode-like cross-section, so all of the layers of grandparents, buried terraces, potsherds, carnelian, oil, and coal are shown like striation in cuts of meat, and then on down to the turbulent, almost unthinkably inhuman, magma heart.

On the surface, a marble temple with delicate fluted columns appears to look up toward the stars.

Ellen's

1.

Turning and turning in the guiding wire.

The phone rings.

Collect, long distance. "Albert it's Ellen I'm in Kalamazoo and singing in the park"

"Kalamazoo?"

"by the fountain. I'm singing by the fountain in the park."

So it's An Ellen Call.

"And the people like it but I'm wondering should I sing for free and sleep in the park by the fountain"

If voices have eyes, these two are round as the moons in a child's drawing.

"or charge for my singing and sleep in a hotel."

"Does your sister know where you're at?"

"She doesn't like my singing oh Albert"

"Ellen?"

"Let's rent a Xerox machine and have a party and Xerox our bodies and make a frieze of all our friends on the wall."

"When you get back. Ellen, what's your sister's number?"

Ellen is in her thirties. It's 1969, she's been my friend three years but I've never seen her depressed. I've never seen those moons' dark sides.

"Albert it's Ellen I was wondering"

"Hey, Ellen, hi."

"if you want to build a raft this summer and float down the Mississippi like Huck and Nigger Jim I know it sounds crazy"

"It sounds a little crazy."

"but I've got the details worked out how to construct it and charts of the currents and navigation laws so don't worry."

Some nights, plenty moonshine.

"No, I'm not worried."

"We could sing songs on the raft."

All of this is serious on Ellen's part, and not without a full comprehension of how it sounds to those of us not touched by the light of her mania: wondrous, stuff-o'-dreams, disaster-bound, retardate. In fact Ellen is the most intelligent friend I have—her IQ an apogee.

My lesbian divorcée single-mother friend Ellen the poet.

"It's . . . Ellen."

Collect (to Chicago) long distance (from Bakersfield, California). I'm living at home. My father extends the phone as if it were powered by fecal matter. His eyes roll up to God, the sign of a kind of cynicism they share.

"Hi, Ellen. What's up."

"Well I'm okay really"

I won't say much until my father leaves, and the stalling is costing him money. His pupils return like a one-arm-bandit's indicating of jackpot. He leaves.

"but I thought Sammy might like to visit his father who lives in California so one day we got in the car with Mr. Bones the dog and just left and *that* was okay"

"Where's Sammy now?"

"but we lost Mr. Bones around Arizona because we ran out of food and he was hungry and *that* was okay because we made California"

"Look, where are you calling from?"

"and when Sammy ran from the hotel room I ran out to get him back of course though I was mostly naked not completely but mostly I had to run out fast"

"Uh huh."

"so when the cop stopped me I hit him."

"Oh, Ellen."

"That wasn't so okay."

Sammy's in the custody of the State of California. Ellen's to remain there, for study. Sammy might be allowed to come back home, to his grandparents . . . will I contact them?

I'll contact them.

I'll make any number of calls in the next few weeks, to any number of friends, all of whom love Ellen.

The cord of the phone, its dozens of spirals.

"Anyway, how are they treating you?"

The long, the very long, distance.

"Okay. They won't let me sing after lights-out though."

2.

"Swervings into fantasy"—a phrase from Kenneth Clark, on the notebooks of Leonardo da Vinci.

He says: "Leonardo was fond of drawing artesian screws and other spiral devices. On a sheet of doodles in the *Codice Atlantico* he had drawn such a spiral for its own sake, and he has endowed it with a kind of monstrous life, so that it changes, like Aaron's rod, into a serpent."

Years later, I can see that spiral as perfectly emblematic of my friend Ellen Dapple's manic (and, as I'd discover, depressive) reactions. Not that I necessarily think that Leonardo shared in her biochemical distress; the records-taking of Ellen's brain, in its secret convolute script, was urgent—and I can't speak for how casual may have been the perceptions of what Clark calls "this interweaving of fact and fantasy in Leonardo's mind."

I only know I think of the notebooks, done in his backwards hand, demanding a mirror: and after ten years Ellen is clear again in my reverie: dear, and diligent, and chronicling my world truly in her head: though in her own special coded reversals.

This essay-of-sorts will turn to Ellen again, a bit later, will . . . well, spiral back. For the spiral's supremacist, though, we need to look to Daedalus: Athenian, mage of mazes, he whose name means "the cunning maker." Michael Ayrton has him say: "I am a thickset man, inclined to run to fat. My legs are weak and I am a little lame in one of them." Gide, in what seems contradiction: "He was very tall, and perfectly erect."—No matter. Here he is really: bunch-browed, bent to the task, his whole face: white light focused through thought-like-a-lens, burning its way to a problem.

Which has been set him, the legend goes, by King Cocalus of Sicily: ". . . a spiral shell, offering a large reward to anyone who could pass a linen thread through it." No sweat. This is the man who devised "the three-legged tables, with golden wheels, which would run by themselves to their owner's side when he commanded." Orderly in his catalogues are weapons of war the size of modern-day battleships, with feasible catapult mechanisms and moat-digging motorized jaws requiring sometimes tens of dozens of grunting winch-turners, sometimes just a kettle of steam; and ladies' intimate devices the size of peas, oh, the size of silver peas in a satin-and-lacquer case.

Today, on a Sicily beach, it's easy. The olive trees bounce sun like thousands of drab-uniformed schoolchildren. A bird cuts a leisurely corkscrew, down, and down. He yawns: a cave of garlic, lemon-brushed squid, a little only, ruby wine. "Drilling the shell at the top, Daedalus tied a strand of gossamer to the leg of an ant, which he induced up through the whorls by smearing honey around the drilled hole. Then he joined the linen thread to the end of the gossamer and drew it through."

You see him? That man, there. . . . "On the beach?" Yes, licking his fingers.

It is told how Minos, contending against his brothers for the throne, would pray, at the day's three Holy Junctures, that the god Poseidon send up a bull from the sea, as a sign of Minos's ascendancy, "and he had sealed the prayer with a vow to sacrifice the animal immediately, as an offering and symbol of service." For many days: the brass bowls on the altars, ropes of incense-smoke. And then the prayer was answered. And Minos was king of the island-empire Crete.

The bull was pure white—as if fashioned from sea-foam itself. The light rode its flanks like epaulets. Minos beheld it—something about the lustrous horns, its bellycurve up to the cock, the cock like a counting-house chute, its almost-goosedown snout. . . . He added the beast to his herd, and on Poseidon's altar substituted a gray-white bull of his own, a good one though, a good one.

And so it's tempting to say: Poseidon's wrath inspired the lust of Pasiphaë, wife of Minos. Who knows? You draw the spiral-line of the inner ear, the cochlea, snailshape whorl on whorl, and finally who's to say on which side falls the voice of the gods, on which the voice of a man's own congenital counselors.

Or a woman's. In any case, one day Pasiphaë beheld the bull. . . .

And brought her need to Daedalus. Which was, in all, a simple need and they say the contrivance was simple.

It's simple today. The gland-man straps them by snout to the ceiling pulleys, cranks them from feed pen to breeding rack. The prepuce is scrubbed. Sometimes the attendant's hand's insinuated up the rectal pudge, and massages away. The slit in the dummy cow's steel rump is scented. That's the important thing. And they /*hey diddle-diddle*/ spasm, once, into water-warmed rubber. They're married to seventeen inches of engineered vinyl and the ring in the nose gleams.

Talk about spirals: 15,000 coiled feet of tubing in the testicles of a bull.

Pasiphaë knelt, all fours, the understructure was ventilated with ribbing and yet cowhide over it all kept most of the heat in. Daedalus measured well: though inches of unlit air surrounded her face, her gooseflesh breasts, her tensed arms up to the shoulders: here, where the worlds would meet and it counted, her rump was flush with the cowskin. And its slit was scented. That was the simple, that was the important, thing.

The offspring was a monster. Birthed in pain, and soon thereafter a painful sight, the Minotaur required hiding. This is the simple story of how a complex thing is done. And it was done. The sun shone full upon it. Daedalus smiled. I think at a sense of completion, something having clicked with the final brick into place. And no sun shone inside it, at all. The smile was short, a hyphen, it connected him to the rest of the day, a workday like all days and so he turned from the world of kings to the world of cogs and counters.

The Labyrinth "commemorates him as the ancestor of all the celebrated architects of the Western world."

And the father, of course, of Icarus.

There were adventures: pourings of blood, semen dried to a knee's-crook, something gold. . . . The world of kings, like cogs, will turn. It tells the time. It tells you when the time is up. For this in one version, for that in another, Daedalus and Icarus, insubordinate, arm-linked, rag-shod, were imprisoned in the Labyrinth.

You know about the wax-fashioned wings. Ellen's sister once did a series of prints, *Icarus Descending*. His face, like that on a coin, starts shining; and then the quick use rubs it blurred. Finally he's sunken treasure; the death gives us Brueghel's painting, Auden's poem. Riding a low safe flight line, Daedalus landed in Sicily, stumbled along the beach, and lay his first night with his arms still strapped to the flap-hinges and his cheek in a puddle of salt. He'll wake grieving. He'll learn to carry the grief. That salt will flavor the rest of his days, though not to bitterness. In Ayrton's novel, he's left as an old man calmly, in a humming garden, listing by way of summation the symbols of one human life spent working out mazes. Here's how I leave him: just taken off, the air a palpable crutch-rest under each arm, his beeswax holding, all the sky become his home, and he's that jointed befeathered scallop-wing figure we picture dangling, working the quills, across the cream-color heavens that's a page from the notebooks of Leonardo.

Clark: "The most curious man in history." He sets aside his sepia schema of man-in-flight, and focuses now on—anything. "Why does one find sea-shells in the mountains? How do they build locks in Flanders? How does a bird fly? What accounts for cracks in walls? What is the origin of wind and clouds? How does one stream of water deflect another? Find out; write it down; if you can see it, draw it." Spirals: maelstroms, whirlpools, screw threads thrust in seasoned wood, and most especially the slippery loops of the human body.

"Leonardo discovered a centenarian in a hospital in Florence, and waited gleefully for his demise so that he could examine his veins. Every question demanded dissection and every dissection was drawn with marvelous precision."

Here: the fetus wrapped in its natal coils, tight as a watch spring readying Time. Leonardo, bent with pen, to the shadowed whorls of the pinna, to the kidney coils, the ampersands lining the lung.

In *Rites and Symbols of Initiation*, Eliade considers the shape, and our necessary confronting of it: "The labyrinth is presented as a 'dangerous passage' into the bowels of Mother Earth, a passage in which the soul runs the risk of being devoured" before it exits—if it does—to a next life.

So. Here's Leonardo, over a bowel.

Here's Leonardo studying the thirty coiled feet of a human gut—which is, itself, a kind of studying: funneling ever finer, bringing it all to a distilled point, deciding what to reject, what to keep to go on with.

Dissection was new. It's worth repeating what we know of the times: no antiseptics, no refrigeration—not running water, even. The stink was almost visible, mucused-over and splotched. He did some thirty bodies. Sometimes he used small blades. He had to know. If needed, his nails.

3.

The very form, if it's to be perceived as a form at all, requires our focus—takes our vision around and, in going around, exacts it. Not, then, that the spiral *inspires* meditation; to see the spiral *is* to meditate. And so the mandala.

This: "In 1902 Fakir Agastiya of Bengal, India, raised one arm straight above his head." In three months the circulation cut off completely. A bird built a nest in his palm. He died in 1912, the arm still raised, and was duly buried that way.

With this concentration, imperturbable, whole, the successful initiate becomes—not looks at: *becomes*—what Giuseppe Tucci calls "an immense mobile mandala." The two-dimensional pattern we know from the printed page radiates from the mystic in blazing foliate-bangled tentacular convolutions: "Shining round about, the divine matrices of things come forth from the center of his own heart, pervade space, and then re-absorb themselves in him."—He novas.

Is he culturally preconditioned to see the expected shape? "C. G. Jung discovered such forms emerging from the psyches of his European patients, the majority of whom knew nothing about mandalas. The production of these mandalas came to his attention 'long before I knew their meaning or their connection with the strange practices of the East.'"

—It's the East. An adept's vision is hovering over a circle of many in-voluting galactic pathways.

Or: a bee, above a full rose.

A lover's tongue at the cunt-lips.

Many bees, and many roses—it's a topiary, the Minotaur done at its center out of alabaster. The visitor's eyes: around, around.

A man drops to his knees. And then his entire body, under desert noon, assumes the tremulous supplication of a kneel. His name is Ezekiel. The Bible says he saw wheels of eyes, saw chariots, flaming, on wheels of eyes. Well of course he did.

He'd been concentrating.

Ellen practiced yoga. Ellen went to The Meditation Center. She had a mantra, and sang it for me. It made the phone's transistorized circuits, a moment only, mandalas in mandalas in mandalas; then the discon-necting click, and the long empty hum.

Jung ends one of his seminal works: "As the historic parallels show, the symbolism of the mandala is not just a unique curiosity; we can well say that it is a regular occurrence." Okay. A history of doodles, shard on rock, Bic pen to butcher paper: thousand-foot serpentine earthworks, Navajo sand paintings, tree rings in ink, green eddies in chalk: a species' history. For Jung, it has many possible guises, and some I'll list later.

For now, though, this. The work that I've just quoted from is *Individual Dream Symbolism in Relation to Alchemy.* One patient's dream in analysis: "At all events the spiral emphasizes the center and hence the uterus, which is a synonym frequently employed for the alchemical vessel, just as it is one of the basic meanings of the Eastern mandala."

Charlatans there were, aplenty, dropping dung in a cheap alembic, muttering Latinate mumbo jumbo, stirring with *this ancyent Philosophers Wand,* then dribbling the gook out to reveal *a Nugget of Gold New-Mayd,* and thence cast as a florin, and wasn't the wonder-maker toasted well and wrapped warm about by the court ladies, wasn't he subsidized with guilders up past the flaps of his ermine cap! (The gold was hidden in the wand, and loosened by stirring.)

There were, too, the other kind—fewer, less florid. *Laboratory* comes from the alchemist's workshop: *labor,* and *oratorium* (place devoted to prayer). For these, "moral virtues were required," their real object was "the perfection or at least the improvement of man"—the maze of alchemical tubing: emblematic of inner refining. The monster. Trying to face it.

It's Texas. The West. A man, one morning, sees his face in the bathroom sink: shimmer, break, collect again, then spiral down the drain.

He walks out, thinking: his friends, their baggage of griefs. A woman he loves, but her face shimmered, broke, and was never repieced. Then it's night. The leaves whirled in the yard. Back home, in bed, there isn't any mandala, just the darkness. Just the darkness, nothing more.

Unless it's the swirl in his navel.

Unless it's his own identity-gyre.

He's trying to face it all, now. He's making this sentence, a word at a time: the spool of the typewriter ribbon: unwinding.

4.

Ellen is huge. Her movements, in their affinities, are birdlike: shy and dainty. Translated up through Amazonian compilings of bone and muscle, they seem to be the movements of bulldozers, pile drivers, airport security systems. You have to look hard to see the nest inside the steel girders.

But it's there, and the bird coos. Ellen collects the folk songs from her Ohio chalk-quarry birthland. She tapes herself to better learn its rhythms—when to hold, and when to let go of, authenticity. Based on this, she's writing a folk opera using the plot of *Deirdre*. And she's a poet. Much of her work is concerned with an Amazon figure, vital, proud, and ungainly. Ellen's eyes and lips, such eloquent sensitized apparatus, are lost in a head too vast—as if a delicate Japanese flower were glazed as the central device of a heavy Amish family-sized serving platter.

Sammy was accidental, at something like sixteen. Soon he was Ellen's alone, and by his prodigious IQ and equivalent shoe size, you can tell. He's twelve. He sits in a circle of beers and drinks his chocolate milk and argues aesthetics. He's tall but short of friends. He's invented conceptual baseball, solitaire, by throwing his key ring. The number of keys facing out, or in, or clustered according to certain rules, the variables of configuration: all this dictates runs about the bases. Ellen's always back by his bedtime. One day they find Mr. Bones, this wasted dog with cat's-cradle hips, and bring him home. They clean up the crap together.

At parties, Ellen's warmth is so intense it solders. There we are, in a circle, dancing, and she's the heat in our hands. She's crowned with a dandelion wreath. She tells the story of when she was young and got the peanut stuck in her nose. She laughs so hard she pees. Later, drunker yet, her urine-soaked boots drying off by the fire, she talks about her theory of circularity in poetic form and alternately sucks on the stems of her dandelions.

Her love life, though, is bleak. For a time she experiments with a group of lesbian poets. A member dances in pasties and a ruby-sequin G-string. When a lover knocks unexpectedly at the back door one midnight, dressed in a forest-green hunting jacket, riding breeches, black leather boots, with a leather crop and a huge fake handlebar mustache, Ellen drops out of the group—these scenes aren't good for Sammy. Later, taking a class, she meets Jerry O'Geary. That really is his name. He writes poems, he carries a key ring more populous than

Sammy's, his one piece of furniture is a refrigerator—that's all I remember. Ellen writes me a letter: she's just bought a sheer black nightie. The whole page sings and blushes.

She holds a clerical job in the Art Department. Part-time, she's completing her Master's Report—something about the prose of Joyce as a geometric figure. Ellen explains, she's concentrating on how the language itself is labyrinth-like—circuitous, many-appendaged, spiraling out and in—while listing all the references to mazes in the text itself. She tells me she gets lost in her work.

The things she tells me! We're sitting on Josh's lawn, near done with a bottle of Portuguese white. He's had a lamb roast, everyone's mouth is greased like a clown's. The carcass is still on the spit and a few of the more determined celebrants still do Neolithic dance steps around it. I'm trying hard not to crack my cracked plastic cup even more. But it's the only thing to fidget with. The stars have come out, like confidants saying it's okay now, and Ellen's explaining her Joyce visions.

When she's troubled lately, he comes with advice. Not bodily, no gray shape from beyond the grave, nothing hokey like that. But say she's been throwing a problem around, from one cerebral hemisphere to another, back and forth. And at the critical moment, Joyce Brothers Movers rounds the corner—its timely van. A random rippling of newspaper pages opens to Joyce Shoes Annual Sale. It happens this way, over and over, she tells me quiet and matter-of-fact, whenever she's troubled she has this vizier.

Sammy's growing truculent. Why not? He's pushing thirteen, and it's pushing back. She tells me, though not in these words, that Jerry O'Geary is losing interest. They still see each other, etc., but he's seeing other women too, etc. You know. We all march against the war. But Ellen marches harder. She sits down in a suburb jail and won't stand up. She studies the papers, you have to *know* your enemy. Black limousines follow her home. She checks the couch for hidden microphones. It's rose-patterned, you could hide anything in it. She doesn't want to hit Sammy.

One morning Jerry O'Geary calls, I think from a pay phone. Ellen's just committed herself to a state-run mental facility. She's asked for me. Would I visit?

I'll visit.

It's ten years later, I live in Texas now. And sometimes I still walk out at night, as I did in the razor-sharp snows of Chicago, and pray for my friends—or myself, in some kinds of darkness it's hard to distinguish sure outlines.

Not an orthodox prayer. A kind of well-wishing made in the small, the personal, mandalas of the skull's two semicircular canals—where we keep our balance.

5.

Androgeus, a fully human son of Minos, was slain by a score of Athenian rowdies. Minos, by then a Mediterranean power, demanded retribution: seven young Athenian men and seven Athenian maidens, every nine years, would be shipped to Crete as tribute, and there given over to the hungers of the Minotaur. In the third such group—it's eighteen years since Daedalus limned the final perfect block in place—is the son of Aegeus the king of Athens: Theseus.

According to one source: "He slew the Minotaur with his fists." Another: "Theseus was able to despatch him, driving the sword through his body and then cutting off his head."—It's been a long while, the Panhellenic sun dazzles the edges of details.

This we know for sure: Ariadne waited, just a step inside the mossed-over mouth. Her breasts were bare, and lightly perspired, and cold enough today to be projection of the rock. Her gauzy skirt: a ground fog. Only one thing moved: the clew of linen thread. It started waist-high and as wide as a pantry door. But now it fit in her hands like an injured bird, unraveling.

—Where we get the meaning usually given its other spelling, "clue."
And Theseus, figuring it out—by the yard, by the great taut length of
attachment, spiral twist and spiral backtwist, literal: figuring/it/out.

There are thousands of versions of the battle, it's difficult *not* to
make it horrific and adventuresome. I refer you to those available in
English; you can follow every acrid desperate slash in the torch-
splashed darkness. What I'm interested in is the memoir found on a
fire-blackened parchment scrap, in Theseus's effects, and bearing
a smudged Athenian seal. It starts midsentence "not as you would
believe, and not as I would have believed had I not seen it. The very
step-in and traversing of the ill-lit fenestration-ways, was a test of
mettle—and truly, as I have recounted, I doubted; my muscles doubted,
my spit; and I was afraid. Long after, the tunnels unwound, to face the
monster was further terror; he was of fierce aspect, and whether it was
courage or simple enervation that held me, today I could not say. And
then the fight, and now you understand why I write this holding my
nib in a grip more scar than flesh. But then the Minotaur died and the
worst came.

"On the floor of the central-most cavern he curled. He said once
the name of the bull and the name of his mother—the voice was a bur-
ble of blood—and then his spirit left. I could study him now, in the
calm. His head was slightly turned and the lips gone softly away from
their living snarl. It was anybody's face—I had seen my own, in many a
standing pool, on many a day, twist beastly more than his. His knees
and hands were drawn into his belly. Having spoken what was un-
speakable of his coming to be, he came to pass, and in death his like-
ness to me—or so it seemed then, after flurry—made me stroke him
once with either hand, a tremble, as if to say one shook in revulsion;
and one with tenderness.

"I ran back to Ariadne. . . ." (*—in rough translation*)

Plucking the thread back up, to the light at the mouth. Their kiss is
famous. She threw the last bit left of the thread to the breeze.

There's a legend: the thread raveled up and flew off. The shape of
a healed bird.

———— 〰️ ————

A man walks Texas, thinks of friends: Carolyn, Micheline, Lune: the last so high once on a manic jag, she masturbated past pain to blanking out. They're all, now, stabilized on lithium pills. The stellar bursts, the vast black spaces: in balance. This makes a working night sky.

And what of the woman, her name I can't use, my ex-fiancée whose griefs were not—and so whose curing couldn't be—chemical. Over a year since I've seen her. Where can she look to. Sometimes I walk all night. Her shrink recommended hypnosis. There are myths in the nervous system.

—The stories, the figures up there that the stars figure out.

The bulls. The spiral nebulae.

6.

Theseus conducts his carnage and coronations in myth. For Philipson: "Leonardo is infinitely more significant as a myth than as a man." And de Santillana: "Leonardo is, precisely, an irreducibly mythic personality."

(But I want to conjecture him callus-footed, worrying a peach pit in his cheeks, and walking the tideline: grumbling, distracted, a funny old cluck, just before dawn and he's the only stick out stirring this soupy air. And thinking: eddies; thinking: whorls. "Leonardo was obsessed by the study of water." "A sheet at Windsor shows water taking the form of both hair and flowers, racing along in twisted strands, and pouring from a sluice so that it makes dozens of little whirlpools." The shape of it. Meditating.)

"Leonardo was an Oriental. His thoughts on art and nature would ravish Indian, Chinese, or Japanese readers." I can't say if that means a mandala pattern was one of his psyche's natural modes of expression. But Heinrich Wölfflin, describing the "dream-like . . . brown, green-blue and blue-green" background of the *Mona Lisa,* chooses to start: "fantastic, jagged labyrinths of mountains."

Then: "They are of a different order of reality from the figure (of

Mona Lisa herself)." The idea of bifurcation runs through studies of Leonardo, unavoidably.

Often it's charged with a dolorous current. Herbert Read refers to a "divided nature" that's "tragic"—Leonardo as artist, Leonardo as scientist, meeting like brothers on different sides in the war. In the notebooks, "we find feelings and sensations recorded in all their poetic actuality, and these same feelings and sensations converted to idea, coldly analyzed and dissected." And this, says Read, is why Leonardo "lays down precepts which were to corrupt the artistic consciousness of Europe for the next three centuries."

And "a man can be at the same time great and disastrous." Even Leonardo's intense admirer Kenneth Clark records the frustration and folly of a world in halves: "In 1503 he persuaded the Florentine Government—probably the most hard-headed body in Europe—to accept his design for diverting the Arno so that it should no longer enter the sea by Pisa, but in Florentine territory. . . . It is typical of Leonardo's mind that his notes on the subject are, up to a point, quite factual; but that when he comes to the real difficulty, a range of hills, he says simply, 'At Serraville I shall cut through'; without the slightest indication how."

From this unreconciled schism, ills by the oodles.

From silliness ("Jokes with which he occupied his time—animals of paste which flew, and a lizard dressed up to look like a dragon . . . no wonder he despaired of ever putting his researches in order.") to blindness ("He overlooked two of the greatest inventions not only of his time but of all time: printing and engraving. . . . How did it happen that Leonardo ignored and rejected all this?") to harm ("The majority of his precepts—to painters—are in effect nothing but formulas for . . . the fixation of emotional cliches.").

—And, finally, to a private sadness. He wrote at the foot of a page of "drawings . . . anatomical of the generative functions": *I have wasted my hours.* A late self-portrait in red chalk, with its "nutcracker nose and sharply turned down mouth," shows an old man, "head on his hand, gazing into the distance, with an air of profound melancholy."

Clark says, almost in disbelief, as the particolor flakes spiral down: "The most scientifically minded artist of the Renaissance painted his two great wall paintings with so little science that they almost immediately disintegrated." Disintegrated. And: inside? *Those* pictures? K. R. Eissler: "Leonardo's basic relationship to the world was a traumatic one."

(He hunkers down on the beach, and by the first thin steak-blood smudge of sunrise, takes his memorandum-book from his belt with his left hand, digs with his right simultaneously for a crust. He jaws it awhile. A duck, maybe lost from the marsh reeds, lands; waddles up, like a low-level papal guard, for a crust of the crust. His left hand busy with a scribblestick of graphite: the wings, the rubbery web-weighted legs. . . . His blue eyes perfectly still. Perfectly still and accommodating.)

Commentary, though, on this divided mind is itself divided. "For in truth great love is born of great knowledge of the thing loved"—from his *Treatise on Painting*. And of that love, and its parent knowledge, precisely *because of* this generous double direction, much of Leonardo study is, as one would expect, salutation.

"The strong and the soft were equally his province," Wölfflin says, admiring the very sense of opposite pulls that so disturbs other critics. "If he paints a battle, he surpasses all others in the expression of unchained passions and tumultuous movement, yet he can catch the most tender emotion and fix the most fleeting expression. Qualities which seem mutually exclusive are combined in him" most miscibly: "the world revealed itself in all its inexhaustible riches."

So, sure, in that treasure trove some stones are smoothed, and lustered. "For Leonardo, delight is the role of the young animal . . . the kittens, playing or licking themselves—the kittens he puts everywhere in his sacred subjects, to the great dismay of his pious patrons." And some stones' edges want blood. "Further on . . . there is effort, tension, monstrosity. There is ugliness and unconscious suffering; above all, there is conscious suffering, everywhere."

For de Santillana: "In all of this, there is a beautiful order. There is a logic, the supreme knowledge of the prime mover . . . which was able to allot to all those powers the quality of their effects in the necessary proportion. The universe has no frustration."

To hold it, all. Roger Shattuck discusses "Leonardo's mental organization," quoting Valéry and Freud, and concludes: "The division we have begun to lament publicly between two climates of thinking, scientific and humanistic, between opposed methods of inquiry, cannot be traced to any corresponding division between regions or faculties in the mind. At the origin is unity."

I can't claim he was a happy man. But I'd like to think so. Philipson: "The fascination of Leonardo's personality rests on this fact: that the essence of self-enjoyment is directly related to the interest one takes in the attractions of the rest of the world—in nature as well as in one's own spirit . . . *all* he did was to *enjoy himself*."

And so I return to his labyrinth-ranges that back his famous smiling model with phantasmagoria rampant: they function. "This is no caprice on the part of the artist, but a means of increasing the apparent solidity of the figure. It is an exposition of some of Leonardo's theories concerning the appearance of distant objects . . . and its success is such, that, in the Salon Carré of the Louvre where the *Mona Lisa* hangs, all the neighboring pictures, even those of the seventeenth century, look flat."

(He's come up from the beach. The land rises, it's mountainous now, he's idly knotting a twist of rope picked up from an overturned hull—he loved knots, and this love I'll speak about later. Now, though, he's lost in convolutions. His eyes took a snail from the sand, his mind's reconstructing it into a spiral staircase—we still have the notes. He's searching for stones, for any kinds of stones, he's poking the gullies and crags of the mandala, wandering—even the pit of it, wanting to find out—even the shadow. He's brought a candle.

"Suddenly there arose in me two things, fear and desire—fear because of the menacing dark cave, and desire to see whether there were any miraculous thing within.")

7.

The Reade Zone Medical Center is west along Irving Park, near where the city boxes itself into suburbs. Just the day for it. Classes are over, I'm with Linda, the sky's the color of cream of potato soup. We joke. It's early fall in Chicago, the roadside weeds—when you're far enough west for such rustic touches as weeds—are like old aerials: gray, telescoping, and bent. We even sing a little. What do *we* know, we've never been near a place like it. And Ellen's committed herself. Voluntarily. We say it a few times, *voluntarily*. How bad could it be?

The grounds are immense, and barren except for occasional wads of litter. The wind has room to accumulate force here; in the parking lot we're almost whipped up with a few crumpled handbills and Kleenexes. As if the Mayor's afraid the ground itself might gather gale impetuosity and take suddenly off, the buildings are squat red brick. Like paperweights, they hold down the crew-cut lawns.

The hall is long, a bilious green. Something sour and something antiseptic court in the air. It's only our first step in, but already at the far end we can see people with a slow stupid shuffle, animal-shouldered, animal-jawed, their blinkless eyes as uniform as their institutional buttons. Even from here we can see, on a few of the faces, anger flash across like bolts of interference slashing a monotone news report. We get closer. These are the orderlies.

We have to sign in. Our names, our relation to patient, the time. As if confessing guilt by association. Then we're frisked. *She committed herself.* The door's unlocked, not without some fussing. *Voluntarily.* It's inches thick and sheeted over in metal. What do *we* know. *Out* is a word a whole panel of doctors has to say.

Well, I've seen places like it since. They make you want to drop, like a stone, to a field, and just let the rain hit. With my ex-fiancée I've entered: the floor where you're dragged like a sack; the floor with blood on the walls, and the old people peeing; the Tunnels, in the basement, where there's easy sex, where two eyes full of needing it fall on two eyes empty of everything. Then the medic comes by and says your hearing's postponed. He says don't worry, the guard will be reprimanded. The night is a needle. The day is a night. The guard smiles.

Linda lets me go first. It's a common room, haphazardly divided by ruptured couches and table-and-chair arrangements. Three dozen people or so, mostly patients, go through their Boschian motions. There's a bunch of frantic pacing, and even the stiller people knit with invisible yarn or pluck at cello-string drool or shake their heads like cans of paint till they hear the metal ball clicking. Ellen stands out by her quietude. She's in a chair by a window, huge as ever, her hands asleep in her lap. A burly red-headed fellow, ringlet-haired and bearded, growls protectively. Warning over, he leaves in a slope-shouldered walk. We sit down. Less a group portrait; more a still life.

"Flipped your coco, huh?"

No answer from Ellen. Her jaw is blue with a coat of stubble. Colorless flowers pattern a shapeless frock.

She's so serene, though. It's hard to be sad. And then her hands lift up, and swirl, like young birds learning.

Slow, very slow: "Albert." And then: "I. felt. a. little. wrong."

We spend a half hour that way. It's disconcerting but never dramatic: Ellen's answers always make sense. They're long in coming, though, as if she's standing back a couple of miles inside herself. And always her hands, her bird-friends, answer first.

Sammy's fine.

They miss you at the office.

What a way to get out of work.

Some great material here.

Do you want your books. Do you want your books. Ellen. Do you want your books.

The window's barred but clean and the light pours in. A few times there's a smile even, clumsily done, as if drawn on her face by a child— in that room, though, it's exemplary mirth and Linda and I hang onto it. We say we'll visit again. On the way home Linda cries. It sounds so healthy, compared to the Center's gibbering. The sky, which for a time had opened up, goes gray again and I drive around a long while, not straight back, in wide consoling automotive circles.

Three dozen people or so, on valium. —Whose mouths are open all day around the *e* in *help* but can't get the *help* out.

8.

"Yellow brick was a common building material in late nineteenth-century architecture." But what Baum does with it! Certain ritual, certain fantasy, pertinent channels of psychic need, allow the common walkways of the world to exhibit on either side (as Eissler says referring to Leonardo's art) "the transcendent through the immanent." By the time Baum's into chapter three, that "hard, yellow roadbed" Dorothy takes will lead us past "neat fences at the side of the road" and "fields of grain and vegetables" to a talking scarecrow, witch trouble, flying monkeys, and a ripping away of the curtain that secrets humbug authority everywhere.

The movie journey is a classic. Judy Garland, in a special corset to flatten her breasts, gives splendid authenticity to Dorothy. Special effects spent a week, picking the proper yellow (in those days some shades photographed green). One-hundred-and-twenty-four Munchkins gather around to the Good Witch Glinda's invitation: "Come out, come out wherever you are / And meet the young lady who fell from a star. / She fell from the sky, she fell very far / and KANSAS she says is the name of the star."

They greet her in all their diminutive flowerpot greasepaint mustachioed pouf-sleeved jester-capped sunbonnet glory. You know what's ahead: the mythic journey: past smudge pot, past axe head, to brains and courage and heart. But I want to focus in now at the start of it all, the genesis-spot of the Yellow Brick Road: Dorothy's ruby slippers taking the first irreversible steps: it'll straighten, and swoop, and follow both the most bizarre and most pragmatic of narrative needs: but first it begins as a spiral.

———— ⋊⋉ ————

So, the common walkways of the world. On the floors of old churches, one can still find stylized pilgrimage trails, done in mosaic design with Jerusalem marked out at the center. "These pilgrimage ways are labyrinths, like that in which Theseus killed the Minotaur. This is clearly spelled out in the church of San Michele in Pavia, where, beside the labyrinth, are the words: *Theseus intravit monstrumque biforme necavit* ('Theseus entered and killed the two-natured monster')." Killed it. Maybe (another way of saying) made it whole.

It isn't strange, by now, to see how many paths partake of the shape—especially those that have to do with spiritual matters, especially those in which the spiritual matters have once been institutionalized. Think of the codified merrymaking swirl about the maypole. Or, austerely but just as ecstatically: the Mevlevi dervishes: turn, and whirl, and turn. "Ancient mazes marked out in turf or with stones are often called after Troy, itself a word apparently meaning 'to turn.' These Troy mazes are connected with dances at places held to be entrances to the other world." For initiation, Australian aborigines are commanded to take to the bush—it's termed a "walkabout," they "wander through the country, hunting as they go, singing and swinging their bullroarers as a mark of their new status," braving the maze of the wilds. "This is why he who knows how to follow or make the diagram has his passport to the other world and resides in the god."

Then it isn't strange that the pagan puzzleway laid out by Daedalus reappears in Christian guise—the floor of Chartres Cathedral "with a pathway some six hundred and fifty feet in length, leading round and about until the center is reached." The French labyrinths "appear to have been called *in lieue* or *Chemin de Jerusalem*; they were placed at the west end of the nave and people made a pilgrimage on their knees."

Nor is it unexpected to find the motif predating Daedalus—the rock carvings in the Camonica Valley, Italy. "A demon is represented . . . as in a labyrinth. The legend of the Minotaur doubtless draws its origins from this kind of concept. Sometimes the monster is pictured within the labyrinth; sometimes he seems to be one with it, to be himself the labyrinth."

A thread through human history—with many looped knots up its length, but running uncut, and always connecting.

And those prehistoric rock carvings . . . from where do they draw *their* origins?

A man in Texas wakes, and shivers, and at 3:00 A.M. is the only live thing in the universe. He wants to make it through. He wants to stare it down, till the sun rises and the world starts. He wants to be new. He stares then, hard: his fingerprints, whorl-in-whorl. *TO this, THROUGH this, OUT again.*

"Or, as John Layard has observed, among many similarities in labyrinth ceremonials and beliefs 'certain facts stand out as being of special import.' The rites invariably have to do with 'death and rebirth.' "

And so they learn their attributes, through trial; and, by way of initiation into this world of newfound knowledge, receive appropriate symbols: a ribboned diploma (he furrows his dirty cloth forehead and quotes the means whereby we formulate the hypotenuse); a ticking heart-shaped watch; a medal stamped HERO. "The men who are broken in body (the Scarecrow, the Tin Woodman) are restored to wholeness, as is the one who is broken in spirit (the Cowardly Lion)."

Dorothy returns to her origin-world, bolstered by her gain: a heightened sense of Self and Place. "In the end, reality and home are restored." Perhaps she slops the pigs now finding oil and water make rainbows anywhere. Few films live as long or as well.

Its thematic concerns are so lightly a part of the whole, and the whole so unselfconsciously jolly, analysis seems at most a violation; and, at least, seems rude. But the delight survives—and supports—interpretation. "The Yellow Brick Road is the path through the chaos, the anchorage to reality like the river in *Huckleberry Finn*."

"*The Wizard of Oz* was published the same year as Freud's *Interpretation of Dreams.*"

A man in Texas will wake from a dream, will shiver with it, but finally feel successfully tested.

The trees of the Magic Wood, the witch's glinting-eyed retainers, doors in the Emerald City irrevocably slammed shut, that lush but oh-so-narcotic field of poppies . . . and then the clear light. The morning, being stronger for the night just spent; the morning and morning's clear light.

Although first it takes being there at the center, a common home of common construction: whoosh through the spirals of cyclone.

9.

They don't manufacture new seltzer bottles—not worth it. Each one extant is an antique "and the handsomest bottles of all, pale-blue or sea-green, with delicate, unseamed, tapered lines, were hand-blown sixty years ago at a glass factory in Czechoslovakia. . . . Because of the pressure in a seltzer bottle, and because of a coiled spring in the head," the shape again, exemplary and commanding wonder, "seltzer stays full of fizz until the bottle is practically empty—unlike an opened bottle of club soda." The bubbles in morning light catching fire, rising like magma red and fresh from planetary creation, here and everywhere: a paean to the shape.

Yes it's morning. The helix of a peeled orange on royal blue china. Yes it's night. The needle in a record, the sweet black jazzy spinning-in.

The Archimedean Spiral "is defined as the plane locus of a point moving uniformly along a ray while the ray rotates uniformly around its end point." Huh? "It will thus be traced by a fly crawling radially outward on a turning phonograph record." Yes, of course, there it is. Not that they notice, the jazz having carried them somewhere into their own postmidnight fleshly definition of the shape.

It shines from high. The Spiral Nebula nests in a telescope tonight, like any many-legged insect safe in a secret chute, and keeping to itself

an other-than-human brightness. It calls from below. "Many discoveries—not one of them more interesting, to the layman, than this: the
dominant direction of coiling of shells of a certain species of
Foraminifera, *Globorotalia truncatulinoides,* changes with some chemical or physical change in the water—probably the temperature." I see
them, coil-left, then coil-right, like the sleek fastidious chorus-line kick-
kick of the millennia.

Amazing, yes? Wherever our stunned sight turns: amazing. "There
is, for example, a small plumed worm called Spirorbis." It secretes
about itself a tube which is "not much larger than the head of a pin
and is wound in a flat, closely coiled spiral of chalky whiteness. The
worm lives permanently within the tube," both snaring its food and
breathing by means of "delicate and filmy tentacles."—This from
Rachel Carson.—There, on the beach, and fitting her morning's dili-
gence to the shape of the chambered nautilus, the Spirula, the
knobbed whelk, the moon snail making its gelid way, the lightning
whelk, the tulip shell, the pink conch, the horse conch, the embryo of
the nudibranch, the umbilicus-shell of the Sundial of Taiwan.

I sing of the "spirals at the Maltese temple of Tarxien" and "those on
a stele from one of the Shaft Graves at Mycenae, c. 1650 B.C." I sing it,
sweet and jazzy. The spring in a cheap tin windup toy's frog-spotted
body, powering half-inch hops. The carried curl of an elephant's trunk.
The carried curl of an insect proboscis. Maybe the record stops, but still
they're making love. At night—they're powering. The metal thread up
a screw. The green spring wound in the cotyledons. Cornucopia.

The new spring drives the new year open. My father goes to syna-
gogue, it's *Rosh Hashono*—"The Head of the Year"—and the first thing
he does, as prescribed by The Book, as performed by the ancients and
handed on down: is coil the black leather strap of *t'fillin* devoutly up his
arm. He pulls it tight. He feels his body's bloodthump tested against
this sign of his adoration, successfully tested, he closes his eyes. He
blesses me. I sing for his spirals. I sing for his phylacteries.

I sing, and I want you to sing, for a couple tonight on the couch,
and what they carry: "the chemical messages of inheritance from

generation to generation . . . DNA." Bronowski: "a sort of spiral staircase, with the sugars and phosphates holding it like two handrails. . . .
It is an instruction, a living mobile to tell the cell how to carry out the
processes of life step by step." It's everywhere, and it isn't stopping.
Yarn, on a room-sized industrial spindle. The Three Little Pigs' pink
curlicue tails. "The airy, spiraling trellis design of this porcelain plate
was created in St. Petersburg for the private dinner service of Empress
Elizabeth I, about 1760." They're done, or they're in between, he's
getting up to turn the record over—she goes for rosé and a corkscrew,
and stops, and thinks of the shape. Let's sing to fill the silence. Rings-
in-rings of her ravenblack pubic hair.

Two eyes lost like two crazed hares in a thicket: a woman studying
scrimshaw.

Rat (like a lonely man's thought) around an experimental maze
(like a lonely man's brain convolutions).

The shape, the shape.

It's Leeuwenhoek, over the world's first microscope—able to pay,
for the world's first time, attention to the dozenfold spiraling "animal-
cules," gray torques, in his glistery spit, in the pastes from between his
own teeth.

"A proton enters the bubble chamber from the left, then knocks an
electron out of an atom (spiral track), and then collides with another
proton to create sixteen new particles in the collision process."—A
lovely physics, some of its microphotography scattered with coils like
the Bahaman sands.

Collision process, renewals between the collision process.—He
walks back from the phonograph, she's in his head like a black sweet
bar of jazz. Though he stops at the john first. I sing of the shape, I sing
and his one gold note in the bowl is accompaniment. "Urine passing
through the slit-like urethral opening is emitted in the form of a thin
sheet that twists and spirals for approximately 100 to 150 mm (four to
six inches)." In this phase, the length of each twist is determined by
bladder pressure (velocity), from "9.5 mm (three-eighths of an inch)"
to "an increment of almost fifty mm (two inches)." The shape, its poet-

ries and exonerations, its citizenry, the shape and its anguish, its licorice-twist esperanto, its blood down the drain, its snakeshape copper bracelet up a countess's olive-tone arm, the shape, its dialectic, the shape, its lore and its lure and its singings.

This set down in the autumn of 1979 in a spiral-bound notebook.

10.

Ellen is released in a month. Her parents' money buys her halfway time in a private facility, the Fox Grove Rest Home.

"Albert . . . hi!" A grizzly-bear hug and a chimp smile. Real talk: would I like a soft drink from the canteen, would I prefer her room or the sunporch. Pointing this out to me, and that.

Compared to the Reade Zone Medical Center, the Home is a luxury spa where butterball girls from wealthy families come to slim. The room is frilly. The roommate's watching TV while her wrist scars heal. Nobody mentions the scars, but we talk about the TV quite a bit. "I can answer three out of four of the game-show questions. I'm thinking in terms of career." The orderlies pass the door like laundered sheets on a clothesline. A bud vase sprouts a jonquil. Ellen's poems taped on the wall. "And my folk opera . . . Albert, when I walk on the beach I sing it to the fish!" There's some excitement in the little box: a schoolteacher's won a trip to Paris and cutlery for a dozen. "I'd sing it to the moon but I can't go out at night yet."

A fact she accepts. They're truly helping her here. They've decided it's lopsided chemicals; lithium will work. The days are spent in analytic chats, in searching for her proper dosage. Purple capsules and a pleated paper cup. At ten o'clock the floor turns out for Pill Line. There are zombie faces, faces like bags full of cats to be drowned . . . it's still, let's admit it, the funny farm. I've still had to sign in. But this time, this place—for up to an hour—I can sign Ellen out.

The Home is at the point of one of those frequent V's in Chicago where a slum and an older wealthy neighborhood meet. One way you wend across the clover-patched grass of a city park, to where Lake

Michigan foams like bacon fat along a strip of sand. But we want hot dogs in steamed buns With Everything On Them To Go, so drive a couple of minutes into a noontime gnarl.

"Albert, stop, look."

There's a man facedown on the sidewalk. I pull over sharp. A dozen people, at least, walk by; some step directly over. He's moaning. A little blood leaks from under his nose, and when Ellen lifts his head we see the blood nets it. He smells like a distillery sieved through an old sock.

"Go 'way." The voice of a mean, hurt crow.

"Albert, we have to help him."

He pisses. It picks up the blood, then the whole wet sheet of it slithers its way to the curb.

It's my father's car.

"Go 'way."

"Ellen, no one who lives here stopped." *You absolute turd, you, Goldbarth.* "Maybe they know best." *You little shmuck.*

"But, he's sick."

We prop him between us, Ellen the Queen of Fox Grove Rest and Goldbarth the Little Shmuck. Then dump him in the backseat like a pair of apprentice garbagemen.

"There's a People's Free Clinic somewhere. They mentioned it in the ward."

"Go 'way."

"Where?"

"Well, I heard about it, but I'm not sure where exactly. Close by. We can stop a policeman and ask."

"*Go 'way.*"

"Should I sing him my opera?"

"Um, let's drive around and find it on our own."

By Lawrence and Broadway he's puked.

"If he'll fit through a window, chuck him out."

"Albert. . . ."

"Just kidding." Down Sheridan maybe? Down Ainslie? "But Ellen, your hour's almost up."

"Albert, he's *sick*."

Uh-huh.

Three hot-dog stands go by. I'm signed responsible for twenty-five minutes of overtime with a runaway lithium loony, when we find the clinic on some block we've done at least twice.

"Doan wanna."

"Up the stairs, come on. I have to see doctors too."

For some reason this convinces him, and the three of us take the stairs with a kind of back-and-forth progress like eating corn on the cob.

Ellen signs him in.

When we're back at Fox Grove after five desperate minutes of speeding, Ellen hums her way up to her floor. Nobody's around. I'm sweating. She does something in between hums to the book. "Let's go for the hot dogs." "11:30" is artfully smudged into "1:30." When in Home, do as the Homans.

"Okay. We can eat them at the lake."

It's so good, seeing her sit on the sand and wave a kosher weenie With Everything On It to punctuate her points.

The lake can look really sludgy. Today it's not so bad, though; when the clouds break open, it's diamonded and torched, and you think with your nostrils. Canada seems to be in the air. Something fresh, from a long way.

"Sing for me, Ellen."

She sings like a poultice. It falls to everything caught with a barb in the palate, and asks to smooth.

She's seen it, she's stared it down with her eyes turned inward, her voice like new skin over a burn. She sings something green and Welsh, and plants it lush by the side of a shanty in central Ohio. She sings from a series of rounds, to be transcribed on Möbius strips, to never end, ever.

Ellen-With-Tilted-Halo-Of-Mustard. "My parents are coming with Sammy this weekend. Albert. . . ."

"What?"

"I think it'll be okay."

I think it'll be okay, too. And then she tells me something, My-Friend-Ellen-On-Her-Way-Back-From-Halfway, she tells me something special.

11.

This is where I leave Leonardo: on a beach, having figured it out. Having brought a problem of stairs to the shape of a snail, having it answered there.

He's standing at the tideline in his white Rhenish linen and deep-red Florentine cape. The cape falls in folds to his knees; occasionally a rough wave reaches the hem, which is soaked for an inch all around. And so he's encircled, as if in a magic space.

He loved the spiral. He drew "ten spiral staircases round a tower," refined the architecture, measured, chalked it in, a knotty problem. He's idly knotting a twist of twine.

"It is fascinating to note that Leonardo da Vinci in describing his proposals for building new towns makes the point that all stairways in the 'public housing' should be made spiral stairs so as to prevent the sanitary misuse of stair landings." He who dissected the bowel.

In one of his graphics, he places his name at the middle point of an intricate hundred-interwoven-knot design "in the same manner as [the names] of various medieval church architects occupied the central points of cathedral labyrinths. The affiliation of such knots to labyrinths is thus clearly established."

I leave him, where the world of land and the world of water sizzle and mix: contented today, a little weary, sure, but content, and watching the first magenta spill of the day on the ocean. He once did a sketch of *Pleasure and Pain*. They're figures of equal size and substance, looking in separate directions but attached a bit above the waist to the same one healthy functioning torso. Which looks as if it's about to take a step, off the page, its four arms in balance.

He never did fly, but he knew where to take his stand.

He steps off the page, this page. Whatever name the monster had, there's only *da Vinci* now calm and assimilatory, declaring shape from the center.

12.

Five-rayed, four-dimensional, golden, hat as—just the index shows the manifold explorations Jung made of the mandala.

It was "the most complete union of opposites that is possible"; it was a "world clock" that "never runs down . . . that revolves eternally like the heavens." It was a fiery wheel "as a concept for wholeness." He cites an alchemical dragon gobbling its own thick tail, a wide-eyed Christ surrounded by evangelical wing-beating beasts, an intricate Navajo sand-painting vortexing vision, an "eight-petalled flower."

"The horoscope is itself a mandala (a clock)." It was "a vision of Paradise . . . seven large spheres each containing seven smaller spheres." It was "the central symbol, constantly renewing itself . . . often pictured as a spider in its web" or "the serpent coiled round the creative point, the egg." It was "a small-scale model or perhaps even a source of space-time." He charts it through 400 patients' dreams.

The presentations, obviously, vary. Their direction, though, is similar, and clarified by others' later research.

Eliade says it's "the Cosmos" given "in miniature" and thus its re-creation is "equivalent to a magical re-creation of the world." When a magician designs it in corn flour at a patient's bed "the patient is immersed in the primordial fullness of life; he is penetrated by the gigantic forces that, *in illo tempore*, made the Creation possible." And it works: "This drawing is preserved until the patient is completely cured."

Or Huxley, on "a process by which a sick man would sleep in the temple of Aesculapius . . . in order to have the dream that would reveal the cause of the disease"—and, that done, the priests could prescribe a cure. "Aesculapius, the god of healing (whose sign was a staff with two snakes twined around it)."

The Aboriginal Rainbow Snake is another spiral—Huxley reproduces a lovely geometricized bark painting. To be swallowed by the snake is to "have been incorporated into a system of knowledge and action that gives a new sense of direction"—to be initiated. Successfully traveling the alimentary coils means a new life of wisdom or ecstasy—you're vomited up "transformed." But "a labyrinth" as Eliade points out "was at once a theater of initiation and a place where the dead were buried," and the rite of initiation was "a passage in which the soul runs the risk of being devoured"—of, using Huxley's version, *not* being vomited up: condemned to the serpent's belly acids.

"The representation of the beyond as the bowels of Mother Earth or the belly of a gigantic monster is only one among the very many images that figure the Other World as a place that can be reached only with the utmost difficulty." The necessary sickness, madness, death. To know it, "able to look the rainbow snake full in its glaring eyes as it swallows him." And then to emerge a shaman, one of those of the tribe who "cure disease, kill enemies by magic, foresee the future, and make rain fall"—life on what Eliade calls "the transcendent plane," what maybe Leonardo called a good day's work. Preceded by a frightening night's self-inventory.

Much of this assumes what Charles Poncé, in *The Game of Wizards,* convincingly argues: that the cosmos is a unified matrix, ordering itself along certain energy fields, and making its ordering principles known through the symbols shared panculturally in the collective unconscious. The spiral is such a symbol for the Dogon, an African tribe in what was once the French Sudan: totality is a "foundation stone on which the earth is created." It's topped by a spinning whorl, and in the Dogon myths, the entire structure descends from the heavens "down the rainbow, in a sevenfold spiral." Huxley continues: "Plato, in *The Republic,* used the same image as the model of the universe, which revolved upon the knees of Necessity, the spindle piercing the earth at its axis, and the rims of the whorl representing the orbits of the sun and the moon, the planets, and the fixed stars.

"Necessity is a goddess—for it is the woman who spins in these cultures. She spins, measures, and cuts the thread of life, which is then woven into the fabric of the body." The spiral holding—the spiral *as*—Existence.

If Poncé is correct when he espouses "the existence of a principle of order underlying the psyche, a principle that has a definite structure and with which the whole of our psychological and biologic constitution may be intimately linked," a "structure of order inherent in the universe, as the base of both physical and psychological realities"—and if it is the nature of the psyche to produce "archetypal symbolism of an impersonal character, more akin to myth," which is expressive of this Wholeness—then, no wonder certain images are ubiquitous, and speak of being Complete, or of being healed toward Completion, or of the terrible fragmentation before the healing takes place.

Poncé, by way of summing up Jung: "After many years of consideration he concluded that in any deep penetration of the unconscious the individual suffers a disorientation of his conscious personality, a decentering." There appears at such times "the psyche's announcement that an attempt is being made at the unconscious level to rearrange and reintegrate those components of the ego that 'break down' or 'fly to pieces.' The visual representation of this psychological process is the mandala."

13.

"I know it sounds crazy"—she's pleased with that—"but all the time I was there, in Reade Zone, I was living inside my Master's Report."

I look stupid.

"Inside my research on Joyce."

I shake my head, but can't tell if it's marking the air with a yes or a no.

"Remember a heavyset guy with red hair?"

"Sort of."

"He was my best friend there. Remember him, curly-bearded and muscled? Every night we stayed up talking. Sometimes we were strapped to our beds, sometimes not. We often stayed up till dawn."

She says this all so nonchalantly, shaping it out of the light beach day with what remains of a hot-dog bun.

"Albert, this is what was in my head the whole time: I was trapped in a maze.

"And he was the Minotaur. He was feeding me clues. And every time I figured one out, I took another turn toward the mouth of the maze.

"Until I was healed."

Many Circles

1. Solid Ground

If only this were about—and this were *only* about—respectably credentialed archaeology honcho/pioneer John Lloyd Stephens. Then it could be—and it could purely be—1839, and I could describe it like this:

He disembarked from the square-rigger *Mary Ann* at the British port of Belize in the Gulf of Honduras. Even with the breeze, it felt like stepping into a vat of something recently molten. The light: *so* bright, it made his straining eyes inadequate, as if he were a creature used to a twilight world. And just for contrast, he'll want to remember this light, and so will we: in only another five days Stephens and his traveling companion, the architectural draftsman Frederick Catherwood, will be in the thick of a forest gloom so dense, so ceilinged shut in jungle green, that not one nickel-spot of this light will fall to the forest floor in the whole of an afternoon.

"Do you have the papers?"

"Yes, in the trunk. There—being unloaded. Now you see to the case with your frame and your crayon sticks."

They had, independent of each other, traveled (some would say "explored" or "adventured") before. Stephens had visited Italy, Russia, France, Poland, Austria, Greece, Turkey, Palestine, Arabia—in the 1830s, a long, long way from his New Jersey. He had sailed up the Nile from Cairo to Aswan, he had lingered as well at other places equally steeped in resonance, Mount Sinai, the Dead Sea, Nazareth, the rose-stone ruin of Petra—in aura, a long way from the law office that he'd once established on Wall Street.

Now, Honduras. He was thirty-four. He'd read in obscure sources,
he had hints, and a whiff of the unknown flared his nostrils. "The papers" were documents identifying him as *Encargado de los negocios de los
Estados Unidos del Norte*: he was ambassador, what entrée to the favors of
President Martin Van Buren could do for an eager attorney-turned-
archaeologist. He was wearing a jacket to fit the post: the deep and un-
natural, beautiful blue of a royal occasion, with eagle-detailed golden
buttons set like coins against that blue, like the beckoning wealth of
the treasures of America (del Norte) come to lavish itself on the laborers of America del Sur.

And then it was folded back into the monogrammed trunk. In a
day, their attire converted to an outfit of the nearly shapeless and ob-
stinately durable native cloth: hat, shirt, and pants that Stephens said
"could take it and take it," *it* being something closer to torture at the
hands of nature than most of us could bear without turning back.

Not us, not La-Z-Boy Explorers & Sons. Our sleek weed-whackers
take us just so far, and not a single deviant, thunder-roughed, hiero-
phantic molecule over the line. Our ski wax. Our hibachi coals. Our
blush-on. Nothing here commits a self to simply leaping into alien risk.
We aren't John Lloyd Stephens.

So if only I *could* chronicle his hardships and his counterforce de-
termination—and leave it at that. If only his story *were* the story.

From Belize, a steamer transported them due south to Punta
Gorda, then on to Lake Izabal. Here they hired guides and a caravan of
pack mules for the strenuous journey across the mountain and down to
the tangled interior of Guatemala . . . war-torn Guatemala, as it turned
out.

Three political parties had recently taken up arms against one another, and belligerent splinter parties soon formed. The heartland was
a mess of operatically swaggering warrior chiefs with overly macho
scabbards and mustachios, and their cutthroat armies. Here, the name
"Martin Van Buren" wasn't worth a spit-up of chicken gizzard. Carbine
rifles skreeled in the always-too-close distance, and howler monkeys
chorused back. A favorite triplet of mine: "Catherwood?" / "Yes?" /

"This is *not* good." This country dissolved the potency of his wax-impressioned documents with the surefire whammy of horse piss showering cigarette papers.

One night, near the village of Camotán, they were attacked and "arrested" by a party of twenty-five "soldiers"—"ragged and ferocious-looking fellows," Stephens later wrote, "armed with staves of office, swords, clubs, muskets, and machetes." In the flickering light of burning pine knots, one of Stephens's men—Augustín—took a head slash from a swung machete, and Catherwood attempted to deliver an impromptu disquisition on the finer points of international legal codes. Before the scowling village alcalde begrudgingly released them the following day, they spent a night in the Camotán jail, guarded over by a sprawl of thugs who drank aguardiente, puked it out, drank more.

But the by-product dangers of civil war had *nothing* on the hour-by-hour rigors supplied by the land itself. Men fainted from the heat and sometimes vomited from a stink of rot that seemed to pace their trail like a living thing. The dimness was oppressive; when the thirty-eight-foot fronds of the corozo plant closed overhead, they felt as if they were festering in the gut of a Venus's-flytrap. They would dream that they were pieces traveling down its long digestion. It was thorny furze and interknit lianas and roots that ran above ground as high as their waists—in a jungle like that, a plant is mainly the Earth's way of making a fist.

The mules sank in swamp over their bellies. Cargo was lost to the muck. Catherwood couldn't draw without gloves, but *nothing* kept the mosquitoes out of one's breathing. Malaria waited for them somewhere ahead, an ambusher. Days were little more than successions of rent flesh; nighttime carried "twinging apprehensions of the snakes and reptiles, lizards and scorpions." That, from a man who'd cheerfully endured the Biblical deserts.

"Every step required care and great exertion. I felt that our inglorious epitaph might well read: 'tossed over the head of a mule, brained by the trunk of a mahogany tree, and buried in the mud.'"

And then they came to Copán, "half a dozen miserable huts

thatched with corn," and everything changed. Across a shallow but turbulent river, they saw a stone wall "in a good state of preservation." A flight of its stone steps led to the clear patch of an otherwise overgrown terrace. And *then*—with the sweatwork required to free it from its centuries of jungle vine—a stela nearly thirteen feet in height, completely squiggled with intricate carvings "unlike anything we had ever seen before." They had arrived.

"Solemn, stern," Stephens said of the male figure carved on one side, "and well fitted to excite terror." He and Catherwood oversaw more hacking away of wrist-thick lianas: one more stela, another . . . eventually fourteen, and the teasing hints of an entire city, platforms, pyramids, altars, heads of fiercely grimacing serpents and jaguars, Stephens working away "with breathless anxiety while . . . an eye, an ear, a foot, or a hand was disentombed."

"The beauty of the sculpture, the solemn stillness of the woods, disturbed only by the scrambling of monkeys and the chattering of parrots, the desolation of the city, and the mystery that hung over it . . . dark, impenetrable mystery."

Even today, in museums of Meso-American art—today, when those glyphs that look as plump as rolled socks, and those hook-beaked, beast-jawed, pantheonic faces, are only so much tasteful room décor and gift-wrap to our blasé eyes—a sudden confrontation with the real time-redolent thing can nonetheless be a powerful moment. How, then, to imagine the awe that Stephens knew when these stone columns more than twice his height, these buried bones of a culture, showed themselves for his rapt attention one lopped jungle creeper at a time? It must have been as if a god had entered his throat just then—something more than a man can take in without gasping.

And the point it all made. . . ! Well, no, not "made" exactly, he was too cautious an archaeologist for that, but surely "the point it all *implied*. . . ."

"Would you agree, Catherwood?"

The draftsman lifted the netting from around his eyes. He looked at the broken-off, figurally busy chunk of cornice he'd been sketching, then at the sketch, then at the original a further time.

"Johnny, the *world* will need to agree."

The world until then had been skeptical (at best). "Most scholars," writes C. W. Ceram, "viewed the American Indians as never having risen above a condition of basest savagery, and the suggestion that civilizations of the highest order had once flourished in the western hemisphere was unacceptable in academic circles." Scottish historian William Robertson was exemplary when he wrote in his well-known *History of America* (1777): "Neither the Mexicans nor Peruvians are entitled to rank with those nations which merit the name civilized." Yes, and here was Stephens, staring at a length of sculptured building-stone as magnificent as anything he'd ever seen in the ancient pyramid tombs of Egypt. He squatted, and let his fingers read the intensively curlicueish surface. Not even the locals, the *descendants* of these artisans, had remembered or cared.

"Well then. The world is going to need to write a more truthful past for itself."

If we can imagine (especially in the wake of his party's sufferings) his exultant pleasure in all of this, then we can begin to imagine the acute heat of his feelings when, just a few days into their excavating, these dormant secrets waiting to be awakened were snatched from his stewardship—worse yet, by someone whose own agenda excluded genuine interest in the ruins.

His name was Don Gregorio—self-styled *patrón* of Copán. He carried a silver-headed cane. He kept his muttonchops sleek in scented slather of fish grease. In a festive mood, he treated the village to gourds of sour wine. And in a heavier mood . . . there was also a more pragmatic cane, with a brass knob at its tip, and every one of his hacienda workers intimately knew the sound it made on human flesh. "Aside from his distinctive dislike of outsiders," says Maya historian Charles Gallenkamp, "he was angered that some of his laborers were being lured away by the high wages Stephens offered them to work at the ruins."

A lesson: the authority of two-bit village big shots is as fervent to keep itself whole and unchallenged as is, for example, that of reigning academic theorists. In any case, a Don José Maria Acevedo (whom Gallenkamp calls "a respected member" of Copán village, and Lionel Casson designates "one of Don Gregorio's henchmen": *not,* of course, that these assessments are exclusive of each other) approached the expedition claiming they were trespassing on land he owned—would they be so kind as to pack their Norte belongings, and vamoose the hell out? He'd be curling his muttonchops shag around a finger as he said this, in an awkward duplication of Don Gregorio's smoother gesture. His boleroesque silver-trim jacket would be ratty around the edges, and yet impressive in this land of mud and hunger.

In private to Catherwood, Stephens scoffed at the notion that *any* individual could think to own a range of this indomitable rain-forest backlands—and, in fact, there wasn't any title to the property that Don José could offer as proof. But the situation was complicated: they were strangers, already the subjects of Don Gregorio's rumormongering, daily treading half-blind over political lines of open fire beyond their comprehension. And who, in this jumble, *was* the interloper? the son of a son of a son of the son who'd patched a shack together in this country generations back, who fell to bed and wife and sleep each night with ten small hills of Guatemalan dirt beneath his nails—and yet who admitted he believed the land was useless, all unworkable root and rubble, who freely said that the "idols," so far as he was concerned, could stay forever lost? or the Anglo alien, here for such a scant, untenable while, but who had claim to real bonds of affection and knowledge tying him viably to these archaeological wonders?

"Ticklish," Catherwood said, "an impasse. This requires some eggwalking, Johnny."

Ticklish indeed. Potentially tragic. And so it would be a fine cliffhanger place at which to leave a stalwart hero, leave him that night sleepless, wandering the stelae, stroking crested juts and topknots of unknowable deities, whorled invaginations of unknowable calendar months, these faces scowling out *death* as grimly as devils, these gigantic stones as shyly exposed from their protective coverings as debutantes . . . we leave him here . . .

. . . but need first to remind ourselves, despite my own fat, lyrical di-
gressions: Stephens was properly moderate, always, in attempts to
guess the lives behind the artifacts; no rhapsode, but a rationalist.
(Perhaps the effect of his studentship at Tapping Reeves Law School in
Litchfield?) And his hope was, as he wrote, to conduct "an unbiased investigation" into those ruins; after all, "we live in an age whose spirit is
to discard phantasms and arrive at truth."

Gallenkamp says of Catherwood's exactingness that "unlike the
works of so many artist-travelers of the period who indulged in romantic
fantasies, his drawings reflected the unerring pen and critical eye of an
accomplished draftsman and scholar," and adds, "Stephens was guided
by the same integrity in his literary observations." Ceram agrees that "he
was a genuine archaeologist, not easily tempted into hasty conclusions."

He wanted *the thing in its accurate self,* and not the thing dissolved
and then remolded in his own speculation. "In regard to the age of this
desolate city, I shall not at present offer any conjecture. Nor shall I at
this moment offer any conjecture in regard to the people who built it;
or to the time when or the means by which it was depopulated; or as to
whether it fell by the sword, or famine, or pestilence.

"One thing I believe: its history is graven on its monuments."

With Ṣtephens, we're on solid ground. If only we could stay there.

2. Shaky Footing

He caught her with her tongue up her therapist's ass, he said. And she
said that she'd seen him at night, when he thought that he was alone in
the house, naked and rubbing—sensuously rubbing—cubes of ice
along his body from his nipples to his balls.

They told me this separately, of course: by then the papers had been
filed and they were living in different quadrants of town. And I realized
soon enough in each case that the instances reported were symbolic:
he was a cold, cold bastard; she was involved in therapy sessions so
bizarre, they were sicker than the neuroses they asked to address ("Although I did lick him. But jesus lord, *not there!*").

In *her* understanding, the therapy helped to clarify their marriage. In *his* understanding, he consistently radiated steady emotional warmth: a human heating unit set for the length of their marriage to level *sufficient*. She says that's crap. He says she's plenty bonkers.

Ah, the vagaries! Let's call them that: Teal and Justin Vagary, friends of mine (and representing, I'll bet, acquaintances of yours). If John Lloyd Stephens here means "solid ground," then these two tellers of ever-shifting, ever-disagreeing pasts—these tweakers of fact, these callers-into-question-of-*the-word*-"fact"—serve as spirits from the land of indeterminacy, where the footing is shaky, and *if* and *but* and *edit* are the road signs.

We'll return to them. (For that matter, just provide them with your e-mail address: *they won't leave.*) But if the subject is shaky footing, let's make it literal for a while. It's 1869 and Augustus Henry Julius Le Plongeon is immersed in the study of earthquakes.

He's born in 1826, on one of the Jersey Channel Islands off the northwest coast of France. He graduates from the École Polytechnique in Paris, and we pick him up next in Chile: he and a school friend, in their own boat on a sight-seeing voyage, are shipwrecked and swim their way to the coastal town of Valparaiso, where Augustus briefly settles, teaching languages and math at the local college. Next, California—the gold rush; work as a surveyor. After that, England, where he experiments with daguerreotype photography, perfecting, under the patronage of Lord Russell, the ability of the process to be of documentary value in the climate of Egypt. "He then may have signed aboard a ship to the orient, working as a navigator . . . Australia, China, Pacific Islands." Then back to California: dealing plots of land. We get the sense of a man for whom a map of the planet's particolor countries holds the rumpleable comfort of a patchwork quilt.

He builds upon the skills he learns. He runs a portrait studio for a while, and learns the then-new glass-plate negative process; he will eventually publish a comprehensive, 200-page *Manual de Fotografía,* and will document Peruvian ruins for a hobby. In San Francisco he "may have acquired medical expertise by apprenticing himself to a physician" ("even his foes and rivals addressed him as Dr. Le Plongeon throughout his life"), and he later establishes a private medical clinic in Lima, Peru, where he uses "electric hydropathy and modulated galvanic currents" to ease his patients' ills. A quack? A visionary?

It's this thread of interest in electromagnetism that leads him to studying earthquakes, sure as he is that surface upheaval is caused by "voltaic currents in flux." ("His writings included observations of animal premonitions occurring before a quake"—a visionary? a quack?). And this is the perfect time in his life for us to join him. He's going to journey again to England, where he'll meet Alice Dixon of Regents Park, and pay court to this nineteen-year-old liberated British woman twenty-five years his junior. He will become her husband; she, his lasting collaborator:

"Please do not forget," he wrote to the editor of the *Proceedings of the American Antiquarian Society,* "that the scientific world is as much indebted to Mrs. Le Plongeon as to myself and that I decline receiving all the honors and see her deprived of her part she so richly deserves. So be kind enough not to publish my portrait unless hers is also published."

Okay. Here *he* is, with his deep-sunk, bottom-bagged eyes and to-the-breastbone, unrolled-scroll-of-a-beard. We can read the intelligence on this face, we could sense it *by Braille*—that, and the pride of the autodidact. And here *she* is, at twenty-two, asquat amid the tumbled-down stones of a vault at Chichen Itza. Her hat is sensibly brimmed for fieldwork, and she wears no-nonsense cotton pants, and a skirt she'll put on *over* the pants: she rolled it up while laboring in rubble, and rolled it down as needed, to meet the standards of local Yucatan women.

She and Augustus are here (this photo is 1875) to excavate these Maya ruins. To mind-meld with the ghosts of their builders.

It was their lifework. Altogether, a breath above a decade, digging remnants of the Maya empire out of its possessive, obdurate ground. And because it *was* their life, and the start of their life together (they were in Yucatan within six months of the wedding), this was also their lovework. Whatever they were to each other, they also were to this idea immensely larger than each other. And because of the years involved, if nothing else, a running tally of their sufferings surpasses that of their predecessors Stephens and Catherwood.

The powder keg of guerilla gunfest hadn't abated; if anything, the war between the Mexican *federales* and the current-day Mayans had inflated since Stephens's visit. Alice wrote, of their initial ocean approach to the Yucatan coast, "The first sound from the land that reached our ear was the shrill of the bugle—ill omen"; and later, that they sweated on the baked land and the wretched flats of spring agave with "Remington always in hand, death lurking for us in every direction." One rebel group took its directives from a sacred Speaking Cross. One took its orders from a general with the resonating name of Crescencio Poot. There are dozens of photos in which the unflappable Le Plongeons and their hired workers pace along some ragged line of stone wall, while a military escort rings the background.

Alice fell to yellow fever within a week of their arrival ("we had been assured that no stranger attacked with the fever that year had escaped death"); later, malaria ("I only regret that it stood in the way of our perfecting our survey"). Her journal is punctuated with dire discomfort the way that other diaries note dates for dental checkups. Sailing in the twenty-ton sloop *Viva*: "Wish the weather would stop. Heavy thunderstorm. Very rough. Extra sick. Wish I was dead." She notes of the local bedbugs: "When they begin to feed on one it is like a needle running in the flesh. A dozen of them will draw an ounce of blood." And simply: "In order to complete our grand discovery, we have been sick to death in places where we could not procure medicine of any description, where, at times, we had not even bread."

Augustus was heartier, yes, but hardly unscathed. Once, a misleadingly steady branch that supported him over a shadowy limestone sinkhole snapped, and he fell to the bottom rocks. A gash entirely traveled his forehead. Alice attempted doctoring it with makeshift stitches like rawlings: "It was a jagged wound, refused to close at first attempt, and bled for six hours. Even after a new skin formed, I needed to cut him open again, for a painful extraction of slivers." Cockroaches feelered over their sleeping bodies. Sharks were their constant companions at sea. At the Temple of the Jaguars, work was halted by a column of locusts *a mile wide* and *seven days long*. The heat was a hammer flattening the mind to sheeted foil.

So tell me: who is this man here, doing a whoop-whoop whirl of dervish dance steps in that tumble of fretwork stone? What is this "grand discovery" Alice uses to keep herself swaddled in healing dreams?

Augustus on a ladder for a ten-hour day of photography, until he's nearly arthritically rigid . . . then back on the ground, and improvising a circulation-goosing hoodoo jig of deep joy in his toil.

"For each photograph the process was the same," write Desmond and Messenger. The collodion syrup was made by dissolving cellulose nitrate or gun cotton in an alcohol-ether solution. Then each plate was rushed up the ladder to the camera before it could lose its sensitivity, "exposed for a calculated amount of time, and rushed to the darkroom for development." This, for *sixteen* seamlessly overlapping stereo views of a wall 320 feet long. In that heat. With the sting of that insect torment. The sweat like teeth in his recent gash.

The result was "pioneering" according to Desmond and Messenger. Also comprehensive: excavations, architectural floor plans and cross sections, detailed photographic records, ethnography, field notes, molds of bas-reliefs in papier-mâché, translations. "The first systematic Yucatan dig . . . ." "Their highly sophisticated photographs are *still* among the best visual records of many sites. . . ." Alice published distillations of their research in such venues as *Harper's, Journal de Société des Americanistes,* and *American History. Scientific American* commended her in 1895, as one of a score of "women in science who have contributed to the knowledge and the culture of our age."

Augustus and Alice: what went wrong?

As almost always, the answer is: the same as what went right.

And their sex life there on the ground or in their hammocks amid the develop-ment equipment and the picks, above that buried vein of another culture, buried vein of another time, their sex life as the little yap-dog Trinity bonked its way around the stacks of tinned food, over the vein of raw-heart-in-an-a ltar-dish, and over the vein of serpent and monkey deities, what of their physi-cal pleasures there in the vampire heat? We don't know. Our talk-show sensi-bilities ask the question, but the answer isn't available. We can only imagine them curled at rest in the same mosquito netting: a single marbled cheese in its cheesecloth.

It's foolish to limit the moon with time. It isn't "an early period Mayan moon" any more than it's "a moon above a Broadway opening." Still, they can't help looking into the night at this full, steady presence, somehow feeling it emoting a special fondness for the world of Mayan kings and queens . . . making them, despite their recent arrival, coeval with that world; making them two of its population.

"Augustus . . . ?"

"Yes."

"Sometimes . . . when I glance at you, as now. . . ."

"Yes, I know."

The journey may be fantastical, but each small, contributing step has a credibility.

When Augustus notes that a shield in a wall mural is distinguished by a pattern of "round green spots"; when he infers, or more *communes with,* more *divines,* that the warrior bearing this shield is Prince

Chacmool, a brother of the regent-queen; when he remembers seeing a ruined mound just a few days earlier, also with that pattern of spots; and when, having thus understood "the signs of the stones," he orders digging into the mound, to find a large reclining human figure five feet long and several hundred pounds, "the Mayan prince himself, he of the Shield of Jaguars" . . . this example of an almost mystical intuition is credible. After all, it happened. There were witnesses. Juan Peón Contreras, director of the Museo Yucateco, said that "by his meditation, he determined the place, and, striking the spot with his foot, he said, 'Here it is, here it will be found.'"

"You know, of course, what the workers say." Alice idly shoos away some insect as pudgy and drifting as a Montgolfier balloon, but doesn't remove her eyes from her husband.

"Yes. I do."

"They may be right, then. They are of the blood—*they know.*"

And when Augustus leads a group of his native laborers to the summit of the pyramid at El Castillo—leads them "with great mystery and ceremony"; and when he points to the profile of a warrior on a doorjamb there, a warrior with a great, low-hanging beard; and when, with grave and florid rigamarole, he places *his* own face beside the *carved* face; when the workers see this, and kneel . . . this tale is credible. There were too many there, to naysay it now. Desiderio Kansal, one of those laborers, later told his grandson how "we saw that these two faces were the face of one. And so we said that night to each other, 'Doubtless they are one.'"

"Augustus, there *is*. . . ."

"Yes, Alice. You as well. I see it when you turn, *so,* in the sun. This is why we met one another, don't you think? You *do* think it, Alice?"

In back, the parrot Fiction (because it never repeated them truthfully) takes *its* turn and, with a twitch and beak-snap, sends the insect (almost as if in a game of Ping-Pong) back their way.

"Yes." Pause. Shoo. "I believe . . . *I know.* . . ."

"We must be sure, Alice."

"*I know.* . . ."

(What *we* know: they were steeped in the Maya experience. Their research and their marriage were indistinguishable passions. "Yucatan was their life; the Maya, their family" [Desmond and Messenger]. Now perhaps if we set their marriage, set the anomalous *themness* of them, in all of its intimate force, against a carving of their arduous daylong fieldwork—we too would kneel, stunned by the congruence, and say in whispers to each other, *Doubtless they are one.*)

". . . We have been here before, Augustus."

There is soil under the soil, it goes down to the unthinkable dot at the center. There is earth in the Earth that hasn't been touched by light for a millennium. There are temples, sleepmats, sexmats, stairs that lead to gods—inside the planet. A millennium! But let that soil be brought to the surface: nothing has been forgotten. There isn't an excavated speck that needs retraining. There isn't a single dust mote anywhere in the dance of light that fails in filling its function with grace.

Steeped in it. For starters, they valued, and befriended, the current-day Maya. They mingled with the women grinding corn (one of their candid photographs shows a woman pressing onto her roller pin in exactly the pose—the same stiff concentration from her shoulders, down her stiffened arms, to the materials she works with—that, elsewhere in this same year, 1875, Degas sees in a robust Parisian laundress). They watched the *etzmeek nylan*, the rite of passage at four months ("Five eggs are buried inside a mound of hot ashes, there to break, and the child thus to have all five senses awakened"), and they'd set aside their shovels and Remington rifles to dance in the long arcaded plazas of Yucatan villages.

Augustus put his medical expertise to work and, at the request of the Yucatan governor, vaccinated for smallpox as they saw the need arise in their travels around the thick-grown forest towns near Uxmal (he was unsalaried in this). Their hearts went out to the Mayan laborers at the sugarcane, cattle, and sisal haciendas ("they live and die in abject misery," Alice wrote, and tried to sensitize the North American press to this plight in a number of articles); in the tradition of Stephens before them, they provided better wages than the hacienda overlords.

They would halt their three-mule wagon at a likely location and, in a snap, Augustus—spade and entry book in hand—would be doing the high-step walk of a heron or a crane, through the knee-tall shrubbery. Sometimes there would be no people at all. Sometimes, distant watchers, with impassive faces—no more easy to read than the faces on weather-smoothed stone. Occasionally, far gunshots. But at other times, the word would spread, and a gathering of full-blood Mayan villagers would greet them with explosively affectionate shrieks and roughhouse banter: the "healer people" were here, the living ones who were like the Old Ones. They would sing as Alice strummed guitar.

And so, in part through predetermined plan, in part because affection carries—and is borne by—language, Augustus and Alice learned to speak Yucatec Mayan. They felt a warranted pride in this, and not infrequently a pushy pride, as they tried to find a home for their maverick ideas in scholarly circles. For the length of their professional lives, Augustus and Alice were *the* only theorists of Maya culture who truly had a living understanding of its language.

Everyone else had endless drafts of colloquium papers and a little brush for dusting off potsherds. Everyone else had death by which to study the dead. Not them, *they* had the words, the breath, the *tick-tick* in the wrist, the mojo, the witchery vibes. They said "here," and the earth gaped wide, and there was the carven eloquence of the ancestors. How *could* any of Yale's or Oxford's illiterates disagree? Desiderio Kansal remembered climbing the pyramid steps to the temple of Kukulcan and, by his candleflicker, witnessing Augustus in a hieratic mutter in front of an earthen vessel, "the kind the ancient ones used in burning incense before their gods."

In the epic poem that Alice published in 1902, she says: *"When evening came, and all from work reposed, / They told the white man why the things inclosed / Were found by him: 'Thou art returned once more / From long enchanted sleep; wast here before.'"* It was credible—wasn't it, Alice? Aren't we, Alice? Doesn't a kind of current zizzle out of these stones, through the air, and into the waiting, ordained empathy-powers of They Who Know the Speech? He took a jadeite tube from an up-dug urn and mounted it in a gold brooch, Alice's "symbol of her spiritual connection with the queen of Chichen Itza." We can see it on her breastbone (it's the only gleam against otherwise flat black fabric) in the portrait of 1885. *"Within a white stone urn in ancient tomb, / Charred heart and talisman lay in the gloom. / To her, he gave the gem.—'Now take thine own, / I pray: henceforth it must be thine alone.'"*

Tommy Albright in Lerner and Loewe's *Brigadoon*: "Sometimes the things you believe in become more real to you than all the things you can explain."

They felt a warranted pride in their exclusive knowledge. It conferred on them a privilege in interpretation. They didn't learn about; they were *intimate with*. They didn't posit; they *knew*.

The animal representations in the murals of the Upper Temple, Augustus "took to be totems." An eagle "which he identified as a macaw" became the totem of Queen Moo, the Maya ruler. A fish, he designated as totem of the High Priest, Cay. A grouping of miniature columns, platforms, and altars at El Meco was the work of "a magical race of tiny people" who, according to local folklore, lived unseen in the jungles. A bas-relief face in profile on a wall at Uxmal is obviously Queen Moo—why else would it be so large, so prepossessing? The fragment of a statue, also at Uxmal, exhibited symbols (*secret* symbols) of Freemasonry. Would you be surprised to hear, then, that Augustus was a Mason? Three triangulated dots that follow his name in all examples we have of his signature are a reference to his membership in the brotherhood.

Augustus "openly stated that he came to the Yucatan with the hypothesis that the Maya were the founders of world civilization." Not surprisingly, all of their labors finally validated this whimsy. Would you be surprised to hear that Maya civilization thrived 11,500 years ago, before the glory of Egypt, Sumeria, Babylon? (This implicitly provided the Americas, not to mention the Masonic order, the great cachet that Graham Clark calls "the sanction of antiquity." A pedigree. The *best* pedigree.) Do you know that Christ's last words on the cross were Mayan?

Oh, yes. *Eli, Eli, lama sabachtani* is merely a phonetic version of Yucatec Mayan: *Hele, Hele, lamah zabac ta ni*, "Now, now I am fainting, darkness covers my face." (A *not* unreasonable statement for Christ to have made, let's admit.)

Do you know that thousands of years ago the Maya predicted the telegraph? Oh, yes. In the town of Espita, a man who was said by most of the locals to be 150 years old, received the Le Plongeons, and was interviewed. In the Akab Dzib, "the house of dark writing" at Chichen Itza, they could find a hieroglyphic text that spoke of a future day "when inhabitants of Saci (Valladolid) would converse with those of Ho (Merida) by means of a cord, that would be stretched by people not belonging to the country." Augustus reasoned that this man, Mariano Chable, given his age and insular town life, had no knowledge of the telegraph. Surely, therefore, something . . . *special* was alive here. Wouldn't you know it? When the Akab Dzib was cleared of brush, and the lintel above an interior door was washed, Augustus "saw glyphs that, to him, represented lightning or electricity" (Desmond and Messenger). Thus, the Maya-Marconi connection.

For all I know, we could justifiably say that Augustus Le Plongeon was a prototype of personal computer technology. Didn't he hack (this time I don't mean a machete) past the veils that normally intercept our human senses, didn't he plug his consciousness into a flashing all-connective web beyond the chintz and toxins of our own more limited world? Didn't he download thought at one end of a cord stretched to the astral computation of the Maya skies?

Oh, yes. Overhead, the days rolled on inexorably, Imix, Ik, Akbal, Kan, Chicchan, and the rest; and the months, from Pop through Uayeb; and over *these,* divinity stared earthward into the Order they created: the God of the Zero; Kinich Ahau, the Sun-face Lord; the Jaguar God of the underworld Xibalba; the Goddess She-of-the-Moon, holding the moon rabbit tenderly to her breasts.

It was against this backdrop of dazzlery that the bloated drama of Princess (later Queen) Moo played itself out: her love for her consort (and brother) Prince Coh (or Cay); his death at the hands of the other brother, the spurned Prince Aac; Queen Moo's escape from the armies of Aac, and her wanderings through Atlantis, India, lands of the Fertile Crescent (spreading civilization the way that Johnny Appleseed spread orchards), finally finding a home in ancient Egypt, where the people received her as Isis; and "after her death she received the honors of apotheosis; became the goddess of fire, and was worshipped in a magnificent temple. . . ."

Each small, contributing step had a credibility. If we relegate this now to the museum hall where phlogiston and phrenology and the homunculus are embarrassingly housed . . . if we "know" "better" now. . . . Still, is the penny-dreadful, mellerdrama saga of Moo and Cay and the sinister Aac any *more* incredible to our own non-Maya ears than the "actual" verified text of the *Popul Vuh?*—of Xquic, and Chipi-Caculha, and Raxa-Caculha, of Black Obsidian God, of the thirteen upper worlds-after-death, and of the nine below; and of the resurrected brothers who did the dances of the armadillo and centipede for the Lords of Death, and tricked them, and so killed the Lords of Death; of Rotten Cane, and the Demon of Pus, and Yellow Egret Woman; and of the priests (this is true) who draw the blood from their ear lobes and penises, using either thorns or swordfish saws. . . ?

For that matter, is the mythic parfait of Augustus and Alice Le Plongeon any less credible than . . . oh, let's pick Stephens's President Martin Van Buren, who campaigned in "a snuff-colored swallow-tailed coat with matching velvet collar, an orange cravat with lace tips, white duck trousers, a pearl-grey waistcoat, silk stockings and yellow kid gloves, and he topped the whole with a large, broad-brimmed beaver hat covered in longish fur" (Paul Johnson)? The picture defies being held in one's skull. It was during Van Buren's vice presidency under Jackson that Samuel Swartwout, Port of New York collector of customs, swindled the federal till of one-million-two-hundred-twenty-two-thousand-seven-hundred-five-dollars-*and*-nine-cents, scooting on to Europe with this boodle. *That's* a good one. Only the subsequent D.C. follies of the twentieth century make of it something the mind can digest.

What *can* we believe? The ostrich was said to digest lumps of iron. What fits and dissolves in our credulousness? I invented the parrot: *I* named it Fiction. Michael Oakeshott: "History is the historian's experience. It is 'made' by nobody save the historian." And Edward Hallett Carr: "The facts of history never come to us 'pure,' since they do not and cannot exist in a pure form: they are always refracted through the mind of the recorder."

True, but the Le Plongeons weren't charlatans smarmily counting up the yokels' ticket money after the midnight show. They didn't knowingly plant the bony knobs of Piltdown Man with a cynical chuckle.

In his study of the poetry of Albert Goldbarth, the critic John Enfield mentions the contemporary quest to find an original (that is, without precedent) wholeness: "If, as seems to be the case in today's world, our experiences of the originary unity must come not through ecstasy but through attempts to puzzle out what lies on the other side of the great divide, a poet can only look for that unity in what he or she finds on this side." Not the Le Plongeons. *They* contained a special resonating nerve that said it connected them, their flesh and soul, direct to

Revelation. Question: What if you *do* know ecstasy, and what if your ec-stasy *tells you* it's substantiated scholarly fact?

Shaky, very shaky, ground. Richter-scale shaky ground.

3. The Experts Beg to Differ

"We're like a little two-of-us island of contentment," one of them said, I don't remember which, or I *do* remember which, but someone else re-members the *other* one saying it. That's how it was with Teal and Justin, they blended. We thought that was good, or even a paragon, a sort of "ultimate sharing" other couples might aspire toward but never truly succeed at. "T and J" they were called by most of us at first, but "TJ" soon enough—"Did TJ get that CD yet?"—as if they made one person.

Maybe that was part of the problem; seen in those terms, they re-duced themselves.

But the first three years?—the smoochy-smoochy yummylove that choreographs itself to schmaltzy violins and mega-adrenalined bass guitars in made-for-TV movies. We just *knew* each cherished the sappy dream of giving up a kidney for the other. We *knew* they'd Done It on the hood of their car (its vanity plate: TEEJAY), the way it happens in those slinky glimpses in over-the-top rock videos for erotic "urban music" hits. "T, do you remember—" and we *knew, of course,* she not only remembered but understood by those four empty introductory words alone *exactly what it was* that he *hoped* she'd remember. It was beautiful (*creepy,* an inner voice said sometimes), beautiful, creepy, beautiful, creepy, beautiful. "J, I just—." "—Yes! Me, too!"

"Island of contentment," they said. We could even forgive them *that*—the goopy, willful adolescing of their love—as we forgave the in-evitability of his nerdy plaids, and overlooked the nasal shrill her voice assumed when she was excited. If anything, we liked them *more* for their sharing these tiny frailties with us—we had so many of our own. But they were the best of us. We'd have bet on them, blind, any time.

So what went wrong? What canker started eating its way across their mutuality, and (this, *this* was, as Andrea said, the real kickeroonie) what

dark perils did it augur for the rest of us, aghast at *their* emotional bol-
lix, and testing, now, our own dependabilities as if they were teeth that
our tongues had discovered were softening at the center?

When it started to happen? Year four. There was fog around them
now, there was a tendency toward barb and accusation. There was too
much of "You did" and "No, I didn't"—as if, in some odd quantum-
physics way, the Earth could hold two simultaneous pasts. Eventually this
became "You did" and "Fuck yourself. You're crazy." And it wasn't far
from that to the night at Amanda's house (it was, I think, her thirtieth
birthday party) that a face was slapped and a glass of wine was flung, and
I remember that Tillie needed to forcibly wedge herself between them.
It was the kind of scene that makes the taste in your own mouth ugly and
alien, simply from watching it. There was no going back.

Once, when it was just us and a pitcher of suds at The Cedar, I tried
to gingerly counsel Justin. He was sweating despite the AC blast, and a
stain in the shape of a person looked like something trying frantically
to escape from his chest—but kept in by the jail bars of plaid. And I
should be accurate: "counsel" really isn't true, who *could*? Because
nobody knew what thing had gone skewed at the heart of them.
Infidelity?—we thought not. Money?—no. *What* then? And Justin
wasn't telling. All he said was that he'd joined an AA group.

"But—you don't drink. I mean, one, two. But Justin, you're *not* an
alcoholic."

"I know." He shrugged. "Whatever, it makes me feel better to be
there, doing the ritual. So I lie. I *say* I drink. I've invented a gloriously
adventuresome drinking chronology."

It was nuts. Or it was a shrewd try at self-doctoring. Or it was a cruel
misuse of other people's real disease—although he assured me he was
well-liked by the group and considered an asset in their go-round of
confession.

And that was all; I learned no more from him and, lacking any target, had no solace I could aim. Mel met a similar failure with Teal. "She
sighed, she sobbed, she said she was 'coming apart,' she kept returning
to romp around in that topic like a dog to its vomit. But all of it was so

vague . . . ," and then Mel's hands made the sign of something evaporating into the sky.

If they needed a visible reason, though—a pole their fog could whirl around, and thereby gain a shape—they quickly got one. Teal started seeing a therapist once a week, then twice, then Monday-Wednesday-Friday, I imagined she'd feed me the Justin line: "It makes me feel better, doing the ritual." He was a charismatic, silver-templed, deep-voiced man I'd seen once give a showy presentation on "the Inner Journey." His name was Adam Mada (get it?): "The patient and I approach from our respective ends and meet in the center." "Adam Made-up," Justin said.

It took less than a month for Teal's "hypnotic regressions" to uncover a year of abuse: an uncle, from when she was five, "in my mouth and my anus, he was careful to leave the rest intact." As you can see, she had no prim reluctance in sharing the ugliest details; and the more she shared, the greater in number (and sadder) the details grew: a friend of the uncle's, a neighbor's dog, a man with a camera, the whole demonic cast of Pederasty Incorporated. The sobbing Mel had seen was only a series of seeds from which this new, luxurious tragic weeping flowered like some extravagant blossom that fed off a bone-rich landfill in Hell.

This might have been a perfect moment for Justin to rise to—set the fiddle back in its case (he played on Friday nights with Country Funk) and take a week of sick leave from his caseload at the firm, and console her. Instead, he told the truth: "I don't believe one word. Not one word."

He'd known Anthony, the uncle, who was only dead by a year—a decenter man you'd never find, etc. He wouldn't believe a mental bruise like that could *ever* be buried into nonexistence for *twenty-five years*—"it's called 'repression,' J"—"It's called bee-yoo-el-el, and I have a row of psychology journals a mile long to back me. People didn't forget *Nagasaki* or *Auschwitz*, kiddo." And also he couldn't believe "she'd do this" to her mother, "it was her only brother," she loved him and relied on him after her husband's death ten years before, and how could it be the mother had no inkling all that while, she and Teal were able to read each other's moods "across a fucking time zone" . . . *everything muddled, everything* turning to conversational drizzle.

It *was* incredible. According to Teal, her mother *had* known, had covered up the filthy secret. Jane herself, as Justin guessed, was shocked enough by her daughter's rampant narrative (and her daughter's distress) to require daily sedation. No, it *wasn't true*—I saw Jane make a fist through her narcotic blur. But Teal's woe was such a monolithic thing, so primal, it could counterbalance gravity or electromagnetic pull. It was like science fiction: Teal had traveled back in time, and altered the history books by her tampering presence. When that happens, of course, the present needs to change.

"J, look: just comfort her."

"*You* look. It's a lie."

"So what? She's your wife. It's real to her, and she's hurting."

"What do you mean 'so what'? If this lie isn't exposed, then there's another lie one day, and then another, and her whole life is a house of cards. Is *that* supposed to 'heal' her?"

The following month, she showed us a monstrous six-inch cut on her forearm. Justin had done it in anger. *She* said. The cut was real enough. The skin around it a rubbery purple. Lucy cried, and Dennis said that Justin *had* looked sheepish that day at the gym, but. . . . But. A razor? *Justin?* This was around the time, before, or shortly after, who knew in the drizzle of their back-and-forth, when Justin claimed she was, as he encryptically put it, "playing Missy Eve Eve to our Mr. Adam Mada." And he repeated the slogan "The patient and I . . . meet in the center," making a certain well-known, unmistakable sign with his hands. She was, she said. Yes, it was true. And then the next day she retracted that.

It was Evan who pointed out the pitiful wonder. He'd passed their house that night, and howling, "I mean *animal* howling," came from an upstairs window, followed by dishes and books, and then a humming—queasy, deep, eerier than even the howls. Teal or Justin? Everyone wanted to know. By then, though, *who* didn't matter. That was the sick,

sick miracle. In their misery, they were like one again, they were an island.

"Oh sure," Tillie said. "Atlantis." And we all looked down, to see if the cracks that run through the planet had traveled from them to us yet.

Nor do the experts agree.

In 1992, Pamela Freyd of Philadelphia created the FMSF—the False Memory Syndrome Foundation—in support of parents speciously accused of satanic or sexual abuse of their children. Was there a felt need in the country for such an organization? "It is currently helping over 9,500 American families."

Immediately, however, the organization, its goals, its methods, its funding, its findings, and its underlying assumptions were reviled by proponents of conflicting interests. *The Politics of Survivorship* by Rosario Champagne "concludes with a critical look at the way in which the FMS Foundation has conducted an antifeminist campaign against incest survivors and their therapists." Joan Shuman and Mara Galvez, in the journal *Feminism and Psychology,* add that "the FMS Foundation emerges as an accomplice of the mental health establishment and a leading force in the heteropatriarchal backlash against women."

Although the Foundation itself has made its official position a seemingly even-handed, objective one ("that whether they are continuous or recovered, some memories are true, some a mixture of fact and fantasy, and some are false": surely, by *anybody's* standards, a reasonable overview), David L. Kalof's article "Notes from a Practice Under Siege" alleges a program of harassment ("invasions of privacy; intimidation of family, staff, colleagues and others; interfering with landlord-tenant relations") leveled at "clinicians, lecturers, writers, and researchers identified with questioning the validity of the FMS hypothesis."

"Hypothesis" here, of course, is intended to damn. And according to John F. Kihlstrow's "Memory, Abuse, and Science," "the data presented to support claims of FMS are frequently extreme misapplications of published research." Also, "dignifying the idea of false memory with the title 'syndrome' silences women and children who are struggling to be believed" (Saraga and MacLeod). An article in the *Journal of Child Sexual Abuse* delivers a solar plexus knockout punch: "There is *no* evidence of a clinically verifiable false memory syndrome."

I could go on and maybe have you thinking there's nearly unanimous opinion on this subject. I *could;* but I would be deceptive; and you, naïve. "There are," as Yeats supposedly said in surveying his fellow poets gathered one night at The Rhymers Club, "too many of us." Accord isn't part of this story. If Chang and Eng, those famous ligatured twins who shared, for sweet chrissake, *their circulatory systems,* didn't live in the same attitudinal world (Chang, a drunkard and knee-jerk bully; Eng, abstemious and thoughtful) . . . then what hope is there for the rest of us, separate and misunderstanding even our own dearests any number of times a day? If Wallace Stevens promenading through the neighborhood was really the brain of a poet and the brain of an insurance company CEO at odds (or intermittently at peace) in a single human body . . . what are the diddlysquat odds that the *national* body politic *ever* will make a choraled-out consensus of its zillion-divisive voices?

The protagonist of John Cowper Powys's novel *Wolf Solent* remembers a moment "his father had made him throw back" an undersized perch: "As it had swum away through the aqueous dimness, between two great branching pickerel-weed stalks, he had had an ecstasy in thinking of that lovely, translucent underworld, completely different from his, in which, however, the pale-blooded inhabitants knew every hill and hollow, just as intimately—nor with such very different associations either—as he knew his own world."

There are always at least two realms.

And so we're *not* surprised a countervoice insists on the validity of FMS, that "in the hands of some therapists, mind-altering techniques create confabulations" (Eleanor Goldstein, *American Journal of Family Therapy*). "That early childhood experience could be repressed but recovered many years later is at variance with established knowledge concerning human memory. The common phenomenon of child-hood sexual abuse is contaminated by many cases that may be re-garded on strong grounds as being false, and have been retracted [as of 1996] in more than 1,000 instances. Repressed memory treatment is also at variance with traditional psychotherapy, which does not en-courage confrontation on the basis of uncorroborated information; moreover, many cases of repressed memory therapy seem to result in deterioration" (H. Mersky, *American Journal of Psychotherapy*). The analysis of recanted "contrafactual accusation" is now its own very busy and detail-laden subindustry. And the left to the jaw (from *Conscious-ness and Cognition: An International Journal*): "It is important to recog-nize that the construct of a repressed memory mechanism, per se, has yet to be scientifically established."

Meanwhile, the files on bogus recall are annually fattened. Patricia Burgus sought therapy for depression in 1986 after the birth of her second son, and Dr. Bennett Braun, a Chicago-based memory special-ist "over time convinced his patient that she possessed 300 personali-ties, had sexually abused her children, eaten human flesh, and served as the high priestess of a network of satanic groups." Later—three mil-lion dollars of her family's insurance policy later—Burgus had second, saner thoughts. "There was no way I could come from a little town in Iowa, be eating 2,000 people a year and nobody said anything about it." And who's saying what about the parishioner of Pastor (and coun-selor) Doug Riggs of Tulsa, Oklahoma, a woman who has "several thou-sand personalities, each possessed by hundreds of demons"?

In the signature case of the Little Rascals Day Care Center in Edenton, North Carolina, children testified to being thrown to sharks, to being cooked in microwave ovens, and to traveling in spaceships— this, although the building was in the center of its little town, and open to frequent unannounced visits by parents. Doctors could find no physi-cal evidence of sex crimes (which included claims of invasion by needles and cutlery); parents admitted using such techniques as with-holding desserts until a child provided, finally, a looked-for tale of horror in response to leading questions, and was rewarded. North Carolina: the state where "parents in Gaston County demanded that Africa and Germany be removed from classroom maps because these places are anti-Christian."

Grist for comedy—except that day-care-center owner Robert Fulton Kelly was sentenced to twelve consecutive life terms. Six other people were also brought to trial (including a man who had no link to the day-care center "but was named by one of the children as the owner of the sharks").

Robert Hughes: "There is nothing to prove these tales, but nothing to disprove them either—a common condition of things that didn't happen." Baloney, he means here: hokum and bilge.

Yet even so, atrocities *do* sear their daily pathway through our national awareness. Debra Robertson *did* scald her children to death (a six- and a five-year-old) by forcing them into boiling water: "she said she had been possessed by demons." Brian O'Rourke *was* twelve when Sister Linda Baisi, a forty-year-old Roman Catholic nun, initiated a five-year love affair with the boy. And Janice Gibson of New Zealand *did* declare she was God, and her husband Lindsay *did* hold down their twelve-year-old son while she beat him repeatedly over the head with a concrete block "to exorcise the devil out"; he died. This human plane of ours *is* truly aseethe with the sign of the beast, and the spawn of the pit, and base abominations.

Sometimes, anyway. And sometimes not.

It gets harder to tell. It gets nuanced and spun. Can the news reporters be trusted? In "Insidious Deception" (Robert B. Rockwell, *Journal of Psychohistory*) "it is argued that perpetrators of abuse and organized satanic movements exert control over law enforcement, legal processes, and the media to distort the facts of satanic ritual abuse and to produce doubts." And what about saucer abductees—those human bubbles of carbonation, ascending those mysterious alien straws? And what about sufferers of Anton's Syndrome?—the recently blind, for whom "the brain constructs an entire imaginary field of vision, leaving them unaware of their blindness"; like "phantom limb," only . . . phantom entire world.

And Teal fits into this portrait—where?

And Justin is somebody's puzzle piece that helps add up to—what?

Elizabeth Renker, in her introduction to *Moby-Dick,* reminds us that "the Sperm Whale's eyes are positioned on opposite sides of his head" and that, as Melville's Ishmael says, he "must see one distinct picture on this side, and another distinct picture on that side."

In south-central Turkey, twenty miles southeast of Konya, in what was once Anatolia, the mound called Catalhoyuk rises sixty-five feet above the fertile alluvial plain. Nine thousand years ago, when Stone Age hunter-gatherers were first initiating those experiments in husbandry, farming, and settled life we term the Neolithic, nomads arrived from the mountains and built the boxes of brick that would house them here. By 6000 B.C., the population of Catalhoyuk had reached perhaps 10,000: a metropolis for its time.

And here, in 1958, one select November evening as the last light licked the ripples in the Carsamba River and made a saffron glow about the boles of the woods, James Mellaart, out of London, discovered a litter of obsidian tools and potsherds; in 1961, he started serious digging. There are summer days when the sun of that plain will try to do to a human face what a kiln will do to clay; but over four years, Mellaart and crew—including his Turkish-born wife and colleague Arlette—dug up 200 houses from the heart of Catalhoyuk.

But the tools and pottery fragments weren't everything. There were also amazing paintings on the plaster walls of hunters (or domesticators?) arranged with outsize deer and boar; molded plaster reliefs of leopards and bulls; strange scenes of headless men surrounded by giant vultures; and fully dimensional, decorated plaster breasts that were molded onto the walls around the skulls of vultures and weasels. "What Mellaart had found were the oldest paintings from the Neolithic, the oldest paintings made by humans on the walls of houses that they had built themselves." To this day, Catalhoyuk remains unique in that way—the richest, densest Neolithic site in terms of artwork: paintings, sculpture, statuettes.

Mellaart loved the site ("he remembered every single carbon-14 date that came out," says Louise Martin, a former student) and he loved interpreting what he'd found there, shaping it into a growingly clear, cohesive understanding of the formative days of city living. For instance, "what looked to Mellaart like an erupting volcano [was] probably Hasan Dag, he decided, which is visible from the mound on a clear day. Under the volcano, the artist had painted a pattern of rectangles that could be taken for the terraced town of Catalhoyuk itself. Mellaart said it was the first landscape painting in history." For him, it wasn't only sweat and science, but beautiful storytelling.

That, as I said, was 1961 to 1965—millennia ago, in terms of academic theory. "In the 1980s, some archaeologists began to question their whole enterprise, to dismiss as naïve the view that you could ever know what really happened in the past." Today the excavation is in the hands of Ian Hodder, and when the two men speak of each other, you can hear the roil of conflict in between the lines of their curtly professional speech. "We disagree," Hodder briefly explains, "about some interpretations." Of Hodder's labor, Mellaart says (a zinger), "I wouldn't call it an excavation."

In his synopsis of this gulf between perspectives, Robert Kunzig writes, "The Mellaarts thought [the artifacts they unearthed] might tell them what really happened at Catalhoyuk," a narrative beyond doubt, like the creation story out of which our own mode of living and sensibility grew, "which is not at all the postmodern spirit." For Ian Hodder, "there is no one objective reality at Catalhoyuk, no single story, but many stories, all with a tentative connection to reality at best."

So, Catalhoyuk was ruled by a priestly elite; unless there was no centralized authority, and life was governed by ritual and taboo. One famous figurine is a goddess; unless it's a symbol of domesticity. The highly decorated rooms are shrines; unless they're plain and simple highly decorated rooms. "What Mellaart saw as a volcano looming over Catalhoyuk, Hodder thinks might be only a leopard skin."

It's a little like watching the Vagaries and their psychojargon armies slinging the mud of Anatolia at one another, at war to claim the past.

Perhaps the ancient Mayans would have known how to accommodate both Hodder and Mellaart at once. "The notion of polarity is often said to be a key to understanding Mayan religion. The gods had multiple aspects and were capable of both good and evil. To this day the Quiché Maya think of dualities in general as complementary rather than opposed, interpenetrating rather than mutually exclusive" (compiled from Nelson and Tedlock).

Lovely in theory, difficult in everyday American household wake-up-and-live-with-it practice.

"Did the priestess have a knife?"

"No. Wa . . . yes, now I can see . . . she held a knife."

4. Generations

Eventually malaria brought Catherwood to the point of collapse. They found him on the viney ground, a kind of toppled column himself. "You *are* an excavated artifact, Freddie—" Stephens said when Catherwood made a boomerang turn away from death and, after an excruciatingly long night, opened his eyes. "—Recovered."

July 31, 1840: the two of them arrived back in New York. In June of 1841 *Incidents of Travel in Central America, Chiapas, and Yucatan* was published—Stephens's account of the journey, illustrated with Catherwood's evocative, precision-point engravings. Its success was stunning, running through twelve editions in its introductory year, and almost immediately appearing in translations, "for archaeologists and historians its impact was phenomenal," "generated a storm of interest," etc., "Stephens is deservedly termed the father of Mayan studies."

And his progeny?—four generations now, of serious Mayanist searchers and researchers.

1876: León de Rosnay "identified the glyphs that represented the four directions," and "six years later an American epigrapher named Cyrus Thomas established the sequence in which the glyphs were intended to be read." Ernst Förstemann, German philologist and librarian to the Elector of Saxony, "liberated two symbols for zero, month signs, gnomic calendrical inscriptions, and the complicated tables for predicting Venus cycles and lunar eclipses" . . . liberated, at last, from the resistant grip of opacity.

In 1897, California newspaper editor Joseph T. Goodman "arrived at a correlation of the Maya and Christian calendars which is still in general use today with only minor revisions." Paul Schellas: matched the gods to the glyphs of their names. Eduard Seler: revealed the glyphs for "red," "yellow," "black," "white," "blue-green." Nothing dramatic here, but the steady and gradual work of daily water, until those stones gave way. Or anyway, in terms of secrets, gave *away*. Some of it in niggled slivers. Some of it, given up as whole as Jonah out of the whale's gullet.

J. E. Teeple, Daniel Brinton, William Gates, Charles P. Bowditch, Hermann Beyer, Sylvanus G. Morley, J. Eric Thompson, Heinrich Berlin, Tatiana Proskouriakoff (at last, as we reach the 1950s, a woman's name makes its way to our list). In 1952 the Russian linguist Yuri Knorozov "became the first to apply computer technology to the problem of Mayan decipherment." In 1968, the Scottish scholar Ian Graham launched the Mayan Hieroglyphic Inscription Study program, under Harvard University's Peabody Museum: "it is aimed at finally compiling an exhaustive inventory of all monument inscriptions" and "the data from this project will eventually fill an estimated fifty volumes."

Meanwhile, as the whorls on stones were being turned to words again—each, a fist with a secret—tens of hundreds of ever-further stones were being discovered and offered to the world. In 1883, Alfred P. Maudslay started on a thirteen-year campaign of exploration in

Mayadom: "accurate" says one source, "systematic" another, "a truly meticulous scientific outlook" a third, and these become—more, even, than the heart-race modifiers we happily lavish on jungle adventure— the mantra of kudos applied to all of those Stephens-successor explorers whose methods and bequests have entered the academic canon.

"It became possible to trace stylistic developments in art and architecture, to define chronological sequences, and to classify the enormous quantities of pottery recovered by archaeologists, which provided a highly sensitive indicator of cultural change, outside influences, and technological advances. Simultaneously, naturalists studied the region's geology, climate, flora, and fauna" (Gallenkamp).

Teobert Maler. Frans Blom. Miguel Fernández. William Coe's people "have been excavating and studying Tikal's 3,000 structures for over a decade." In 1952, Alberto Ruz discovered the subterranean burial crypt at Palenque—"the Maya equivalent of King Tutankhamen's tomb." Exhumed from its 1,300-year-old dark hold was, for example, a death mask in jade, its eyes of shell, their irises and pupils of volcanic obsidian.

Yet *more* atmospheric is Balankanché, for which we'll need to twist down a tunnel-like cave, through a maze of underground vaults, and up a precarious rope against a wall of slippery rock, to a great domed grotto, its ceiling mini-nubbled by millions of tiny stalactites winking in tiny waves in our headlamps' pencil rays, its central space defined by a gigantic natural pillar (who knows *how* many grouped stalactites in communal agglomerated descent over *how* much time?), and a deep niche in this pillar "which might have been the throne of some god."

There, the Tulane University–National Geographic Society effort led by E. Wyllys Andrews IV uncovered a fabulous series of ritual chambers carpeted in a clutter of pottery offerings and ceremonial censers, some from as long ago as 1000 B.C. But first (the "atmospheric" part), Andrews and his men—who had, by entering this sacred arena, violated the precincts of the rain gods—were required to appease the offended deities "not only to avoid retaliation on themselves, but to insure against possible suffering of the whole surrounding native population."

Soon after dawn the next morning, Andrews entered the cave with the whole of his scientific staff; with Romualdo Hoyil, a *h'men*—a Mayan priest—from nearby Xkalakoop; and with thirteen assistant priests. They bore the necessary offertory goods: one turkey, thirteen hens, thirteen black candles, thirteen jars of honey, plus anise, corn, cloves, cumin, tobacco and copal incense. The assistant priests held candles (it was the only light allowed in that nearly strangulating darkness) and they kneeled in a circle about the central pillar.

Then seven small boys entered, who had been trained to skillfully imitate the croak and click of frogs and tree toads—harbingers of the rain gods. And for twenty-four hours straight, there in the bitter, thinning oxygen, as the suffocatory heat and the heat of packed-in, strung-tight bodies thickened . . . there, while smoking incense lapped as solid as surf, as black surf, at their ankles, waists, and throats . . . and as the candle glimmer seemed to make their sweated bodies flicker, seemed to turn them into bodies of static jittering in and out of this world . . . there, the *h'men* led them through the incantations of twenty-seven rites . . . and the gods of Chac did hear, yea did hearken, and attend, and lo, did accept of the humans' offerings, and were pleased.

We *know* this. This is verifiable. We *know* how the Maya positioned their highest stones to make a systematic survey of the stars. We know they could diagnose cancer. Dysentery, *kik-nak,* they would cure "by taking the tender tips of the guava plant and stirring this with the excrement of a dog, a little tapir dung, and some honey, and boiling this mixture." We know their steam baths and their ball courts and the patterns on their jars that held the blood of victims' hearts. We *know,* and we're sure that we know, and we're sure because of the slow and tested, tested and repeated, and empirical, uncaffeinated, thorough and authority-consensual nature of how we've come to know . . . the lineage risen out of John Lloyd Stephens and Catherwood.

But the legacy of the Le Plongeons is a mightily contrary thing.

(From their aggrieved perspective, Stephens was "a tourist," note-taking "hurriedly.")

A sympathetic view of their approach appeared in 1948, in Manly Hall's "The Maya Empire" in *Horizon*: "It was impossible for them to be in the presence of so many wonders without doing a little wondering themselves." Although as explorer Edward Thompson put it, "Dr. Le Plongeon evolved a Mayan theology which is either inspired or the result of a mentality unhinged by too great labor." It isn't easy to meet the heaped-up zeal smoldering in the eyes of the later photographic portraits.

When, in *Queen Moo's Talisman*—Alice's epic poem—the spirit of Prince Aac asks to be reborn through Alice ("*To her he turned again:—Forgive! forgive! / Earth-born thro' thee. Ah! let me once more live. / My crimes and victories, my soul's defeat, / My anguish and remorse, wilt thou repeat....*"), her self-deluded and yet sincerely intended transports only serve to validate others' later (and more knowingly con-game) fancies.

When Augustus, in misguided but genuine theorizing, dates the fullest flowering of ancient Maya culture to a moment 11,500 years ago (a moment when "this great civilization seems to have extended its influence to the remotest parts of the Earth, . . . Asia, Africa, Europe"), when he sees Queen Moo in her perilous exile wending her way to those Atlantic islets that are remnants of "the Land of Mu, the Glory of the Ocean" ("In one night it had suddenly disappeared, engulfed by the waves, with the majority of its inhabitants"), his work becomes a matrix that the mystico-guru school of snake-oil peddlers has been profitably seeding for a century now. The humbug kings and queens. Flimflammers.

This Mu of the Le Plongeons is often conflated with that other fabular realm-of-the-unprovably-proto-, Lemuria, which enters the annals of pseudophilosophical thought in 1888, as described with mumbo-jumbo embellishment by Madame Helena Petrovna Blavatsky, former bareback rider, pianist, and medium, then founder of the Theosophist movement. She could slaw the cabbage, that's for sure; her volume *Isis*

Discovered (not her only authored text) is 1,500 pages. For her, Lemuria was the home of the third of six (some books say seven) "Root Races" of humankind. The Lemurians were hermaphroditic, egg-laying giants who had a third eye in the back of their heads. After they discovered sex, they gave rise to subsequent branches of the human species, including American Indians; also, they interbred with Lemurian beasts, thereby creating the apes. Space travelers from Venus (you could sense them waiting fidgetingly in the wings to enter this story stage-front, couldn't you?) taught the Lemurians the arts of agriculture, metallurgy, and fire-making.

Her work is still in print more than a century later and, "despite factional disputes, splits, and changes of emphasis, the Theosophist Society remains active with a worldwide membership of about 35,000."

Exactly twenty years before those published revelations, one James Churchward (later self-styled "Colonel" Churchward, although paranormalist Peter Tompkins says that he was simply a civil servant) worked in India, where he had the chance to befriend a Brahman priest by providing "relief aid" during "famine time." In return, this man showed Churchward "ancient tablets" in a language "which my priestly friend believed to be the original tongue of mankind, that is, the Naga-Maya language."

Churchward mastered the reading of these ur-texts (as one book says, he claimed to have a "mystical ability to interpret all ancient symbols. If he stared at them long enough, the hieroglyphs would 'speak' to him in the original language of their creators"), and it was true: these told the story of Mu, "the cradle of the human race, the source of all human civilization." (Atlantis itself was only a long-ago colony of Mu's—as was, by definition of "cradle" and "source," *any* inhabited place on the planet.)

In 1926—after nearly forty years, he claims, of research—Churchward published his flagship book *The Lost Continent of Mu.* By that time he was able to say he'd been "dear friends" with the Le Plongeons, to whom he repeatedly, obeisantly indicates intellectual debt. Augustus was wrong, though, in a basic assumption: Mu was *not* in the Atlantic. It was a continent bordered by the current Hawaii, Fiji, and Easter Island (all of them, tiny chunks of Mu). And there, 200,000 years ago, existed "a tropical paradise inhabited simultaneously by dinosaurs, an assortment of modern animals and birds, and exactly 64 million humans of advanced scientific and technical prowess."

Detail after detail, we can watch him inflate this flimsy rubber ball until it's a very large and solid-seeming planet.

"It was over 5,000 miles from east to west, and over 3,000 miles from north to south, a beautiful tropical country. The valleys and plains were covered with rich grazing grasses and tilled fields, while the low rolling hill-lands were shaded by luxuriant growths of tropical vegetation." Is that real enough? If not, then:

"Over the cool rivers, gaudy-winged butterflies hovered in the shade of the trees, rising and falling in fairy-like movements, as if better to view their painted beauty in nature's mirror. Darting hither and thither from flower to flower, tiny hummingbirds made their short flights, glistening like living jewels in the rays of the sun." There's much of this verbal buttersauce, from "little feathered songsters" to "the roaming of herds of mastadons," all of its substance purportedly gleaned from Indian, Mayan, Easter Island, and other age-aura'd records.

As for urban Mu, and its socialities, and their party life: "Broad, smooth roads ran in all directions 'like a spider's web.' Great carved stone temples without roofs, sometimes called 'transparent' temples, adorned the cities. The wealthy classes adorned themselves in fine raiment with many jewels and precious stones. During cool evenings might be seen ships on pleasure bent, filled with gorgeously dressed, jewel-bedecked men and women. The long sweeps with which these ships were supplied gave a musical rhythm to the song and laughter of the merry passengers."

Who were all, it turns out, Anglo. "The dominant race in the land of Mu was a white race, exceedingly handsome people." There were also races of yellow, brown, and black, but "they did not dominate." It isn't amazing that Empire was a major consideration of these merrymaking people: "Colonies had been started in all parts of the earth."

"Le Plongeon," Churchward tells us, "found records in Yucatan that state 'the Hieratic head of the Land of Mu prophesied its destruction; some, heeding the prophecy, left and went to the colonies, where they were saved.'" Hence Mesopotamia, Babylon, ancient Egypt, etc. Hence *us. We're* the descendants of those who escaped when the gas beneath the land built up, and cracked the surface asunder, and there were "roaring flames three miles in diameter" and "the doomed land sank. Down, down, down she went, into the mouth of hell, into a great abyss of fire."

This book's bestsellerdom demanded a subsequent industry, and Churchward was evidently pleased to comply. *The Children of Mu. The Sacred Symbols of Mu. The Cosmic Forces of Mu*, volumes 1 and 2. Since the initial title's first appearance, some version of Churchward's opus has been continuously in print. I'm looking right now at my 1998 edition. Under its title, an island gently formed of teal-green hills upholds a many-miles-tall, Egyptian-style pyramid that beams forth rays of light which, in their airbrushed deployment, are clearly laden with mystical wisdom. Playing in the waters are two dolphins that look as if they yearn to swim to the proper human ear and whisper illuminant adages as old as the composition of the stars. The scene is as balanced as a masterful platter of sushi.

Churchward's unsupported revisionism (no one else has ever seen the mystery tablets that started it all, or been shown where, or met the Brahman priest) not only has its advocates, but is canon enough to squabble with, in the fight over New Age marketplace turf. "I find myself disagreeing with Churchward," Murry Hope dares to say in *The Ancient Wisdom of Atlantis*, "as regards the colour of the ancient Mu-an people. These, I feel, were the original red people."

Senses-boggling: Colonel Churchward as a referent authority. From here on, we're afloat in a weightless marzipan soup of telepathic centaurs, pegasi, unicorns, sky-carts drawn by flying serpents, anti-gravity saucers slathered in the overly busy scrollwork design of gypsy-patent medicine wagons, sci-fi towers rising by thousands of floors above their cityscapes and managing to look both deco-sleekly futuristic *and* like watchtowers on some caliph's ornate pleasure palace. Dashiki'd and raygun-toting warrior princes. Gauzy-corseted temple priestesses. Hinted-at Evil Powers swirling like lava-lamp gel at the center of elf-mined diamonds. All-sentient angels. Elvis as Jesus. Neverland.

Stephen F. Hickman's 1988 *The Lemurian Stone* is forthrightly a paperback fiction, categorized as "fantasy" on its spine. *A demon's sword! An empire's sorcery!*—that's the cover's breathless beckon, along with something about *the tidings of Pharazar's doom.* Inside, such prose as this: "The names he came across rang in his imagination: Adenekel Sha-Kronon the Traitor; Trenk Dar-Aroz the Hero, and the Battle of Thumunzuluum; Houses Sah-Tran and Ket-Anor of the Black Flame, fierce and proud. . . ." And also dialogue like this:

" 'I now beg leave, Princess Tara Wing-tzu, on behalf of the Empress of Pharazar, to do battle with the forces of her enemies!'

" 'You have my leave to go, Sideon of Archaeron, and the blessings of your comrades go with you!'

" 'Then I cannot fail, my Princess, for truer comrades have I never known!' He bowed to them; then, grasping the sheath of the Great Sword just below the hilt, held it forward, saying"—I'm sure you get the idea by now, but I can't refrain from telling you what the courtly Sideon says at this moment:

" 'Behold! even as the great Lord Yngor in the halcyon days of the Third Realm of Kulos, I go forth with the Sword Izilazog, an Avatar of the Light, for the honor of my sacred trust!' "

Three-hundred-and-forty-two pages of that harmlessly pneumatic make-believe. Then what to make of this self-pigeonholed *non*fiction published by Signet Books in 1975? The cover come-on of Craig and Eric Umland's *Mystery of the Ancients: Early Spacemen and the Mayas* tempts our browsing eyes by promising "Startling new evidence to solve the riddle of Earth's lost civilization," including "why decoding the Mayan hieroglyphs is the goal of a secret strategic military race between America and Soviet Russia." Yup. We're a long, lost way from radiocarbon dating and symposia.

Well, Mayan study has *always* seemed to attract the impeccably serious and the wackoid—inextricably patched. Of Nobel prizewinner Richard P. Feynman ("the greatest physicist of his generation, ranking with Sir Isaac Newton and Albert Einstein"—in *Q is for Quantum, An Encyclopedia of Particle Physics* by John Gribbin), a quote I scribbled over a latté one day in a Barnes & Noble tells us that "his other passions included playing the bongo drums, painting, frequenting strip clubs, and deciphering Mayan texts."

She struggled against her captors, but to no avail. The honor guard of the Lamiph of Mu was trained to effectively wield the Lamiph's stern, sure justice even to the barbarian hordes of the Outer Wastes; the Lamiph's niece, a lone maid of sixteen, could not escape their grip.

They carried her up the alabaster staircase of the lamiphry. Already, ashes that shot forth from the maw of Volcano Mother floated down to soot the carven gryphons on either side of the walkway. But her captors didn't halt; they had their orders. Not her pitiful twists and moaning, and not the nearing sound of the splitting earth, could stop them.

They reached the top of the stairs. Her uncle, the Lamiph, awaited them there, a look of leering triumph in his eye. He pointed rigidly to a set of ivory-inlaid doors. Then "Bring her to my chambers," he ordered.

"Yes, I did. I had a past life."

"That's horse doo."

"Why are you always so dismissive? I'm *telling* you: I *remember* being a temple-virgin of Mu."

"Oh, great. You couldn't even pick something *slightly* credible? Ancient Rome? The Han Dynasty? How do you *know* you were there?"

She can only mimic him, he's so ridiculous. "How do I 'know'? How do I '*know*'? I remember it. I REMEMBER IT."

In a certain sense, what we are—in a certain sense, *all* that we are—*is* memory; is DNA remembering the phenotype, from womb to tomb, for each of the (truly) hundred thousand billion cells of the body. The forming fetus is instructed to repeat the lizard, the bird, and the fur of the four-legged beast, like a schoolboy reciting his lessons. The body sloughs, then it replenishes, in an unlost ongoing image; the body loses, then it regenerates; by death, the human body will have replaced every one of its cells some ten to twelve times, but will still be itself, its fingerprints and its irises having remembered what they needed to be and, time and again, unfailingly having become it. DNA is the species' mnemonic.

Rupert Sheldrake's book *The Presence of the Past* even posits a "field" of "morphic resonance," a living, evolving, invisible something-or-other (an earlier science might have called this thing the "ether") that's exterior to (and yet includes) our human selves, and (here, I *try* to synopsize nearly 400 challenging pages) that's a storehouse and providing-place (a register of sorts, a global "community mind" of sorts, an "awareness" structured into the cosmic weave) for the ways in which life changes; and we breathe and sleep and screw and dream our hallelujah dreamy-dreams in a sea, in an overgoverning gestalt, of constant memory—occasionally in our consciousness, *always* on the level at which the fundamental dots and sines of the universe "remember" the laws of physics. If our cytoplasm had its own thesaurus, "exist" and "remember" would be synonyms.

In ancient Rome's academies and medieval universities, the student was encouraged to imagine a "memory house," the rooms and spatial relations of which would be familiar and unchanging; and in this structure, he could array what required remembering—a limp squid, in a puddle in the foyer; Lucretius's theory of how vision works, in an airy, windowed attic; anything, really, from a grocery list to Aristotle's descriptions of spontaneous generation—and, by close association with a pattern already mastered, every squid and every furrow-browed hypothesizing sage would be adroitly recalled in succession.

In the Renaissance, devotees constructed actual—that is, physical—"memory houses" of wood. (One way of understanding the mythopoetic compartments of Joseph Cornell would be to see them as separate rooms from a twentieth-century version of this architectural project.) The most extravagant, done in the early 1500s by Giulio Camillo of Bologna, was large enough to hold two people "and was a mass of little boxes and carved images, variously designed to represent eternal truth from the birth of the universe through all the stages of creation."

In 1958 a go-getter by the name of O.W. "Bill" Hayes ("currently vice-president and coordinator of sales for the American Desk Manufacturing Company of Temple, Texas, president of the Temple Rotary Club, and official lecturer on memory exercises for the hostess-training school of Braniff Airways") published *Your Memory—Speedway to Success,* in which his (registered trade name) Auto-Magic Memory Method offered a contempo "memory house": the car. If you need to buy some bacon this evening, picture a rasher impaled on a spiky hood ornament. Work your way backward through nineteen possible stages (nineteenth, the license plate), with the finalmost possibility, twenty, "seen in the rear-view mirror." One could position all ten commandments, seven dwarves, and the individual Tolkien trilogy titles that way.

At first I thought that it would make sense to extend the arrow of Auto-Magic Memory's numbered placements to a twenty-first, the cloud of exhaust at the tailpipe. But no, a cloud is too iffy; it can't be tagged. And the only purpose behind this exercise we've been doing for over 2,000 years is to make our memories small and hard and containable things, systematized and beyond change.

Ha. Good luck. It roils away like smoke, it shape-shifts, it will try to sell you the Brooklyn Bridge. Mark Twain: "It isn't so astonishing, the number of things I can remember, as the number of things I can remember that aren't so."

A sixty-four-year-old engineer from Surrey, England, has—five times over eighteen years of intercourse—entirely lost his memory for thirty-to-sixty-minute spans, while making love to his wife. "What time of year is it?" he'd ask her, "What time of day is it?" and—my favorite— "What are we doing?" This condition is common enough to have earned its own term, "transient global amnesia," and its own acronym, "TGA," but no support group or inveigling body of lobbyists—yet.

For every outré amnesia, there's a countervalent act of super-charged remembering. Jeanne Marie Calment was interviewed in a re-tirement home in Arles in 1998, on her 121st birthday. "She remem-bers selling coloured pencils to Vincent van Gogh and watching the Eiffel Tower being built." One week before, she'd recorded a four-track tape, *The Mistress of Time,* in which she recounted her memories over a musical background of techno and rap. "I have only one wrinkle," she told her interviewer, "and I'm sitting on it."

Perhaps one day we'll all have perfect access to the neuro-files. A team of British researchers is exploring the possibility of a microchip that would be attached to the optic, auditory, and olfactory nerves, recording their electrical-impulse exchange with the brain—storing, that way, an individual's memories. These could be replayed at will (first, for the individual involved, "straight into the brain": direct electric-to-electric transmission; for anyone else, through some sort of decoder). Theoretically, these memories "could even be implanted in another person's brain." This might "be possible within another thirty years."

The future is going to be one very memory-intensive place. Already, a Syracuse University research team is developing a 3-D optical mem-ory device in which the storage capability is supplied by a protein in common saltwater bacteria: an organic-digital wedding. Also, there's talk of using DNA in computers that could then be just a few molecules in size. I can put my mind's science-fiction predicto-sight to work, and envision the memories of a city, or of a human generation, engraved on dust-sized motes in an eight-ounce jar in a government Hall of the Past, Retrieval Division.

But if it's freeze-dried, then reliquefied; if it's *outside* of the body; if it's cyber or steel or powered by the circuitry of an earthworm in a bio lab . . . *is* it "memory"? What's our definition, anyway?

When a sample of the yellow tunic worn by Christ—the scantest fleck—is lifted from the canvas and, beneath electron microscope expansion, is a geologic-looking wall of strata ("which dated the painting to before the year 1750") . . . can we say that this is a "memory," locked inside a painting's chemistry, then 175 years later given release? Or when a fissure in South Africa gives up "the first complete skeleton of a 250-million-year-old beast called a gorgon (a cross between a lion and man-eating monitor lizard)" . . . is the planet herself becoming newly conscious of something buried in her subliminal long ago? Someone has "transplanted elephant ovarian tissue into mice." And when "the mice produce elephant eggs" . . . aren't the cells, aren't the gravid awarenesses that pass for thought in oviduct cells, "remembering"?

It will try to sell you the Brooklyn Bridge. It will tell you that no, it never did. It will have you awake after fifteen years with a proof-of-ownership paper in your hand, in a language you can't understand, from a life that you can't recall leading.

When Anne Bristow-Kitney, forty-three, a BBC producer ("I was born in Chelsea, west London, and brought up in Cheltenham and Gloucestershire") awoke in a London hospital after undergoing cerebral hemorrhage, "she spoke French with such a good accent that the hospital staff assumed she was French." Six days later she suffered a stroke and awoke from that with a Scottish accent. Stewart Rayner, a London policeman, fractured his skull in an automobile crash and awoke "with a deep Southern U.S. drawl." A Norwegian woman, bonked on the head with shrapnel during a German raid on her village during World War II, fell into a coma and woke up with a perfect German accent. The dilemma is Foreign Accent Syndrome (FAS); though rare, about fifty cases are known to exist in the medical literature.

Following her 1990 heart-lung transplant, Maria Lafferty found she had somehow developed a taste for ice cream and candy, also a newfound interest in toys. When she researched her anonymous donor's identity, she discovered it was a ten-year-old girl. Recipient of a new heart, Maureen Mitchell assumed new preferences. "I used to love coffee, now I can't stand the stuff. I used to love butter on toast, now it makes me nauseous. My favorite food is tomatoes, which I never really liked before."

Those, however, are innocent confusions. What if a hint of duplicity complicates the mixture? The famous crystal skull was allegedly discovered at the Mayan ruin Lubaatun in 1927 by Anna Mitchell-Hedges, adopted daughter of British explorer Frederick A. Mitchell-Hedges. It's the life-size replication of a human skull, in transparent quartz. "The surface is smoothly polished (a microscope shows no scratches or tool marks) and it may have been worked by rubbing down the original quartz block with sand. If so, it would have taken as much as 150 years of constant effort by several generations of artists to complete the work." In both material and perfection of craft, it's singular among Mayan remains.

When light shines through, the two eye sockets collect it, and flicker—some would say they *spookily* flicker. Anna Mitchell-Hedges claimed that, as her father unearthed it, "300 Indians who were working on the dig with her fell to their knees and kissed the ground, and that they prayed and wept for two weeks thereafter." An art restorer, Frank Dorland, who conducted tests on the artifact for over six years, said that it sometimes emitted an aura; that it created the silvery sound of high-pitched bells; that sometimes images of other skulls, and of faces and mountains, floated in its depths; and that it could seize hold of a standerby's moods, and darken them. You won't be dumbfounded to hear that it's since become the object of fuzzy mystical pop-psych speculation.

"However, evidence has emerged to suggest that the skull was bought at a Sotheby's auction in London in 1943, for the sum of 400 pounds. There is no record of the discovery of the skull in contemporary reports of Mitchell-Hedge's expedition to South America, nor are there any photographs of Anna with the skull during the expedition. According to close associates of Mitchell-Hedges, he never mentioned the skull prior to 1943, nor did he refer to it in the lectures he gave in the wake of his expedition."—Which is suspicious; and yet, it in no way—even if true—addresses the ultimate authenticity and origin of the skull.—Which leaves us . . . where?

Or the story of Rigoberta Menchu . . . where? Her published autobiography—a narrative of growing up poor and illiterate among the Mayan Quiché, and of that people's brutal treatment at the hands of Guatemalan security forces—was her stepping-stone to a Nobel Peace prize. Sixteen years after its publication, anthropologist David Stoll of Middlebury College says that the book is "largely untrue." For example, Menchu's brother Nicolas had *not* starved to death while working on a coffee plantation; in fact, in *real* fact, he's still alive.

As a result of Stoll's investigation, Menchu has tried to distance herself from the book: "I am the protagonist of the book, but I am not the author." *I, Rigoberta Menchu* was written by one-time Che Guevara fellow traveler Elisabeth Burgos. *She* claims: "Every phrase comes from what Rigoberta Menchu said."—Which leaves us . . . where?

To torque it one notch further, almost everyone—even Menchu's critics—admits that the book is flimsy in fact but not in spirit: Menchu and her family, and the Mayan Quiché in general, *have* suffered under the Guatemalan elite.—Which leaves our common understanding of "real" . . . where, and in whose dictionary? How long can a person circle over "true" and "false," awaiting clearance to land on either one or the other? Isn't the talky Scheherazade as accurate as the evening news? Sitting there at the feet of the king with her pet chameleon Metaphor in her lap and, on a bare delicious shoulder, the parrot Fiction.

I, Rigoberta Menchu. I think of Ernest Hemingway's statement: "All good books have one thing in common—they are truer than if they had really happened."

How about a lurid book? How about a foaming-over, cheaply join-dered, lurid fiction? Can't it too be an accuracy, in the sense in which memoirist Mary Clearman Blew refers to accuracy when she says to us, "I struggled for a long time with the conflicting claims of the exact truth of the story and the emotional truth as I perceived it."

Say a girl is nine. Her uncle is creepy. Oh, maybe he's not creepy in the way I'm assuming that you're assuming: "inappropriate touching" and all of the other testosteroid, don't-go-there transgressions. Still, he's creepy. She's been sent to stay with him for most of the summer, and *everything* is . . . well, creepy. His breath, his clothes, the stupid things he talks about from his creepy throne on the dark side of the creepy moon. And his friends, too, and the women who visit. And then he locks her into the study, so he and these women can be alone to-gether and be weird together. Like now: she's locked in. She can sense an alien power, and muffled alien noises, coming from his bedroom down the hall.

Her only options for an hour are to pick up where she's left off in a book of his from the study's shelves, or to do her Miss Dizzy dance around the room, maybe "accidentally" knocking down a vase or a pile of papers. She does both, in crazy alternation. I'm Miss Dizzy Dizzy, I hate my uncle, I hate my uncle, I hatey-hatey-*hate* him, up and down and left and right in a blurred conjumble and then, the cosmos still aspin, another chapter from *The Lamiph of Mu*—so many uncles in the world! They're all alike. Miss Dizzy Dancedancedancer la-la-la, the book and the room, the then and the now, the uncle and the uncle. I'm Miss Teal, I'm real, nobody else is reeeee-al, dizzy-la-la-la.

And a year goes by, and a hurt goes by, and a pleasure goes by, and the grass grows. And the leaves fall, and then new leaves (only it may as well be the old leaves) show themselves in the circle of light and dark. And a parent goes by, and an open susceptible girlishness goes by, and then a man goes past, and then a new man (except it may as well have been the previous man) goes past. And the grass is forever and thick, and the hills hold stones nobody ever sees, and the past is a Mayan ruin untouched by any finger of light for centuries, you could think it was dead, you could think it was buried under the grass and dead, if you could think of it at all, and only the sky above that grass is like a mirror above the lips of the here-but-barely-here, its barely-breath a thin fog saying, *Yes I'm here, I'm here to be discovered again, I'm here to be repieced and reinterpreted, come find me, here in Tikal, here in Uxmal, in a skull, in a study, here in Copán and Palenque, here in Tulum and Chichen Itza.*

5. Stem Cells

Martin Van Buren's progress toward the presidency included his wooing of what was then the largest single bloc of American voters, those in small towns and rural communities. To this end, he associated himself—in the slogan-hungry understanding of that electorate—with Kinderhook, New York, the rural environs of his birth. He campaigned shrewdly under the nickname of "Old Kinderhook" and established scores of booster clubs that urged the public to "Vote O.K." That this is the derivation of our word "okay" is [MARK ONE] True ( ) or False ( ).

How soon we forget. How quick we remember last year's sitcom script as part of our own untampered-with lives. A sophomore English course has told me Winston Churchill signed the Declaration of Independence; the Allied and Axis Powers are Roller Derby teams; Mahatma Gandhi had a university dorm named for him: Tajma Hall.

The answer, by the way, if I can trust my source (a book by Vernon Pizer: *Take My Word for It*) is "true." So much escapes our nets from year to year, so much is devoured greedily by Chance for its between-meals snacks, it's a wonder anyone bothers writing fantasy "alternative histories" (just recovering our losses from a single agreed-upon history ought to be sufficient labor). But they do: if the South had won the Civil War, if Brazil had colonized the moon, if we were descended not from apes, but dogs, or bears, or felines. *That* would be a heady, thunderboltish project, with ideas the size of oil tankers, and great, combustive events! And yet for me right now, it feels like enough to return to the years of Martin Van Buren; to relocate just one shard of that time from where it's been hidden under the busy hiss and zoom of human doings; to hold it still in the travel of light.

The lush and sluggish khaki-color river wrinkles sun along its back, and so catches the eye first. Then the banks, and then the plain itself, and its monuments, so squat at the base, so eloquent of tonnage, although they still ordain that the eyes go up, to where the gods discuss our lives. Since Copán is the easternmost of the ancient Maya city-states, the Maya themselves considered it to be on the fringe of the universe. It seems, of course, the opposite to Stephens—a place where a universe was revealed to him, where it vibrates slightly under its layers of camouflage brush, with the willingness to be known.

Here, King Yax Pac erected the altar that shows his royal predecessors, fifteen kings deep. Also here, the stela depicting King 18 Rabbit in the guise of gods and of avatars of the World Tree. For example, one in which he wears the costume of the maize god, and holds the double-headed serpent bar. We know that he was captured by King Cauac Sky—captured and sacrificed. Those altars were often damp. We know that later, King Smoke Shell commissioned what we've now labeled the Temple of the Hieroglyphic Stairway (there are over 2,000 glyphs on its steps). We know so much. We've honored these people by studying them so diligently. Their notion of Hell. Their festivals. What foodstuffs wore their teeth away. It's all there on that day in 1839, incipient, eager to rise toward Stephens's freezing abracadabra. If only.

"I'm afraid we've got a granite hymen, Catherwood."

"Johnny. Are you quite all right? A *what*?"

For a minute it seems he doesn't hear. He just keeps staring out forlornly at the beckoning, difficult green. Then—"That's my idiotic idiomatic American, Catherwood. Sorry." With one finger he makes an invisible line in front of them. "We can't get through. As you put it yesterday afternoon, 'an impasse.'" And his whole face says that extra units of gravity—some special, tailored penance of his—have taken draggy hold of it.

Because (remember?) Don José Maria Acevedo has sneered out scorn in their direction. He says they're interlopers, unwelcome ones; and nobody's *not* about to back up this two-bit local grandee in his two-bit duded-up gauderie. Yes, Stephens can see it: the laborers loathe this arrogant representative of the doubly loathesome Honduran-Guatemalan gentry (in this way, the spirit of Rigoberta Menchu's book *is* unassailable, and traceable back at least to 1839), but *no one* is going to argue this man's wishes, and everybody twelve and above has access to a machete. Acevedo strokes his jacket's fading silver trim as if to clean it of fly-grime. The implication is clear: he will rid himself of these foreigners with a similar easy swipe.

And if he does . . . ? An entire people will never be reborn. The promise in this ground will disappear further, year by year, to the chemical hunger of the soil. Acevedo's only loyalty is to status quo, and to neither the past nor future. Stephens could undo his sturdy explorer's demeanor and weep.

"Come on, Johnny: stiff upper lip, if you won't disallow *my* nation its idiomatics." Catherwood claps his friend's shoulder. "Also, that regimented tribe of mine knows that a freshen-up and a change of attire will do you a world of good."

It does. It's with this statement that Stephens sees the gleam of his only hope. Threats won't work. An appeal to any sympathy is useless. Even a forthright offer of money would only be spit upon. But—a change of attire! And Stephens's lawyer-mind is already sorting his haberdashery possibilities.

That night, in a ring of extra torches and campfires added especially to lend a grandiosity to the occasion, Acevedo returns—for what he's sure is the foreigners' announcement of departure—with a knot of flunkies around him.

"Welcome, gentlemen"—Catherwood chats with them, about the crops, the weather, as if this is a formal state function. And then—

—from the opaque dark beyond their ring of fire, Stephens steps solemnly, even commandingly, into the wavery light. He's unfolded his blue—his bombast-blue—attaché jacket, brushed it off, and polished its golden buttons with the eagle embossings into a row of hypnotizing, fire-lit moons. The torn and muddied work pants and the water-eaten boots can't dim his ornamented presence. And the gold braid on his shoulders looks like something fallen into this world from the smitheries of Parnassus. In this place, and at this moment, Stephens outranks Acevedo in garish aplomb by a good Honduran mile. In his right hand are his papers of presentation (also a contract he's drawn up with Catherwood's input) and he's augmented these with a last-minute series of handwritten rose-swirl arabesques and impressed red splats of candle wax. And—

—it works! What Don José Maria Acevedo wants is respect! Respect . . . and money! Money . . . and pomp! Lavish, preening, over-weening, peacockian, ceremonial pomp! Spectacle! And whiskey! And cigars! And then more pomp!

From Stephens's own account: "The reader is perhaps curious to know how old cities sell in Central America. Like other articles of trade, they are regulated by the quantity in market, and the demand; but, not being staple articles, like cotton and indigo, they were held at fancy prices, and at that time were dull of sale. I paid fifty dollars for Copán. There was never any difficulty about price. I offered that sum, for which Don José Maria thought me only a fool; if I had offered more, he would probably have considered me something worse. He seemed to doubt which of us was out of his senses, the property was so utterly worthless!"

That's how it happens. That's where we'll leave Stephens—at the head of a drunken conga line of the villagers of Copán, that jungle night of mutual celebratory whoop.

Those golden buttons, that I planted in this narrative so early . . . they were the seeds. From them, the serious study of Mayadom has grown to continuous flower for (at the date of this writing) a solid, un-broken 160 years.

But the story of Augustus and Alice Le Plongeon has a different end: a dead end.

Augustus died in Brooklyn, December 13, 1908, at the age of eighty-two, a weary and disillusioned man, dismissed (or worse, perhaps, ignored) by the archaeology establishment. He had dragged the exalting visions born of his fieldwork into the first eight years of the century, only to see them serve as objects of the world's derision. Alice charged her husband's academic nemeses with his physical decline. As early as 1900, a letter of hers describing his painful angina pectoris said that, "He is unable to take solid food, and should have an immediate change of climate. [None was forthcoming: they had been living back in the States for years 'with very strict economy.'] He is the victim of conservative opponents, and his condition is undoubtedly the result of prolonged disappointment and anxiety."

True, a few of the secondhand faithful lingered, making anemic pleas for the Le Plongeons' obvious history of sincerity and dedication. Some implied they had martyred themselves for the sake of their fantastic interpretations. Willis Fletcher Johnson, in his 1923 article titled "Pioneers of Mayan Research," was willing to list Augustus among that handful of the chosen; four years later, in the *New York Times,* John Opdycke, an old acquaintance of theirs, bemoaned how "there can be no doubt that the modern school has been indifferent, not to say professionally discourteous to these two good people, who were the first really great experts in regard to the ancient Mayan peoples. The Le Plongeons were scientists not only, but they were, as well, artists and philosophers in the field of archaeology. They touched nothing with the hand of scientific research that they were not able to adorn with rational, albeit artistic, interpretation." In the coming days of larger-scale, institution-funded expeditions, a few remembered what it must have meant to be alone in those jungles, funded only out of the driving thump in one's own marrow.

But that hasn't been enough to keep a functioning flame alive. A Theosophist publishing firm has *Queen Moo and the Egyptian Sphinx* in print (my copy leaps from page 16 to 108, then backward from there to page 17, at which point 109 picks up). A smeary and cheaply spiral-bound "edition" of *Sacred Mysteries Among the Mayas and Quiches* is available from something called "Health Research" in Pomeroy, Washington (its address is placed via mailing-label sticker on the copyright page). These quickly fading half-lives are hardly a testimony to scholarly endurance.

Nor is oddball W. Gordon Allen's "Pacific Lemurian Society," which in 1958 "was interested in unraveling the mysteries of the alleged ancient continent of Lemuria, but also maintained a burning interest in flying saucers and anti-gravity." Donna Kossy, in *Kooks,* refers to Allen's "'I Field' theory, 'a FOUR FIELD CONTINUUM under constant movement thru an N number of dimensions and states of reality from waves thru universes,' developed to explain UFO electric 'ETHER PUMP' flight behavior."

Augustus's conclusions sounded that nuts to his contemporaries. As Edward Hallett Carr points out in *What Is History?,* effectively quoting Dickens: "The nineteenth century was a great age for facts. 'What I want,' says Mr. Gradgrind in *Hard Times,* 'is Facts . . . Facts alone are wanted in life.' Nineteenth-century historians on the whole agreed with him." Or, as an article in *Discovery* observes of the changing attitude toward Mellaart's digging in Catalhoyuk, "Scientific archaeology had arrived, and with it a preference for the quantifiable over the symbolic, for testable hypotheses over stories."

Augustus's overreaching dates for Maya civilization?—this was a "preposterous proposition [which] was received with the Homeric laughter it so richly deserves" (Arnold and Frost, *The American Egypt*). "His lurid imagination made his writing almost valueless" (H. E. D. Pollock, *The Maya and Their Neighbors*). "Arrogant flaunting of his own ego" (Wauchope, *Lost Tribes and Sunken Continents*). "A master of self-deception" (Miller, "A Re-examination of the Mesoamerican Chacmool").

And if ever these vigilant guardians of the Gates of Truth should hear that the dreaded Augustus Le Plongeon rustles in his grave with a returning vigor, threatening to burst forth and contaminate the record anew . . . they need only obtain a copy of the adventure video *Stargate: Hathor* (one of a lively series of "Stargate" flicks), released on July 1 2, 1 999. Its tempting box copy says that "the evil Goa'uld, Hathor, escapes from a Mayan Pyramid in Mexico. At the Stargate facility she seduces the men into helping her take over the world. Can Samantha and her female colleagues defeat her?" They will hammer this for a discrediting stake in Augustus's troubled heart, and he will obediently crawl back to his grave and blanket himself with oblivion forever.

Alice's death followed his in two years. She was only fifty-nine, but emptied-out already by life in Yucatan and the grinding-away of the subsequent days in America. "I was the only woman," she wrote in 1 900, "who had explored the Yucatan Ruins and accomplished something in American archaeology." This was true, and her obituary made it into the *New York Times* and the *New York Evening Post.*

But her attempts in those two years following Augustus's death to fan the ideological embers of Moo *et al* did their already tottering reputations little good. Her romantic prose "veered ever closer to, and finally arrived at, pulp fiction"—so say Weeks and James in *Eccentrics,* comparing her style to that of Tarzan's word-hyper Edgar Rice Burroughs. In her novel *A Dream of Atlantis,* which began its two years of serialization while she still was alive, Alice related the tale of Atlanteans ("Old Maya stock") who, prior to the island's famous sinking, "returned to the fatherland, in these days named Yucatan, and there founded a new empire"—happening to be the one that she and her husband had excavated. Epic battles. Love affairs. Skullduggery. Capture. Escape. Recapture. Low blows. High dives. Alice . . . in wonderland.

Of course, who *doesn't* sometimes wish admission through wonderland's portals? In the hill land in the wilds of the medulla oblongata, and in the sticky central matrices of the heart . . . who hasn't dipped a cup in the same stream from which Alice Le Plongeon kneeled to drink so immeasurably? As Weeks and James opine about the range of "eccentric theorists" in their study, "Even if they *are* inventing the whole thing, is their myth-making essentially different from that of Plato in his writings about Atlantis? Everyone dreams." At the foveal pit in the eye in the back of the eye in the back of the pineal gland, everybody Quixotes.

I can remember my father, from when I was ten or eleven, struggling over the family accounts book—rent, and grocery money, and all of the equally importuning needs—and every now and then the rigorous, mathematic glare of his face would suddenly soften, and his eyes would stray to a place where "rent" wasn't part of a life's vocabulary, and "raise" wasn't something you bellycrawled for, and "family" came to a man without a hod of bricks for every name; or maybe it was a place where matters of love and economics were as ferociously depleting as they are in the here-and-now, but he'd at least be acknowledged a hero for his battles with those abstract foes.

But my father *knew* that this was airy poof. ("I go forth with the Sword Izilazog. . . .") The statement from Weeks and James is longer than I first indicated. "Everyone dreams; it is the eccentrics among us who sometimes fail to distinguish between the dream world and waking reality." What if your dream and your certainty are the same one thing? if you could knock against your dream and hear a sharp, undeniable rap, and feel your knuckles sting? if you took a long drive in the Auto-Magic Memory Method car, and the figure that everyone said was a ghost-shape of cigar smoke at your side was someone who licked your neck and slapped your cheek and left the open tine-scrapes of raked nails (look, *here*) down your arm? A woman in Sean Russell's *Beneath the Vaulted Hills*—a novelist—says, "If you believe it—it is real."

And so the Le Plongeons fade more, every day, away from our practical, data-bedizened selves.

It reverses a natural order. We can stride into a hundred public museums and ogle well-lit Maya artifacts in their catalogued, captioned displays. We can finger our way through some of the Mayans' most seminal secrets, in thousands of bookstores and libraries worldwide—*tens* of thousands—and we can lounge in bed and conjure them onto the Web. They've risen into the easy recognizability of a Disney *Uncle*

Scrooge comic book: in "Crown of the Mayas," that plucky duck explores a Mayan sacrificial well (and needs to outwit a duo of hooligans, Slyviper and Foulcrook). Yes, and the Chacmool statue that was Augustus's most splendid find, now serves as the image of Mexican and Central American tourism, on a jillion posters, postcards, and brochures. The Maya are here, are ours.

But Alice and Augustus have been buried under by time, erased almost totally from the archaeological record—a fable, a whisper of carbon and calcium in the depths of our cultural past.

And the lozenge of jade that Augustus rescued from a stone urn and that Alice so happily wears on her breast in the portrait of 1885?— is lost again, a covered-over artifact again, a snooze of elements in the overwhelming flux, reawaiting discovery.

December 1998 "saw major advances in cultivating human embryonic stem cells," according to *Scientific American*. This is exciting news for biotechnologists, and filled with hope for those who suffer certain medical ills, but *all* of my friends are in a general way intrigued with the notion of "stem cells," glad that they've entered our layman's lexicon, along with "quarks," "black holes," "the red shift," "the subconscious," and the rest of our excitedly (if often sloppily) bandied terminology.

Stem cells "can become any of the body's tissues"—they aren't delimited as future spleens or retinas or the spongey topiaries inside of the lung, or what-have-you. Their promise is 100 percent, and everything, even what we might think of as contradictory things (the neocortex, say, and the anal lining), are here in simultaneous potential. It's like the light of the First Day. Nothing is "fake" yet. Every line of direction is equally "true." The limbs of the body are here, and so are the pinprick "phantom limbs." As Su Tung P'o wrote: "Joy and sorrow are in fact / Only aspects of the Void." They're partnered here, unprioritized, in the stem cells.

A friend says this is like Steve Cooper's singular trove of comic books. Unlike other serious comics collectors, Cooper doesn't acquire by genre (superhero, romance, etc.) or publisher (Marvel, DC, Dell) or even favored artist or writer (Carl Barks, Marie Severin, Walt Kelly . . .). Instead and amazingly, Cooper's decided on what he calls a "synchronic collection"—over 200 titles, scarce or common, belovéd or even ridiculed, that would have been for retail sale on comic-book racks across the country in April 1956, when he was eleven and *Strange Adventures* #67 "inflamed my imagination."

Here it is, its cover loudly, proudly pitching the feature story, "The Martian Masquerader" ("It's midnight! Unmask everybody, and reveal your identities!" *Uh-oh*. "I'm trapped! I have NO mask to take off—I'm REALLY a Martian!") And so it forms a sensible kinship group with *Forbidden Worlds* (its cover showing "Mr. Miggs from Mercury"), *Journey into Unknown Worlds, Strange Tales of the Unusual,* and *Mystery in Space* ("LOOK—There's our destination—EARTH! But one-half has been sliced away—as though by some giant blade!")

Yet from the same month, on the same shelves, in an equalizing gesture of a thoroughness that no socialist state or democracy has implemented, these extragalactic forays into the future are joined to *Daniel Boone* and *Robin Hood* and *Frontier Fighters featuring Davy Crockett*. While someone M-15's a row of bloody carnage on the cover of *Battle,* and someone elsewhere lobs a grenade at a tank on *Fighting Forces,* three ants spread a teensy picnic blanket and hold their feast on the bouncy, bulbous nose of the eponymous *Nutsy Squirrel.*

The Black Knight lifts his gleaming, un-nicked shield against "The Invincible Tartar!" and meanwhile, love is a difficult thicket on the cover of *True Bride-To-Be Romances.* "Mr." brings us *Mr. District Attorney* (bravely raising his dukes against the city's underworld thugs) but also *Mr. Frog and Miss Mousie.* Here are *Donald Duck, Zaza the Mystic, Tarzan, Little Beaver, Red Mask, Rex the Wonder Dog,* "all scrambled together in life's careless fashion" (Poul Anderson, in his science-fiction novel *Three Worlds to Conquer*). Stem cells: all of the options, in one, and at once.

If this describes the original level of undifferentiated omnipossibility . . . what we do, we humans, is mold a pinch of its substance into specificity—what we'd call an "era," a "culture," on the largest scale; a "worldview," on the personal. *The Incredible Opinions of Justin. Teal's World of Fantabulous Claims.*

Or, set in the terminology of physicist Edward Harrison, the Universe (with a definite cap-U) is unknowable—always has been, always will be. There are, however, endless lower-case-u universes, "models of the Universe. They are great schemes of intricate thought—grand cosmic pictures—that rationalize human experience. Each universe is a self-consistent system of ideas, marvelously organized, interlacing most of what is perceived and known. Whenever we find a human society, there is a universe; each universe determines what is perceived and what constitutes valid knowledge, and the members of each society believe what is perceived and perceive what is believed.

"The people in the past, as we know, had other outlooks and ways of viewing their world, and lived in, or thought they lived in, a different kind of universe. The universes of the past—Babylonian, Pythagorean, Aristotelian, Newtonian, to name a few—were all different, and none was like the modern physical universe. But it does not take much imagination to realize that the people in the past believed in their universes just as firmly as we tend to believe in the modern physical universe. A particular universe might not be rational by our standards, or those of other societies, but is always rational by the standards of the members of its own society.

"The universe in which a person lives is always real—verifiably real."

Of course, Harrison also recognizes that no matter how conformist any culture is, still, "every person possesses an elaborate belief-system, . . . a 'personal theory of reality.' We seek always to impose our [individual] will and shape a universe to our desire."

Not that really *any* of my aerosol expostulating, not that *any* gassy prolixese, can at the end explain away a single hurt in the lives of my friends.

Hurt notwithstanding, somehow we strive onward with our petty pleasures marbled through our blocks of bedrock angst. When I saw

Justin in the week beyond the divorce, he was drunk on his misery, and miserable in his drunkenness, scrunched up in a corner, "I can taste how fucked-up I am in my own saliva, man," he said by way of explanation, "I can smell my sadness rise up like a genie from my piss in the bowl," and when I extended a hand to give his shoulder a pat, "No! Don't! My bones could turn to powder." But when I saw him only a month after *that,* he was out on the town, all grins, in love with a fast-track blonde-from-a-bottle he introduced as "Miss Nicole."

"And buddy," he told me, *"this* time it's the real thing." I think I can understand the immediate sensory pleasure he took in her. She was groomed for fun, from her suck-me pedicured toenails to the bounty above her underwired bra, and her one clear signal was to look at him with a sexual hunger close to atavistic. Beyond that, I couldn't tell much about Miss Nicole; the feeling I had was some pixels were missing, the picture kept shifting in and out of focus as we sat there in The Cedar.

Although *something* she said . . . or a stare that passed between them . . . . Later, when I was alone with Justin for a moment I asked him, truly now, tell me, man, were you involved with this Miss Nicole *before* things started publicly going so rotten with you and Teal?

"No way," he said, taking showy offense. But I kept pushing—*had* he been seeing her?

"Well," he finally said as she reentered our conversation from her respite in the ladies room, "it depends on what you mean by 'seeing.'"

And so I gave it up. I didn't want to know. (Was she a fan who slept her way through Country Funk? Or was she—this suggestion came from Mel—the reason his AA meetings were so appealing? I didn't *want* to know.) There were truths behind the legends behind the inventions behind the truths. But he was happy, he'd said, and I had to accept that. This is how it ends for him—he's happy.

So is Teal. Her live-in lover, Renee, is fascinatingly hobbied-up (skiing, gourmet vegetarian cooking, volunteer work on the board of the health foods co-op, arts photography, gardening, amateur veterinary). And the good thing is—the refreshingly new, good thing, as everybody in Teal's currentmost support group knows, is—women don't hurt women. Good-bye to all of the doubt and pain.

Except there are stories. You know, "stories" that "one hears." Renee steps into this plot from her own corrosive mixture of dozens of previous plots, and one of them has to do with a woman, Pam, or once it was told to me as Jan, who calls Renee "The Snake Queen," and has rudely healed scars on both her wrists from their own years-ago en-counter. Of course, there are always such tales, many of them un-founded. In this case, though (remember the "arts photography"), there's supposedly hard evidence of the Pam-or-Jan connection to Renee, and to the destructive link between them. Unless those photo-graphs are imaginary? In either case, that's the past. This is now. Renee left the room to spatula me my second slice of her silken mushroom quiche, and Teal shyly confided, "I've never been this happy." She gave me her Knowing Look, her Piercer. "Never. *Never.*"

So if anyone appeared damaged from all of the psychodrama brouhaha, it was the mother. Jane still valued her brother's memory—the dead, disputed uncle of Teal's saga; Jane was lost, alone, in a post-war war-zone landscape of emotional debris. "It's like she's not my daughter anymore"—whether this was out of loyalty to the brother, or a lingering affection for Mr.-Perfect-Son-in-Law Justin, or a mother's conservative, homophobic confusion at Teal's new happiness . . . who knew? "I'm going to Sacramento to live with my other daughter," she said, and then she was gone, with no forwarding info. *Zzzip.* Except, in the years that we'd known her, as well as known Teal, we'd never heard of another daughter. Would there be "another daughter" under sodium-pentathol questioning? Is "another daughter" a metaphor for someone? Who? For something? What? Too many questions. Time to let go. You excavate a mind, you'll find a sacrificial victim. That's that. You dig up an altar, you'll find a torn-out heart.

I dreamed I was in a court of law. The light was pleading its case before the presiding judge: that it was all particle. The judge listened, and was convinced; I listened, and I was, too. And then, from the other side of the room, the light spoke up, and persuasively argued that it was all wave. I saw the judge nod yes;

*and so did I. It was a strange court of law. No verdict was handed down, or even
expected by the opposing parties. In fact, there weren't opposing parties. There
was only the light, the one light. It won its case and it lost it.*

"But all of those things she claimed—*were they true?*" Lael asked. Of
course, it would have to be Lael; the rest of us wanted to leave it all behind. Were they true? (because there was more, much more, that I've
vetoed for use in this essay). First the yes vote flooded in ("You don't
just script such horrible stories like some kind of Hollywood hack. I
can tell—it was true."), and then the no vote ("Teal was always more
alive in some dilemma than in contentment. Trust me: she needed to
feel more alive, at any cost, and created the circumstances.") and then
I chimed in by quoting Sean Russell's *Beneath the Vaulted Hills* for a
maybe-yes-a-little-bit vote:

" 'It is only a story,' Banks said, the disdain in his voice less than con-
vincing.

" 'All stories have roots,' Anna said."

These days, when I think of the immiscible stir of assurances that inform the Vagaries' story, I'm reminded of what Dennis Tedlock writes
about the combo word *mythistory*: "For the ancient Greeks this term became a negative one, designating narratives that should have been
properly historical but contained mythic impurities. For Mayans, the
presence of a mythic dimension in narratives of human affairs is not an
imperfection but a necessity, and it is balanced by a necessary human
dimension in narratives of mythic affairs."

There's a murky Guatemalan scene of a woman with a child at her
hip and her body busy in the rhythm of grinding corn, while overhead
the gods Blood Gatherer, Corntassel, and Dark Jaguar shake the heavens with kinds of pleasure and wrath that, if they came near us, would
fry us. Then that scene thins, and behind it—very gradually replacing
it—is a man at a desk, an executive. He folds away the day's columns of
numbers. It's early in the evening now. He opens a drawer and puts
away the lists of his clients' cases. He switches the lamp to off. And then
he takes off, too, the self that attended all day to the clients and the
numbers.

Now he dons another self (although it lives in this same world). Or would the phrase "another self" automatically make it be "another world"? But no, it's still Connecticut. It's still Rhode Island. It's still the Camembert moon. And Wallace Stevens, who's a poet now, walks into the darkening indigo air, and frowns, and hums, and considers his lines.

> *When the blackbird flew out of sight,*
> *It marked the edge*
> *Of one of many circles.*

Worlds

1.

In 1907 my grandfather landed on Mars, he'd come so far from his village in Poland. The water lapping the pilings: that was Mars, the wharf itself was Mars, the Mongol rampage of rats was Martian rats that led, by alley shadows and vats of impossible stinks, to the jammed, flat-broke and flash-o'-diamonds flush, fat, flammable, wholly contradictory and madcap heart of New York: the capital city of Mars.

A dockside conniver had offered to turn his meager crumple of Polish paper money into "'Merica *gelt*"—a chiseler bogused-up in a black silk skullcap.

Here my grandfather stands, some zomboid creature lolling on the trolley tracks, immobilized by too much Mars too fast. The trolley's stalled, of course, and clanging at him as if he were a cow. He's less than a cow. He's a dumbshit Yid, with Hope and Terror frozen in a polka-step in his breast, and half-a-handful of chump change trickling out of his fingers.

That night he slept beneath an overturned clawfoot bathtub, in a dump behind the warehouse district. At daybreak, when even the garbage shone majestically for a moment, he clambered out, as warily as a hermit crab.

"So. You're Jewish?" A man was standing right there, he spoke in Yiddish. "I come here every morning." He gave the tub a dull kick.

"Three days out of four, some greenhorn's spent the night here. Come, you need help?"

He was wearing a black silk skullcap. Once, alright—but not twice: my grandfather threw a loopy punch at his jaw, that he barely sidestepped.

Then, as if he'd practiced this for hours already, the man hunched, swiveled, and neatly tripped my grandfather into a mushy pile of restaurant trash. He held out his hand. "I tell you: come. You need help."

It turned out that he was legitimate—the Hebrew Immigration Aid Society. They walked away, like a father leading his mesmerized son.

And *that* night my grandfather slept in a bed.

It was one of ten beds in the room, in an HIAS hospice that looked like a caved-in orange crate done up to the size of a boardinghouse. A week, they said he could stay here; not that he even knew which day it was. His nine bed-brethren were already sleeping, filling the dark with their heavy-as-sandbags breaths. An elderly woman had led him here by the skimpiest pinch of candle—now by touch alone he opened his oilcloth sack, removed his pamphlet with the text of the *shachris, mincha,* and *mahriv* prayers, and placed it delicately beneath the slab of newspaper meant for a pillow.

At 5 A.M. he leaped up screaming, and ran for a broom in the corner. *"G'vald! G'vald!"* his roommates heard him shouting, *"Geshtroft! Tshepeh zich op fun mir!"* (Help! Accursed thing, get away from me!) Watching him, their protector, beat the alarm clock into a pile of springs and glassy powder, until it was stilled.

He had a lot to learn here.

And he'd prepared, in his nowhere sticks-and-baling-wire village: had perfected his Polish-inflected Yiddish once a week in "immigration class," in the shack out back of Oyzer the cheesemaker's; and had learned "yes," "no," "hey buddy," and the names of seven presidents starting with Vahsheenktun. But nothing could prepare him for the series of spirit-deadening jobs. He learned why everyone woke at 5 A.M. He learned what they suffered before returning fourteen hours later.

First he became a roller—this meant standing for the whole shift, in a windowless, unventilated room. One day, the draggled end of a day, he did his last cigar and couldn't uncrimp his fingers. After that, he scavenged rags; there was a company that cleaned them in benzene, then trimmed and pressed them. When he worked up to being a trimmer, he was given a space on the fire escape; it was early December, thin snow started falling, and the shop boss wouldn't let him back inside until he'd filled his daily quota. After that, he shoveled horses' shit. The company even brought him out to the racetrack, it was like getting a promotion: shoveling better horses' shit. "Hey buddy—c'mere." He delivered back-and-forth the envelopes by which races were fixed. He wasn't proud of this; but he wasn't starving.

By now it's 1911.

"Hey Louie—dipping your dingus lately?"

My grandfather startled up from reading his pulp adventure magazine. He could read—a little. He could shoot the shit with the knockabout guys—a little. Even so, a kind of shameful concern was written over his knobby features. Here they caught him galloping over the novelette-length Wild West, but once again he didn't even know the local argot, from the corner of Forman and Hester.

"Louie, Louie, Louie," with a pitying nod of his richly pomaded temples. Then he made the little universal sexual mortar-and-pestle sign with his fingers. "Louie: getting any?" A wink, a manly clap on the back.

They were at Jake's, the candy store—the traditional roughneck hangout. In a neighborhood of tougher necks than Jews, it would have been the pool hall. Here you wouldn't go to find the rabbi, or the penny-a-page *bar mitzvah* tutor: no. The shoe-shined streetwise congregated here, the wisenheimers and two-bit racketeers, the Jewish cabbies and tough-stuff welterweight prizefighters, even a big ward boss's sharp-creased, pinky-ringed vizier.

Hello, Mister I-Own-All-Of-Forman-Street, thought my grandfather.

What he said, though, was, "Oh—yah, yah, the sex," and grinned sheepishly, and loathed himself for it. But, hey: these were the boys with the easy *mezuma* folded in rhinestone clips, and they were walking their slice-of-cheesecake smiles straight out of these broken streets, on a beam of American moonlight.

And the pamphlet of prayers, of *shachris, minchah, mahriv?* Did its ghost form ever flutter, a transparent moth, among the racks of racing gazettes and copies of *Amazing Adventure?*

"Louie," he said, "don't kid me. I bet you got the hot pants for some little *tsatchkeleh,* right?" He didn't wait for an answer. He poked his finger at the cover of the magazine—a rugged buckaroo and a supple Indian princess sped their horses over the plains. "You can shovel their shit your whole life, Louie, you listening? Or you can ride one."

Louie wasn't sure what language this was, but he knew he'd better apply himself assiduously to a study of the licorice nibs and jawbreakers.

"Louie, you listening? We got a little job."

And Louie did have the hot pants. He'd met Rosie at the Sewing Sisters Association *balln* (a ball, a dance). She had a solid peasant modesty, when posing at the punch bowl, with her friends; her hair was tied in a bun, as tight as a fist. But she could dip and slink a catty Coney Island dance step that you'd swear would call down fire from the sky, and *then* she shook out a luscious tumble of frizzled hair. He wanted to swim in that hair, die in that hair, like a salmon.

What she saw in him . . . who knows? The world is full of smooth-move wooers. Did she understand that knobby face would give a woman something she could hold to?

They were born not more than twenty miles apart. Yes, but they needed to come to America to meet! Can you imagine! Etc. The moon was out, as big up there as a catcher's mitt. He watched her ankles skitter about the shadows of her skirts. They seemed to have minds of their own, like small white creatures in undergrowth. He touched her, and she stopped his hand, but she didn't walk away.

"Is nice—yah?" She was looking up at the full, lush, scoop-of-butterbrickle moon. "In Poland, I see this moon. Now here, I see this moon. Not so much makes from the changes."

"Some t'ings. In Poland, I don't know *you*." This was a major romantic speech for him, and she recognized that.

"Louie, promise me—nobody else, you'll vant?"

"Rosie, Rosie."

"Louie, a name is not a promise."

"Rosie, yah, alright already, I promise."

"A promise lasts, you know this. A promise . . ." searching for a definition ". . . is bigger than all of the miles."

"Rosie, I know vhat's a promise, believe me."

What was she reading? His heart? His dick? She took a quick breath and decided.

"Come—my friend Rebecca, her *zaydee* raises chickens, they haff this little room for the chickens." She grabbed his hand. "You dun't mind chickens?"

No, he didn't mind chickens. He wouldn't have minded a herd of mad elk.

That night he didn't dip his dingus; she was carefuller than that. But it began, that night. The more they talked, the more they met to sweatily clench in chicken *dreck,* of course the more they had in common. Eventually a look across a room was telegraphically charged. Yet there is no perfect congruity.

There's a panel in one of George Herriman's exemplary *Krazy Kat* comic strips, where Officer Pupp is smitten under the lunar orb, and batting goo-goo eyes at the Kat. They say, in their Herrimanesque patois: "Ah-h, 'Krazy' I wonder if yon 'moon'—yon 'June moon'—yon 'love moon'—does not suggest something to you?"

"Sure it do 'Offissa Pupp',—chizz—swiss chizz."

Some nights, rolling away from him, she'd peek back at his snoozing gnomish features and be panicked by the *alienness* of somebody not herself, with his own containing skin and hungers. She had always believed you built a future stone by stone. She was practical, she kept a piled list of her grocery purchases and their prices going back to shack life in Poland, every morning she scoured every fleck from the hall sink. Her three scarves, which were her treasures, she always hung away in what she perceived to be their proper chromatic order.

And he —! A *blonjenkop,* a "lost head," a dreamer. He was forever shlepping the sack in somebody else's tycoon scheme.

She had a brother, Nate, he managed the shop where a silent row of hunched-over Jews ground lenses for glasses. "*Shpeckatickles,* Louie," Nate explained, and with his thumb and forefinger made a circle of each hand, at his eyes. "Pree-SISH-un vork!" And they were booming, too, Louie could see that: orders slopping over the desk (it needed Rosie's touch) and the grinders bent to their wheels and fussy buffing sticks from just past sunup to dusk.

"But vhere to go from here? Vhat is our FOOCHUR? Louie, ve need someone," and now his arm around Louie's shoulder, "to t'ink big new t'ings, ve need somebody inDOOStrious!" And Nate would splay the fingers of his free hand, slowly arcing it across the air as if, in its wake, the lineaments of a glittering and unstoppable Tomorrow could be seen.

But Louie didn't think he was indoostrious. He didn't really know *what* he was, most days when he woke he barely knew *where*. And Rosie kept mentioning Nate's place increasingly, bringing the topic to bed with them, confusing it with the sweet beast scent of their mutual explorations—a woman whose wants and visions and hillocky, billowy body might have been, for him, the complete relief map of another planet.

I mention this now, in 1990, long after my grandfather's yielded bones are gelatin and a calcium cloud, because it explains the trip he took, vacationing away from the city, trying to clear his "lost head" of conundrums. Some of his friends pitched in: a train ticket, first class ("Got you kless number vun!" said Alfie Sprintzer).

This is what did it, finally; this was the straw:

"We've got to start you out small, you understand that, Louie. But this could be a big-time operation."

Jake had gone in back to count a new shipment of jelly beans. He understood when his ears would best be clean of certain talk.

The man who owned Forman Street possessed, and knew he could rely on, a confiding, persuasive voice. That voice, those gesturing hands at the ends of their fancy uptown double-starched cuffs, had won over aldermen down at the Hall. Kid pickpockets basked in that voice, no less than city development entrepreneurs. Now it was Louie's, all Louie's, lotiony and gold.

The plan was simple: they were organizing, and none too soon, the sharpers down at the docks. Louie would be in charge, the captain. All of the fakes out there, the money changers crying out their "'Merica *gelt!*" and wearing their black silk skullcaps?—they would report to him, to Louie, the maker and shaker, the *alta kocker,* the Kingpin of the Wharves!

He looked down to his magazine cover: the uncomplicated air of the West, with a yee-ha! and a yippi-ai-yay!

In 1907 George Herriman arrived in New York, from L.A., with a five-cent shine on his shoes and a dollar's-worth of sketch pads. Yes and by 1912, he was being sent by Hearst himself to do a series of comic slice-of-life reports from west of the Mississippi. He'd been impressed by Herriman's earlier coverage for the *Los Angeles Times,* especially

UNIDENTIFIED AIRSHIP SIGHTINGS
HAUNT IMPERIAL VALLEY
Monster Soars Through Air
Makes Clicking Noise and Carries a Light
Should Salt Be Put On Tail Of This Fly By Night?

with typically Herrimanesque illustrations. Hearst would see that doors were opened, and jaws of importance oiled for talk. All Herriman had to do was—well, react like Herriman, and mail it back for relishment by an eager New York readership.

Hearst couldn't have been more emphatic, and Herriman couldn't, in any case, have been more eager to revisit the land of butte and Navajo hogan he'd come to love when bumming the rails twelve years earlier, a punk cartoonist wanna-be with inky stars in his eyes. (Well, now it's a first-class ticket and six clicking bottles of Hearst's own private-brewed ale.) He'd written, "Those mesas and sunsets out in that ole pais pintado . . . a taste of that stuff sinks you—deep." (Well, now it was: next stop, Arizona!)

And he'd have time, as over half the continent clacked on by, to scratch away at some ideas for this new strip he was going to juggle room for, some time next year. It's night. The side compartment lights are on, a light so yellow it turns his eggshell sketchbook page to saffron. He rolls a smoke, with one hand, from his shirt-pocket pouch of

Bull Durham; with the other, he keeps idly scribbling . . . what does the mouse say now? . . . then what does the bulldog say? . . . then Krazy Kat.

This isn't the place to insist on the screwball, skew-all genius of that thirty-one-year run of hi-jinks, low-jinks, and oh-so-sly-winks vaudevillian philosophy: I've paid homage to it elsewhere, as have others more knowing and eloquent than I am, in the history of such stuffs. As Gilbert Seldes said in his banner-raising essay of 1924, "*Krazy Kat* is, to me, the most amusing and fantastic and satisfactory work of art produced in America today. With those who hold that a comic strip cannot be a work of art I shall not traffic." With his lopsided (or, with Officer Pupp a participant, a truly *kop*-sided) triangle (ever-ingenue Krazy; villainous Ignatz Mouse; and Pupp of the local konstabulary), Herriman created a krackpot kosmos that transcended the limitations of its form, and became, in all of its antic variety, a single sinuous rhapsody of comic meditation, mythopoetic and simply heels-clicking high-spirited at once.

What I need to mention now, though, is "Herriman's language, Joycean before *Finnegans Wake*—the words all working, bouncing, and playing off one another, veering from a bop rhythm to a dazzling poesy. As Ignatz Mouse said, 'Plain language, but in a higher plane.'"

So says *Krazy Kat: The Art of George Herriman,* and points out that the "alphabet soup" involved here included "Victorian prose, the lowest street slang, onomatopoeia, Spanish, French, the alliteration of Navajo names and"—*mais oui* ("Of cawss you may," the Kat might say, "be my guess")—"the Yiddishized diction of New York's Lower East Side." When Krazy arcs her flapjacks backwards, then presto catches them standing on her head, her self-approving comment on her adroitness is, "Oy, a trix—fency."

I belabor this because, as the miles rattlingly pass, George Herriman sits there, doodling, with his lumped-up swayback Stetson hat pushed so far back on his head it's nearly a memory . . . sits there fascinatedly eyeing this fellow across the aisle, who's reading a richly garish-covered issue of *All-Story,* moving his lips along with the English as if grazing it, stopping every now and then to argue vehemently with the open text, with frequent punctuations as the hero faces imminent demise (or love-hugs): *"Oy!" "G'vald!"*

But when Herriman tapped him lightly on the shoulder and wordlessly offered him a room-temperature beer, my grandfather rose to the lingual occasion. "Hey buddy, man, hokay by me, Mac!" He'd had nothing to eat since Ohio, when the last of Rosie's sandwiches ran out; and there's a Yiddish saying, *Beser toyt shiker eyder toyt hungerik*—Better dead drunk than dead hungry.

Louie raised the sweating bottle to his benefactor: *"L'chayim."* It was gone in four pulls.

So they talked. They shmoozed, they chewed the phoneme fat together long past the world-revivifying rise of the next day's sun. Life. Women. Betting the ponies. Legendary New York dandies. Those airships (after Herriman explained them). Dreams. Death. Dipping the dingus. What's suffering for. The grand themes, newly girded and gilded to match these far-flung temperaments.

Herriman opened his sketchbook gingerly, and my grandfather studied the whole incipient anthropomorphic cast, including Joe Stork and Gooseberry Sprig the Duck Duke. "Don't vorry," he said encouragingly, with all of the friendly largesse he could fit in a smile, "you vork hard, you gonna gets better." Herriman found this a real hoot. "Lou-boy, you tickle my buzzum," he told him.

And later, passing pastureland in the slumbrous touch of the noontime sun—"MOOY!" my grandfather shouted, and in explanation pointed at a cow. And you can see her, lowing out that bovine Yiddishism, in panel 6 of the April 23, 1922, *Krazy Kat.*

But this is 1912.

Night's circled back again, George Herriman is snoring, and Louie studies the huge, close clock face of a full moon, and the innumerable stars, as many, as painfully lovely, as when he'd look up at the sky from the rural darkness of Poland. Where was he running to *now*, and why? He'd told Rosie he'd write. How complicated does any one life become in always refolding itself?

The Kat will also wander her gaze "among the unlimitless etha." The Kat will also sing a runaway's tune: "Press my pents/ An' shine my shoes/ Gimme twenny cents/ To pay my dews—/ For I'm goin' far a-waay—/ Tidday." But that's still in the future. For now, it's my grandfather, watching the night-black sand, and the nearly touchable desert sky, go streaking through his head he sees reflected in the window he looks out from. It's almost as if he's watching his own brain first inventing these things: the desert, the wheel of the zodiac, such admirable creations . . . . And his constellation, The-Stars-Like-Stones-In-A-Chicken's-Gizzard, grinding another night away. . . . He sleeps. . . .

Next stop, Arizona.

2.

"Is The Master Unit ready?"

"No sir. Not yet sir. But. . . ."

"But?" Lowell is indignant. Or *can* a person be indignant with a machine? He shrugs, he loses the prickly edge of his exasperation. A night is only so long. He has work.

He was named after Percival Lowle—and his pedigree is traceable back unshakably to this nominative worthy who, in 1639, age sixty-eight, in the considerable company of his wife Rebecca and fourteen others related by blood or business, boarded the *Jonathan* at London, and nine weeks later arrived at Newbury, forty miles northwest of Boston.

In general, the Puritan settlers of Massachusetts Bay "were more affluent, better educated and of a higher social class than any other large group of colonists who came to America." Their intention was to establish a society of saints, as an exemplum for the future, and so their settlement "in the eyes of Puritan leaders . . . appeared to be the most significant act of human history since Christ bade farewell to His disciples." Categorizing the simultaneous settlers of Virginia, Massachusetts Bay Governor Winthrop dusted off his saintly thesaurus and referred to "unfit instruments—a multitude of rude and misgoverned persons, the very scum of the people."

The Lowles were a specialdom even amidst the Massachusetts elect: "Percival Lowle, Gent." bore the heraldic ensign of knighthood (it was the family's since the fifteenth century): educated richly, he could speak Italian Mantuan, and read Ovid in the original. At twenty-six, he had been Assessor of Lands—an inherited office—and, later, a prosperous import/export merchant prince.

Not surprisingly, Lowle, with this advantageous background and his own ambitious savvy, throve in America. He lived to write a 100-line elegy for Governor Winthrop. He died in 1664, age ninety-three; from then, unbroken, the family stock continues, privileged, meritorious, nearly sacrosanct: "the Lowells speak only to God" becomes a common comic trope, and for three generations about the textile town of Lowell, Massachusetts, "Lowell" and "millionaire" are properly synonymous.

In 1854, Augustus Lowell married into another Boston Brahman dynasty, and his wife, the former Katharine Lawrence, bore three children: Amy, the youngest, the Imagist poet; Abbott, the middle, the president of Harvard; and the eldest, Percival, born in 1855. "I came into this world with a comet, Donati's Comet of 1858 being my earliest recollection—and I can see yet a small boy half way up a turning staircase gazing with all his soul into the evening sky where the stranger stood."

And all of this brings us down to autumn, midautumn, of 1912. He's at the 24-inch telescope, a man of fifty-seven as straight and staunch all night as a styptic pencil. He's looking. He's in his eighteenth year of looking, of studying Mars in each red flange and dander and follicle. Some nights Mars wants to cloud its face like a flirt, but Lowell won't take no for an answer, not from his own unwavering eye, and not from one of the 70 million miles. He's going to see each crimson pock, and its rim, and its shadow.

Although, in truth, tonight he also has another urgent project on his mind. "Oh, Mr. Tolliver . . . ," and in a flash Mr. Tolliver is here. He's the perfect associate for Lowell, almost archetypally so: his greatest passion is astronomy; his singlemost allegiance is to Lowell's maverick theories; his hair is a series of bright gray military cleats. Like most of the staff men here, he's abnormally methodical, and clippish in speech. Tonight he seems more soft than that in his manner, however—abashed, perhaps.

"Mr. Tolliver. Is it functioning yet?" *It* is The Master Unit, a showy telescope with an 84-inch lens, inset with a thermopyle and mounted with a single-prism spectrograph of Vesto Slipher's invention. While the eyepiece is a dainty thing like a jeweler's loupe (and calculatedly so: the Master Unit is intended to woo the favor of a list of high-profile, influential visitors) the barrel is about as big around as a subway tunnel (this is also calculated for effect). The whole thing comes, by various metal waists and accordion pleats, to rest on four diminutive feet, like those of a portable tray-table. Yet the total effect of the massive, levered, and socketed main section, is that of a major city skyline tilted upward at the stars.

It's an impressive contrivance, surely; and so it dwindles Mr. Tolliver all the more when he says, "No sir. But we're working at it. We're checking the section relays now."

At this, Lowell snorts—a well-bred snort, but a snort. They've checked the circuits and the beam-struts and the inloads and, with something like thirty-six hours remaining, he doesn't see now why massaging the goddamn section relays is going to do one batshit dash of good.

But all he says, composedly, is, "Mr. Tolliver. Please be aware that the press arrives in little over a day. Some may be . . . hostile to our position. We are intending to overpower them, you know, by the plain cold facts of it we hope, by bulk and showmanship if necessary." Mr. Tolliver nods, because he knows this, and because Mr. Tolliver always nods when Mr. Lowell speaks, and energetically nods: as if he's checking off a list of orders. "Please, Mr. Tolliver. Have the men persevere." Mr. Tolliver leaves.

And Lowell is alone again, slumped, fuddled for a moment. Over eighteen years he's made of himself a serious, professional observer of the heavens; though he knows he can be colorful, espousing his ideas, he's no sideshow barker. Yes, but with the constant and indeed increasing volleys of rebuke at his ideas. . . .

But then—he *is* Percival Lowell—he squares his shoulders; also, one time, flicks them, as if shooing off a gnat. And now he's back to his looking, back to his ever-finer-resolving vigil, as still, as steady, as a concrete gargoyle set on this bench. No, that's not true: the eye at the lens is alive, is at its task with a ravenous basilisk-fire.

And what would Louie have been to this man with the family crest and the white wing collar so stiffly starched it might be bas-relief sculpture? Very little. Less than little. Antipathetically little: unrestricted immigration appalled him; once, at least, he spoke against it at a public forum. My grandfather would have been somebody meant for brooming the floors and freshening the cow-barn hay, if that; and only then, if hired thirdhand by a recent office lackey unacquainted with the ambience.

And still I need to praise the Lowell genealogy here, and enable it forward. Not that his marriage at fifty-three to Constance Savage Keith brought any biological issue—no. But in the metaphoric way in which we use the term, he was the "father" (*he* would have disowned them, but he was provably the father) of the Martians (the "Barsoomians" to use the indigenous language) in eleven novels by Edgar Rice Burroughs— and so, unwilling, the patriarch of the sturdy green line of every insect-eyed, antenna-waving, raygun-wielding extraterrestrial from the saucer-fied 1950s to date, that ever landed and indicated "take me to your leader."

And *Lowell's* "father"?—was Schiaparelli. The respected, keen-eyed Giovanni Virginio Schiarparelli. With the usual collaterally ancestral and second-cousin voices offering background provocation:

Bernard de Fontenelle is opining as early as 1686, "The Earth swarms with inhabitants. Why then should nature, which is fruitful to an excess here, be so very barren in the rest of the planets?" Why, indeed!

Huygens writes a volume of speculations on the citizens of other planets. Kant considers that Earth and Mars, as "the middle links of the planetary system," have inhabitants "that stand in the center between the extremes of physiology, as well as morals." The eighteenth-century astronomer Johann Elert Bode, however, computes by a lucid system of mathematical proportions, that the Martians are considerably more spiritual than their counterparts on Earth. "It is the opinion of all the modern philosophers and mathematicians, that the planets are habitable worlds"—Benjamin Franklin in *Poor Richard's Almanack,* 1749.

In 1784, the King's Astronomer, William Herschel, correctly concludes the whiteness visible over the polar regions of Mars is cap ice—going on to guess that the beings of Mars "probably enjoy a situation in many respects similar to our own." (Herschel also believed the sun is "richly stored with inhabitants.") In 1892 the French astronomer (and toast of the town) Camille Flammarion claims "the present inhabitation of Mars by a race superior to ours is very probable." Three years later, the *New York Tribune* reports a scribble of certain dark markings across the Martian surface spells out the words "The Almighty" in Hebrew. Could Mars be attempting a conversation with Earth?

Then don't just revolve around silently! Plans proposed (and often by highly regarded minds of the times) include, for instance, the Pythagorean theorem drawn to half the size of Europe on the wastes of the Sahara (or better: *dig* the theorem, fill these trenches with water, pour on kerosene, and set the theorem gargantuanly on fire); mathematician Karl Friedrich Gauss suggests a *vaaaaast* wheat field, the size of many Rhode Islands ("wheat because of its uniform color"), shaped to be a right triangle, bordered by pine trees, in Siberia.

It's an age of scientific optimism and mechanical cockiness, writ large. The completed Suez Canal is considered "a wonder of the world," and every day in the press the progress of the Panama Canal is debated. Gods are tottering, and the astronomical jots they leave in their vacated places take on burning meaning. Bricklayers, bartenders, bottle washers: everyone's a dabbler with an ephemeris, and the *wunderdabbler* sons of the rich especially. Lowell brings a 6-inch telescope when he travels as a young man to Japan.

In 1893 he returns to the States with this objective: "nothing less than to build, equip, and staff a major new astronomical observatory in the best possible location," to continue the work of the ailing Schiaparelli.

It's now sixteen years since that night in Milan when Schiaparelli witnessed the geometric pattern of lines he properly labeled *canali.* "Channels," it meant, though overnight a world gone hungry for worlds was making "canals" of it—those *engineered* things.

He is conquering Mars; and he is Mars's vassal. He is stroking that face like a lover, like a proper Victorian lover, with his gaze alone, from afar. He is the obliging amanuensis, to whom Mars dictates its lines. He is Lowell. He is tired. He is sitting at his bench with the pride of a rajah in his howdah. He is reading the varicose scrabble of that face. He is tired. The night is tired. The deeply burned lines of Mars are holding it, like a cheese in a net. He is Lowell, he is the alpha dog here, he is going to look, and chart, beyond being tired, what they call "the Red Planet"—yes, that tabasco-glint in his eye.

Eventually—and repeatedly—he would see, and exhaustively sketch for his *Annals,* 700 canals: "a mesh of lines and dots like a lady's veil." The astronomical language is lushly evocative at times—"a twilight arc on the terminator," "limblight" "gemination," "albedo and density"— but data was arrived at in a systematic, dutiful shift at the heavens-scanning tubes.

He was indefatigable, and his legacy is as serious as his intent. His early insistence on the importance of atmospheric conditions to findings soon became seminal. His "velocity-shift" technique for spectroscopically determining the composition of other planets' atmospheres became a recognized practice. He was confident a "trans-Neptunian planet" existed, "Planet X" he called it; and the first two letters of Pluto stand for Percival Lowell, its harbinger. Under Lowell's influence,

Lampland began his attempts at direct photography of the planets, and Slipher conducted his observations of spiral galaxies that enabled Hubble's discovery of the universe's expansion. Lowell, everywhere. Lowell at the lectern, in the headlines, by the elbows of the sky-beguiled.

"The Roosevelt of astronomy," the *New York Times* says, in 1907. (And later, when Pluto had been discovered, the *Times* quotes Keats's sonnet: "Then I felt like some watcher of the skies / When a new planet swims into his ken."—And so Keats enters this essay, a moment only, but he'll be back.) Uranus! Meteor showers! The mysterious rings of Saturn!

But it's Mars on his tongue tonight like the holy wafer, Mars his un-curable bloody cyst. He will helix its skin clean off it, like the sweetest freestone peach. He will devour it like a temptress's cunt. He is Percival Lowell, and this is his Grail. This is his weight, as Earth was for Atlas. This is his weight, he will carry it into clearer understanding. He is Percival Lowell, his telescope is his pool cue, he will strike this ball dead-on and watch the sparks collect in his pocket. He is tired. Some-times he is very tired. He is its Boswell. He is its weary retiree walking it on a leash of pure vision. Cherry tomato. Pimiento. Slice of cayenne pepper irritating his nights. Sometimes he wakes, he's been scratching a rash across his chest, where his heart is, the color of Mars.

He saw the canals.

"Think back on '07," said the *Wall Street Journal*. "What has been in your opinion the most extraordinary event of the twelve months? . . . not the financial panic which is occupying our minds, but the proof af-forded that conscious, intelligent human life exists upon the planet Mars."

He saw the canals, he labored. "Lowell's plan of attack was emi-nently pragmatic. He intended, in effect, to lay telescopic siege to the planet." In 1907 alone, Lowell and Lampland "obtained 3,000 images" of the Martian disc with their early ratchet-and-squeeze-bulb camera.

He saw the canals, he proselytized: *Mars and Its Canals* (1906), and *Mars as the Abode of Life* (1908). He said, "I believe that all writing should be a collection of precious stones of truth which is beauty." (And so a whisper of Keats is heard amidst the apparatus: Lowell's sister's influence. Amy.)

He saw the canals, he understood the message in their webwork. He said, "It is by the very presence of uniformity and precision that we suspect things of artificiality. The better we see these lines the more regular they look. The intrinsic probability of such a state of things arising from purely natural causes becomes evident on a moment's consideration. That life inhabits Mars now is the only rational deduction from the observations in our presence. Think of the intelligence and far-contrivance necessary to execute and maintain a system of irrigation worldwide!"

He saw the canals, as when a child at Miss Fette's Boston school for the Brahman heirs, that lady of strict comportment leaned above him with her lavender-gargled breath and said, "This is very charming, Percival, but here where you tell us *I fell down* you employ the word *down* gratuitously: one cannot fall up," but he knows better, every night since 1894 he's fallen, helpless Alice, up that wonderland rabbit hole without bottom.

He saw the canals, his namesake Percival Lowle also pioneered "the New World."

He saw the canals, in 1907 the London *Daily News* said, "He is the greatest authority on Mars we have" (the year my grandfather Louie woke up mapping in his travel-baffled head the *dreck*-infected streets of the Lower East Side of New York).

"These delicate features," said Percival Lowell. These are the canals, chimeric and none the less quantifiable, for which, in 1894— in the Arizona Territory, near Flagstaff, in sight of the San Francisco Mountains, on a mesa at an altitude of more than 7,000 feet, in

Coconino County, on the Coconino Plateau, "far from the smoke of men"— he built a "fitting portal to communion with another world."

The gods are wind and death and thunder and the buttery slime of birth, the gods are light and perception, light and darkness, darkness and fires-inside-the-flesh.

In 1907 Natalie Curtis published *The Indians' Book*. She says, "At a Navajo healing ceremony in some hogan where there is sickness, the steady rhythm of the medicine-songs pulses all night long. These songs ('Hozhonji songs') describe a journey to a holy place beyond the sacred mountains where are everlasting life and blessedness. The Divine Ones who live in and beyond the mountains made the songs. . . ." And made *this* world, of fevered skin and thinning game and corn and wolves and ambitions and spittle and burials and pollen, a world interpenetrable with Theirs.

And for the Hopi, as well, the deific dwells in the mountains. "The Kachinas are somewhat analogous to gods or nature spirits," says Edward T. Hall. "They live with the people for half of the year and return to their home in the San Francisco Mountains (north of Flagstaff, Arizona) for the remaining six months."

Do the Hopi make love? Do they sob? Do they stand on their sandstone mesas, mazily lost in regarding the star-beaded black cloth of night? Of course. And yet their universe is fundamentally *other* from mine. "No past, present, or future exists as verb tenses in their language. Hopi verbs have no tenses, but indicate instead the validity of a statement. Hopi seasons are treated more like adverbs. Summer is a *condition*: hot." There is no word that corresponds to "time" and Hall describes the Hopi as "living in the eternal present."

Now the maidens have gathered wild sunflower petals from the mesa at the lip of the kiva, the underground ceremonial chamber. Now they wet their faces. Now they dust themselves with golden powder ground from the petals. Now the Lagon and Oaqol dances begin. . . .

The gods touch our lives: the sky is a membrane. The gods announce themselves: our dreams are a hearing trumpet.

> *Call the Great Ones down from the Mountain,*
> *Call the Great Ones down*
> *From Sisnajinni, from the Chief of Mountains!*

—"communion with another world."

This is the place, the spirit, that moved Herriman so deeply, its presence is verbally homaged and clearly if cartoonily cartouched throughout his other, more daily love: the *Krazy Kat* strip.

"Herriman made many trips into the Indian country of Northern Arizona. He stayed at Kayenta, on the Navajo Reservation, with John and Louisa Weatherill, at the trading post they had opened there in 1910. Through them, Herriman came to know the country in all its moods and facets. *Krazy Kat*'s Coconino has the spaciousness and airiness of the high northern desert. In this vast space Herriman places indigenous mesas, buttes, lunatic cacti, tumbleweeds, blue bean bushes, rock formations, adobe houses, shifting and changing like mirages. He scatters pots, rugs and Mexican and Indian decorative devices; the latter even appear on trees, clouds, or other props necessary to his stage. One Sunday page depicts Krazy sleeping next to a traditional Navajo loom, on which she has just woven a 'febric.' 'That's the country I love,' said Herriman, 'and that's the way I see it.'

"He said that when he passed on he and his dogs would roam that place for a thousand years."

In whatever atemporal pneuma exists, that holds the populous Native American pantheon in its travel from the San Francisco Mountains to the beckoning of women and men . . . the Healers, the Beneficent

Ones, who hover about the path of the Great Corn Plant (Sun Bearer, Talking God, even little Dontso the spirit messenger-fly, and the rest) are being called by the ancient chants, to the sick boy's side and, having arrived, being immanent now in the world of tooth and salt, they start their supernatural doctoring. . . .

And Herriman has Krazy say, simply: "In my Kosmis, there will be no feeva of discord."

"Mars Hill" as Lowell dubbed the mesa. "Site eleven" is what it had been in the earliest days, when he was also considering "1) The desert of Gobi 2) the veldt of the Transvaal 3) the Samoan Islands."

The seeing here, it seems, has always been good.

We know that in 1054 A.D. a supernova appeared "just above and to the left of a crescent moon," as Evan Connell puts it. "European intellectuals failed to report the guest star" but "a pictograph showing a cross with a crescent moon just beneath it and to the right" (datable by potsherds to—correct!—the eleventh century) "was found on the wall of Navajo Canyon in Arizona."

1912. It's dawn. Well, it's a little before: the air along the desert horizon isn't yet touched by light, no, but is emptying itself, by imperceptible gradations, of darkness. Lowell hasn't slept. He loves this moment, when the Earth becomes as real for him as Mars has been, and he packs that latter planet away inside himself like a red corpuscle. Lowell, his 'scopes, his entry books.

We know, we tell ourselves we know, the universe is infinity foliate; nothing should surprise us. Yes, but can it *be,* that the mesa of the Navajo gods, and the telescope-poking "site eleven," exist coeval in space-time, with their separate dreams occurring on this same one physical sandstone x? . . .

The scholar of Edgar Rice Burroughs's Martian novels, John Flint Roy, says, "Carter's description of the planet differs in some respects from that given by our Earth scientists. Thus, we feel compelled to assume that Barsoom and Mars are not one and the same; rather, that the former occupies the same place as the latter but in another dimension—the Barsoomian dimension."

Seated at home behold me,
Seated amid the rainbow,
Seated at home behold me,
Lo, here, the Holy Place!

Another night of observation is over. Lowell rubs his face, as if his hands were roughly nubbed towels. A cup of hot tea is waiting for him, and a shaving of Boston rum cake.

"Mr. Tolliver is making a final check just now." It's Langland speaking. His eyes rove toward the door. Beyond it, Tolliver is desperately attempting to placate the obdurate coven of gremlins that are fucking up The Master Unit. Lampland smiles—Slipher the Elder is to his left, Slipher the Younger is at his right, and they smile as well. But Lampland's voice is a sieve out of which all hope has dribbled.

"Gentlemen. Very well." By now it's full-tilt dawn, though these four men are oblivious to its mercurial silvers and desert tangerines. They're grouped in Lowell's study. He plays with a rumpled telegram on his desk; its greeting peeks out, HAIL. His fingers crease his lower lip. It's like watching an I-beam fidget.

"It may be in the next few hours Fate will reward us with greater luck. For now, however, we best had expect disappointment. You know, of course, our visitors sent from Mr. Hearst arrive at noon. And scheduled for later, at three," and now he glances at the telegram, "my sister arrives on the afternoon Atlantic and Pacific stop. . . ." and he trails off, unsure of what to say. Perhaps they need preparing for this?

"My sister, gentlemen. . . ." Yes? They wait. A look of mingled love and embarrassment suddenly shadows his face. And then he says by way of explanation—he's speaking to three grown men who live alone in a dome in the desert counting planets and stars like fireflies in a jar—he says, as if he were speaking to any middle-class family at its breakfast table, "You should know . . . my sister Amy is . . ." almost, he pities them ". . . *truly* an eccentric."

3.

The president of Harvard University, Abbott Lawrence Lowell, is at his desk. The desk is a fine-grained wonder, about the size of a small-town plaza, and as lustrous as a mountie's boot at dress parade. Even the desktop humidor is expansive, it could coddle a couple of preemies, and its lid is ivory and cloisonné fretted into a Byzantine pattern. From the walls, the money and minds of two generations of stiff-necked Boston patriarchs stare down unblinkingly, stern (if money), owlish (if mind). The phone looks like an obsidian monument, freshly waxed. And the man behind the desk is the man—his every gesture says this: he is a Lowell—who is capable of answering such a phone.

"President Lowell. . . ."

"Yes, Miss Supwich."

"I have a caller here," and Miss Supwich's voice says that this is a call she's accepted the way she might a rotten kipper, by two reluctant fingers with her nose averted, "who claims an emergency. Shall I. . . ."

"Yes. Please transfer the call, Miss Supwich. Thank you."

"Yes sir." *Click. Mmph.* "Go ahead, sir."

"Right. Y'er Mr. Lowell?"

"I am, sir."

"The *Haaahvard* Mr. Lowell?"

"The same, sir."

"Well then. I'm out the Bay Roadway by Lowsley. Rummle. Eb Rummle. I repair cars, and I've jest repaired a Pierce Arrow broke down here early this mornin. The lady driver is a big fat dame who says I should charge the bill to you—she bein your sister. So. Do I have yer permission?"

Let me interrupt this anecdote for a minute. Let's look at that scandalous and battleship-plated woman.

She was nicknamed The Postscript—Percy's idea. She was the last of five, by a lag of twelve years, so the sobriquet was a natural. Now there were seven Lowells under the roof, and they named the manor in Brookline, Massachusetts, "Sevenels." Here she was born; and fifty-one years later, here her ruptured body let go of its cantankerous tanklike ghost.

This was the house of America's homegrown aristocracy, and in its rooms she comfortably grew into her birthright privilege. The private schools. The private coach (the coachman let her hold the reins once she was three). The subsidized publishing of her fairy tales. Lessons at Papanti's, the—no: *The*—young ladies' school of dance in Boston. The European tour (she was eight). At a dinner party, when she was five, Longfellow "carried me round the table in a scrap-basket, and the recollection of that ride is as vivid as though it were yesterday."

The adult who burst from this chrysalis was, not surprisingly, lavish and willful. "To argue with her," Carl Sandburg said, "is like arguing with a big blue wave." The day she stood at the forum to veto retaining a cherished but senile school-board member, she was hissed, but she was hearkened to; no other Lowell woman had ever spoken in public before. And when she lectured on "Some Musical Analogies in Modern Poetry," Amy Lowell became the first woman to give a talk at Harvard. Maids were tossed away like matchsticks. Waiters vied in predicting her wants like adepts at the Buddha's side.

Her father died in 1900; she bought Sevenels and began its Amyfication. Chinese wallpaper. Whistler. Monet. Commissioned Egyptian scenes. The sweeping central staircase that was "carpeted in glowing crimson stair-silk woven to order." Every doorknob on the estate was sterling silver. Japanese stone carvings. Persian rugs. Venetian masks. A sixteenth-century crystal chandelier. Enameled snuffboxes (Paris), elfin music boxes (Lausanne). Two huge white cast-stone lions standing guard at the gate.

Her English sheepdogs (whelped from Ringlow's Sultan, a "champion of record" and Flo) were awarded free run of this rarefied domain; each day these seven ate ten pounds of top-round beef with flanking mounds of fresh mashed vegetables. After dinner, gathered about the fireplace in the library, guests at Sevenels were ritually handed Turkish bath towels, as an interceding between their laps and the freely offered slobber. Her custom-built Pierce Arrow limousine (which we've encountered, waiting repairs by Lowsley) was maroon, and her chauffeur and footman were consequently liveried in maroon to match. Magenta, though, she abhorred, and "no magenta flower was ever allowed in her garden."

She wrote all night, and woke in her third-floor bedroom at two in the afternoon. And then she'd ring a series of bells for the downstairs rooms, beginning the daily Sevenels procession: Ada, her live-in love, with the mail; the housekeeper, bringing a pitcher of ice water; Amy's wardrobe maid; the parlor maid (bearing packages); and the kitchen maid with the breakfast tray. Additionally, the staff included seven undergardeners (watchful, one supposes, for the least magenta interference), a laundress, and the aforementioned blendingly uniformed chauffeur (or sometimes two chauffeurs) and footman. One biography adds: "A man came weekly to wind the clocks."

This ambience of retinue and particularized itinerary accompanied her on her travels. "She always refused to stay at private houses, but put up at the best possible hotel, where she required a suite of five rooms, in addition to a room for the maid somewhere else in the building. All electric clocks had to be stopped; all mirrors and other shining objects were swathed in folds of black cloth; the housekeeper saw that exactly sixteen pillows, chosen for plumpness, were perfectly set across the royal bed." Once, when the pillows were flabby some gastrically restless night, "she ripped two of them open, and transferred the feathers from one into the other." On a train to Milwaukee, wanting fresh air, she "made the porter bring and hold a ladder while she clumbered up and broke one of the small glass panes near the roof."

Her ideological luggage was of a piece with this imperiousness. The industrial looms of Lowell, Massachusetts, enabled her family's philanthropies. The pattern of her life, in a sense, was woven by the arduous, humpbacked, fifty-four-hour work weeks there; and this, like the seasons, or gravity, was something fit and unquestioned. "Haughty, class-conscious, high-minded," C. David Heymann calls her. She believed the Lowells among an elect "who had the right to carry their coat of arms." She gave up smoking a pipe, in part, because of its association with "shanty Irish women."

Union organizing was in the air, and the Suffragist movement. But Amy Lowell could blithely refer to "the ignorant proletariat." She's on record declaiming, "I have no patience with the new-fashioned woman and her so-called rights. I believe in the old-fashioned conservative woman and all of her limitations." She spoke against retaining the maiden name in marriage. Wobblies were monsters. London bobbies were, above all other duties, for hailing her cabs.

Outmoded elevation, her view has become the one poets rally *against*. It leaves her with her verses, on a promontory, crooning to the Muses, while the rest of the planet turns willingly back to regarding its inequities and fractures.

She "devoured," one source says, Dickens; "all of Dickens," says another. Presumably she enjoyed, she agreed or she thought she agreed, with Dickens; it's impossible to picture someone finishing those many thousands of tightly grouted pages as an exercise in argument. Yes, but—what did she think, when all of his smudged and crumpled-up children entered another demeaning day of factory work? when all of those wadded and tossed-away women, nearly bruised to the look of maps, slipped into the night from their laborers' shacks? The mansions of England, like so many termite queens, are clearly being fed by the energies of some of the author's most charming (and most pitiable) protagonists. What *frisson* ran through her, reading these things? What necessary obtuseness keeps a world undefiled by neighboring worlds?

She was five, and lonely. Her father was forty-nine, and remote. But Percy, at least, played jacks with her, and lifted her up to pat the row of carved animal heads, or looked in on the dolls made out of chicken wishbones with sealing-wax faces. Compared to the other, stiffer Lowell males, he was streaked with occasional playfulness, and he became a combination idealized-older-brother-*cum*-supervisory-parent (later, her earliest urges toward a published book would be "to emulate and surpass" his *Mars*).

"I dare you!" Percy said at a family party. Amy was eight. She'd zested her way through a giant plate of rice pudding, and now was eyeing a second plate—which also disappeared, and when it was time to leave, her coat wouldn't button across her middle. "And," she wrote, "it never buttoned again."

Oh, she was ponderous! At twenty she was barely five feet tall but weighed 250 pounds. Oh, she was a ponderous, square-rigged, bunker-built thing!

—A glandular, uncorrectable condition. She needed to twist her body when rounding the turns of the spiral stairway. Alice Lowell remembers being a child at a family dinner when Amy barged in "perfectly enormous in a vast gold dress cut tent-style." And biographer Jean Gould: Amy was "a female Henry VIII," she had "the soul of a sylph but the body of a hippopotamus." "Hippopoetess," Pound said (Witter Bynner, in another version): cruel for its being lopsidedly true. "Squat," "swollen," " stunted," "barrel-chested" . . . this chapter of her life is little more than a thesaurus for her bulk.

It shows most painfully in the diary she began to keep in 1889. She's fifteen, self-tormented, disclosing to its pages, "I am ugly, fat, conspicuous, and dull. Oh Lord please let it be all right, and let Paul H. love me, and don't let me be a fool." But "Paul H." didn't love her.

None of them loved her; the world was full of swan-necked debs. "I don't think that being all alone, in here, is good for me." And "I am doomed, for how can it be different—to see the man I love marry somebody else." And "I am doomed to be a dreadful pill; doomed to visibly blush, and waste my sweetness in the vicinity of the wall." And "I was a fool—as usual! a great rough masculine thing! But Paul! Oh! Goodnight!"

The entry for January 13, 1889: "What would I not give to be a poet. Well day-dreams are day-dreams, & I never shall be. . . ."

"And nightly," says the very chunky study of her by S. Foster Damon, "she recorded faithfully the phase of the moon."

Whatever darkness ran through her life was somewhat alleviated by this lifelong, literal lunacy.

A full-plate moon with a garnish of cloud. . . .

A Camembert's rind. . . .

A cameo. . . .

Many nights it must have been the closest face she knew.

Her best friends in her childhood were her books, and "dearest of all" was the one called *Moon-folk*. Here, "a lonely little girl makes the acquaintance of a chimney-elf"—and under his guidance, Rhoda drifts in a dory away to sea, then to the moon, where "all the persons of child literature, even to King Arthur and his knights" declare her welcome. It's easy to see why this was antidotal.

From then, the moon is a benign and serial punctuation. In California "I woke up in the night and the moon was beautiful." In Venice "We are having a moon, the very best moon that ever was, and we 'gondle' way out into the lagoon." In Egypt her boat, "a little dot of a thing only 75 ft. long"—a *dahabeah*—is named *Chonsu*, after the God of the rising moon, and "the moonlight on the Nile is more beautiful than any I have seen." It cuts its zags of liquid silver in the river chop, and each one for an instant is a chain, a badge, a ritual scimitar blade, for this devotee.

Its totemic presence lights her work from the first poem of her first book (". . . the moon / Swings slow across the sky, / Athwart a waving pine . . .")—*athwart?*—to the posthumous Pulitzer-sanctioned collection ("A red moon leers beyond the lily-tank. A drunken moon ogling a sycamore, / Running long fingers down its shining flank . . ."). The poems are steeped in moon-brew. Quite likely, the poems would not have been written without the moon.

Because in 1891, when she was seventeen, and crying out with the ripeness of being seventeen, ajumble inside and neglected . . . the moon introduced her to someone.

O Moon! old boughs lisp forth a holier din
The while they feel thy airy fellowship.
Thou dost bless every where, with silver lip
Kissing dead things to life. The sleeping kine,
Couch'd in thy brightness, dream of fields divine . . .

. . . and the "nested wren," and the "patient oyster" . . . everywhere, that utterly transforming, magisterial touch.

It's Keats, of course, in *Endymion*—a moonray is stirring his psychic quick into a rich Romantic lather. Douglas Bush reminds us "that poet and *persona* are one" in this poem, that "from his boyhood the moon had represented and consecrated all that Endymion loved and aspired to—nature, wisdom, poetry, friends, great deeds. . . ."

She had a confidant now, a mentor. They shared the secret sign and handshake. She's walked out holding the moon in her eyes, this needy budding woman-child, and found a fellow cultist.

Jean Gould: "The effect of *Endymion* especially was like balm to her turbulent spirits. The erotic narrative clarified for her the relative values of the physical and spiritual in love and, fusing the two elements into one, showed her that both are essentially pure. The love scene in the second canto affected her for days: 'How many boys and girls have found solace and joy in this passage!' Her literary discoveries freed her from the prison of her body."

The format of her own first book was copied from that of Keats's 1820 volume *Lamia*; the title, *A Dome of Many-Coloured Glass,* is brazenly taken from Shelley's elegy for Keats; and two poems frankly conjure him— "He spurns life's human friendships to profess / Life's loneliness of dreaming ecstasy."

"I do not believe," she said, "that there is a person in the world who knows John Keats better than I do." Eventually she amassed the largest collection of Keatsiana in private hands, including the first edition of *Lamia* inscribed "F.B. from J.K.," Keats's presentation copy to Fanny Brawne, and—just as examples—the first drafts of "Eve of St. Agnes," "Ode to Autumn," and "On First Looking into Chapman's Homer."

Damon claims that her monumental biography of Keats "took four years of her life and hastened her death." Overdramatic a statement or not, it's true that by then she was being broken apart by obesity, high blood pressure, hernia, sporadic gastritis, retina deterioration, and cardiac trouble. She finished the volume only after blood vessels burst in both of her eyes. Two volumes, actually: a total of 1,300 pages.

In her posthumous collection he's still with her, still the champion who healed her with his *Endymion*:

> Well John Keats,
> I know how you felt when you swung out of the inn
> And started up Box Hill after the moon.
> Lord! How she twinkled in and out of the box bushes
> Where they arched over the path.

How she pecked at you and tempted you,
And how you longed for the "naked waist" of her
You had put into your second canto.

Did he lay his fevered head against hers, although he'd been dead for seventy years, and the fluid moon poured back and forth between them, as if from one flask to another?

Yes, he lay his fevered head against hers, although he'd been dead for seventy years, and the fluid moon poured back and forth between them, as if from one flask to another.

Ask Louie, ask Rosie, they'll tell you: you can't talk moon, without dragging in the battered, baggage-filled heart.

After Egypt she visited Rome, to see the house in which Keats died, "and worshipped in true disciple form before its barred gateway." It's tempting, too, to leave her here—a white-robed keg-shaped pilgrim at the Temple of the Moon, performing her devotions.

But the anecdotes about this high-tone moxie-powered swaggerer of poetry are too, too good. My favorite occurs on the *Chonsu*: seventeen experienced, toughened Egyptian sailors are taking five supposedly helpless American women up the Nile. It's the job of the seasoned "cataract Arabs" to haul the *dahabeah* over the dangerous rapids. And this, with much rolling of eyes and imploring of extra bakhsheesh, they do—until the especially hazardous rapids near Philae, on the downriver return—and here they balk in a histrionic donkeylike show of recalcitrance. Let the squawky American she-sow empty her purse, if she wants this done! And what the American she-sow does?—she rolls her sleeves up, glowers fixedly at the *dahabeah* as if it's a bad dog needing a firm newspaper whack across the snout—

and then she "stepped out and hoisted and hauled it to shore herself."
Now *that's* Amy Lowell!

That, and the stogies. In a world in which the smoking of even cigarettes by the distaff sex was rigorously taboo (and, under New York's
"Sullivan Ordinance," illegal) Amy Lowell was famous for publicly and
profusely puffing away on her trademark Manila cigars. When the
threat of a World War also threatened to halt her regular supply of
these, she ordered a special humidor built, something like the casket
for a Pope, and stockpiled 10,000 at once.

Well, Abbott Lowell asks by way of logical ascertainment, what's the
"big fat dame" of a lady driver doing at the moment?

"She's across the road here, sittin on a stone wall, smokin herself a
cigar."

"In that case," President Lowell informs Mr. Rummle, "you may
charge the bill. That is, I assure you, my sister."

In 1913 the "International Exhibition of Modern Art" will open at
Armory Hall in New York—the "Armory Show"—and the staid, com-
placent surface of America's taste for realism will shirr and besquiggle
and muckle itself in disturbing (and irrevocable) ways: Cubism, Post-
Impressionism, Futurism, the fleshy glissando-like cylinder-glide of
Nude Descending a Staircase by Duchamp, Brancusi's simplified fetish figures, Matisse's jazzy patterns. . . . Slurs and lauds! Excitement and con-
tumely! Nothing will be the same again.

And as a footnote to these artsy upheavals of 1913, Amy Lowell
(and maid and limousine and chauffeur) will travel to London, there
to take up residency in the posh top-floor retreat of the Berkeley Hotel
(as always, masking her pangs with swank); and will visit (her singular
purpose in being here) the tiny second-floor flat at 10 Church Walk,
where the expatriate American Ezra Pound conducts his bohemian
poetry masterminding.

He will already have heard of her coming: she has stormed herself into the offices of Constable's, the publishers, and demanded to know, in her brassiest manner, why she doesn't see copies of *A Dome of Many-Coloured Glass* in the bookstores here. She thinks she will remain in the publisher's offices until the books are found, unpacked, and distributed, thank you very much.

And she, of course, will have heard of this thorny spade-faced American maestro of "the new poetry," who had almost single-handedly invented (and is frenetically busy proselytizing) Imagism, who one night read a sestina for the "Poet's Club" at a restaurant in Soho "whereupon," said Glenn Hughes, "the entire café trembled." She will want the secrets to Imagism; will suffer his wheedling funds from her, and his cant. He will prune her writing of those *athwarts,* he will chill it clean with a dose of the hard no-nonsense brook-ice of his credo. She will read a new poem of hers at a dinner party, and at its most aqueous moment ("Splashing down moss-tarnished steps / It falls, the water; / And the air is throbbing with it . . .") he will enter the room with a miniature tin bathing tub for a helmet over his head. She will call him "thin-skinned." He will say, "Aw, shucks!" and brand her poetry "putrid." They will flatter and snipe and fortify their respective sides of what Heymann slyly calls "the ongoing skirmishes of the great poetry war."

Meanwhile, the other world, with its butcher saws and tribunals, continues its spin. The Archduke of Austria is assassinated. Austria-Hungary issues its forty-eight-hour ultimatum to Siberia, and five days later declares war. In a few days more, Great Britain follows.

Amy Lowell will see it all take place: "A great crowd of people with flags marched down Piccadilly, shouting, 'We want war! We want war!' They sang the Marseillaise, and it sounded savage, abominable. The blood lust was coming back, which we had hoped was gone forever from civilized races." It turns out, the worlds of our little day-to-day love and competitiveness are gerbil wheels in larger wheels, in infrastructure of cosmologic proportion, not Ptolemy, Einstein, or Hawking can wholly cartograph.

She will come to know and befriend the British poet Rupert Brooke ("perhaps the most notable British poet of his time"). She will attend his reading at London's Poetry Bookshop ("Louder! Louder!" she calls, at his indistinct delivery). Two months later he'll be dead in the trenches in France.

But that's all in the future, though the immediate future. Right now it's 1912. Robert Frost is sprawled on the floor of his temporary home in rural England, winnowing poems from the raggedy sheaf of poems that will be his first book. Robinson Jeffers, Vachel Lindsay, Joyce Kilmer, Elinor Wylie, Ezra Pound, and Edna St. Vincent Millay are first breaking into print.

In Paris, Picasso and Braque are busy upping the ante in a private back-and-forth in which they're making the very small but revolutionary step of incorporating printed commercial lettering and design (for instance, cut-up newspaper headlines) into their paintings: Picasso's *Table with Bottle, Wineglass and Newspaper* (each of the first three drawn, and the fourth a pasted patch of actual front-page newspaper). Gopnick and Varnedoe say "the private innovations of Braque and Picasso's little conversation in 1912 became, by a few intermediary steps and within a decade, a signal part of the official public language of a nation."

And, in Chicago, Miss Harriet Monroe is piecing together the initial issue of *Poetry: A Magazine of Verse*, that will appear September 1912. Ezra Pound is on the masthead as "foreign editor." Eliot, Williams, Hilda Doolittle, Stevens will soon appear in its pages. Amy Lowell receives a solicitation of money and poems.

A Dome of Many-Coloured Glass is published in 1912. Its first year out, it sells just eighty copies. Louis Untermeyer, writing in the *Chicago Evening Post*, says that the book "to be brief, in spite of its lifeless classicism, can never rouse one's anger. But, to be briefer still, it cannot rouse one at all." That year, the textile workers of Lawrence and Lowell stage a record-breaking two-month strike. The Lowells are painted as money-minded, whip-wielding robber barons. The State Police kill two mill workers in cold blood. Everything's shattering, each day is a rare plate thrown at the wall. She locks herself in her third-floor bedroom, hugging her walrusy self, ashamed that she's weeping—but weeping. It's midnight and she stares at the sky with the emptied-out face of a wax museum statue. Gloom and griping: barrel-chested Amy going over the falls. . . .

But she knows someone who—guaranteed—will rejuvenate her, someone she hasn't seen for years, and never in his own far headquarters; someone who can rub away this recent sickly moss. She sends a telegram: HAIL MARSOLEUM STOP EXPECT YOUR SCRIVENER SIBLING SATURDAY 3 PM TRAIN STOP IN NEED OF A FAMILY FROLIC STOP WILL TRADE YOU STANZAS FOR STARS STOP POSTSCRIPT.

Maybe he'll even show her her moon.

But Percival Lowell isn't sure that any of his guests arriving later this afternoon will be able to see so much as a hard-boiled egg held three feet away from The Master Unit's unresponsive eye. He stares at Slipher and Slipher and Lampland, there in his study, from the middle of a mood that's slumping quickly into despondency. Then, from the observatory, they hear a tinny shriek.

Tolliver rushes in: "It's working!" They gape at him in disbelief.

"Mr. Tolliver . . ." he's almost afraid to ask it directly ". . . am I to understand that you have repaired The Master Unit?"

"Yes sir! Well, no. *I* didn't repair it," and now some hesitancy stipples poor Tolliver's uniform rush of pleasure, "but *somebody*. . . ." Tolliver looks from Slipher to Slipher to Lampland; none of the three responds. "Well, *somebody* shimmed it, sir, and now it's working, I tell you!"

"*Shimmed* it, Mr. Tolliver?"—as if he might be saying in public *masturbated* or *butt-fucked*.

"Uh, yes sir. Shimmed it. You know, sir: like when you set a chip of wood or a matches box beneath the uneven leg of a. . . ."

"Yes, Mr. Tolliver. I understand the concept. Gentlemen," waving his hand like a gracious host on a house tour, "let us see."

Yes, there's the observatory. There, in its center, probing toward the heavens like an altar unto the gods, is The Master Unit. And under one of its dainty, exquisite legs is the current issue of *All-Story*.

"Under the Moons of Mars!" the cover blurts. June 1912.

"Mr. Tolliver."

"Yes sir?"

"*Would* you be so good as to bring the custodian's assistant in here?"

4.

"At once, upon hearing the blood-chilling scream of a female voice in that haunted scene, I commenced to bound across the crimson sward of those dead sea-bottoms with the giant leaps allowed my Earthly muscles by the weaker Barsoomian gravity. At the first, my longsword was in my hand, prepared for any contingency, no matter how savage, for mingled with those piteous screams I had heard the exultant, throaty growl of the great white ape of Barsoom.

"The growls continued as I neared the toppled, overgrown columns and crumbling public walls of the ruin of one of those long-ago abandoned port cities that sporadically dot these wastes. The woman's screams, however, had ceased, and I feared that, even now, I might be too late to free her from the fate that awaits the luckless Barsoomian maiden who falls prey to these beasts. The thought that she might be, was almost surely, my beloved, increased both the fear and the urgency of my mad dash.

"The two moons, Cluros and Thuria, leant their eerie double shadows to the night. When at last I had frantically searched through what seemed to me to be half of the caved-in buildings of that formerly glorious city, I came upon my objective. The great white ape was towering above the curled-up form of a woman whose sheer, ripped silks revealed a body bruised and scratched, but quivering yet with life. Her face was turned from me, but who she was, and how she came to be here, were questions that needed their asking delayed, for now I confronted this interrupted, thus doubly-enraged, representative of the most feared of the dead-sea-bottom creatures.

"The great white ape stands ten feet tall, hairless except for a shock of bristly fur upon its head. Its snout and teeth are not unlike the Earth gorilla's, although millennia of cruelty have given these an especially devilish aspect. An intermediary set of arms is located midway between its upper and lower limbs—altogether, a very unpleasant opponent. This one carried a cudgel, and no sooner had I entered the vast ruined hallway where it had dragged its prey, than its club and my sword were adversaries swirling through the night for blood.

"The details of that battle I cannot recall, so swiftly and confusingly did they take place. I know I was wounded once on the shoulder, and I know I gave back more than I received. When it was over, and that giant body lay damp and still at my feet, I leaped to the corner, and kneeled worriedly at the side of the terror-struck woman, and then turned her face to the moons' light.

"'Louie Louie Louie. Vhy do you think soch thinks?'

"'Rosie?'

"'Yah, of course, *Rosie*. Who else? A Princess from outer spaces maybe?'

"'Oh no, no. . . . But—kvick, before more of the apes return, I must rescue you!'

"'Louie. Look around, Louie. *You're* the vun needs the rescue. Yah?'"

My grandfather milked the cow. Her name was Venus, a patchy thing of white with licorice spotting. He liked her fleshy good looks, she had Poland written all over her. Satellite, the calf, explored the fenced-in demipasture in woozy figure eights.

The milking shed was cool. On days when the sun was like a red injection of army ants under his skin, he'd come to the grayly lavender shade of the shed, and press the dented tin of the empty pail against his forehead.

He'd hum. He'd squeeze the ivory withes of milk from her udder, and pretend it was a bagpipe of a sort, and he'd hum some popular tune he'd picked up in town, "The Inky-Tink Song" or "A Soldier's Light" or "Gay Plantation Slippers," or sometimes a Polish children's counting-rhyme, "Chicken-Cabbage-Chicken." But the love songs, either *au courant* or folkloric, he refrained from humming. He didn't want to think about love.

And even so, he daydreamed. Sometimes her face was so tightly pressed against his own, and he was so open to this, that when something startled him out of that world, he thought he'd find himself impressed like dough or wet clay. And occasionally—not often, but occasionally—a female guest stayed overnight at the Main House: men are men, after all, he reasoned, even if they *do* devote themselves to something so fantastically diddleheaded as counting the stars.

He was too polite and (let's face it) unwanted, to sidle up to these slim, pastel, frilled visitors for a drinking-in of their otherness. But he'd see them from the tool shed or the pasture as they breakfasted on the piazza. Then, the usual hobnailed sentences that stomped through the air of Mars Hill—"Oh, dammit, Lampland, I told you the arc declined by seven degrees!" —became the silkier, trilled communiqués of "Do you *haaave* to get back to those silly charts?" (the eyelashes almost audibly batting around the words, like a flock of birds) or "Honey, you can stop looking—I found the hat pins!"

Hot pants, my grandfather heard.

O sovereign power of love! O grief! O balm!
All records, saving thine, come cool, and calm,
And shadowy, through the mist of passed years:
For others, good or bad, hatred and tears
Have become indolent; but touching thine,

One sigh doth echo, one poor sob doth pine . . .
Etc. etc. etc. Ask Louie. Ask Keats,

Who looks back to his page now and completes
These lines from *Endymion* (that I quote above
To demonstrate the brotherhood of love).

His room in what they called "the netherworld" of the enclave was small and spare, but fit his purposes. By its very plainness, it was like blank canvas; every day, in his mind, he tried to paint a believable future across it.

Every evening, when the work was done and the last free-floating smatter of the mesa's sun was snuffled by dusk, he untied the satchel in which he kept a "barbershop magazine": its cover featured a famous New York dancehall girl in a wasp-waist corset, her stockings were unrolled to the knee. He lit a cigarette, and leaned lazily back. His smoke became the smoky air of the hall in which she performed. . . .

And every morning he lifted out, from beneath his pillow, the pamphlet of *shachris, mincha,* and *mahriv* prayers. You could barely say it still existed: he could hold it to the morning light and see his fingers through it, like fish in turbid water. But the Word of God had been poured forth from shakier vessels than this. It served its secular purpose, too: as once it connected him back to Mother Poland, now it kept him tied to those earliest days on the Lower East Side, when the skin of his skin was goosefleshed alive every second with misery, burning hopes, and lovetussle over a floor of chicken feathers. . . .

It didn't matter, the barbershop girl or the Holy Word Itself, he came to see it all led back to this Rosie. More and more, want to or not, her face was painted, in his mind, over the blank walls of Arizona.

Smuddle was his immediate supervisor; Smuddle was "grounds-keeper," he reported to Meacham, "observatory assistant." Meacham reported to C.V. Tolliver. The men liked Louie, he was "okay." A little too foreign, yes, and he kept to himself. But he could take a joke. His accent alone was a rootie-toot hoot that could lilt the most boring of conversations. And he could fix anything—*anything*. Smuddle told Meacham, and Meacham told Tolliver, how this Louis fellow had never *been* behind an automotorcar's wheel before, but Smuddle unfolded the Dracula's-cape-like hood of his dormant machine and this what's-his-name, Louis, intuitively knew, he *knew*, and fifteen minutes later it was running again. So I gave him a package of cigarettes.

What Louie thought of *them*? In a way, they were lesser gods serving The Great God Lowell. Louie would daily see him in the Mars Hill garden, tending with a paternal air to his justly famous, robust squashes and pumpkins (Louie wasn't allowed in the garden, but would keep its row of tools in clean, tight, regimental readiness). Taxis swooped down for these people like golden chariots out of clouds. Photographers begged for admission. They seemed to live in some ever-scintillating effluvium, spangled with planets and stars. They made The-Man-Who-Owned-All-Of-Forman-Street look like a shoeshine boy by contrast.

And yet, they were children. They laughed at such simple things, they bickered like boys in gymnasium choosing up teams. They could use the two-gauge tightening swivel, then set it down, and it would be lost for hours ("Slipher, have *you* seen . . . ?"). They lived in dreams, their heads would disappear in the sky for days on end, like creatures out of fable, or like five-year-olds under the tablecloth, in a magic domain, thinking nobody else can see them. My grandfather knew, *Der kholmer iz a nar*, The dreamer's a fool. He shook his own head, he *tsked* at them fondly.

Meacham offered him cigarettes. Mostly, he was ignored. They gave him little more heed than he gave the turquoise gyroscope of flies around Venus's rump. He wandered, benign himself and unmolested in turn, past windows, through offices, around the Black Forest of dials and wires that fed the observatory, he watched them cater like priests to the needs of The Master Unit. Tolliver told him a joke once, a woman and a bear. Once, Meacham tried to initiate him into the orthodoxies of poker. And Smuddle taught him to drive.

Each week he made the trip into town, with their list of miscellaneous items. And he would check the rack at Larcher's Necessaries! & Quiddities! for the latest *All-Story*. He couldn't get enough of John Carter's splendid deed-filled adventures on Mars.

It was published as "Under the Moons of Mars" in six installments, starting in February 1912 (retitled *A Princess of Mars* for the book, in 1917). He signed his opus "Normal Bean"—to tell the world, this flimsy escapism came from someone "normal in the head." (*All-Story* understandably read the written signature as "Norman Bean," and this became the byline.) Fifty-two years after, the series was still being gobbled by an avid worldwide readership (*John Carter of Mars*, the eleventh book, was published by Canaveral Press in 1964) and, through its imitators, had virtually defined a science-fantasy subgenre.

An enlistee in the Seventh Cavalry, Burroughs had spent two bleak years in the Arizona Territory (1895–97: the formative Mars-espying years of the Lowell Observatory). Surely this accounts, in part, for the heartfelt (though repetitive) portrayal of the desert in his framing story, that sets us up for John Carter's being spirited to Mars.

"Few western wonders are more inspiring than the beauties of an Arizona moonlit landscape; the silvered mountains in the distance, the details of the stiff, yet beautiful cacti form a picture at once enchanting and inspiring. . . ."

But—Arizona; and then a protagonist mystically whisked to a Mars striated by engineered canals? It can't be Burroughs's early cavalry days are enough to account for his choice of these two emphatically rendered locations. John Flint Roy: "That Burroughs read and made use of Percival Lowell's books *Mars and Its Canals* and *Mars as the Abode of Life* cannot be denied."

". . . My attention was quickly riveted by a large red star close to the distant horizon. As I gazed upon it I felt a spell of overpowering fascination. It seemed to call me across the unthinkable void, to lure me to it, to draw me as the lodestone attracts a particle of iron. . . ."

Green men. White apes. Red dunes. It begins.

And Arizona, to Louie? He had hours to fill as he pleased, too insignificant a worker to be time-clocked. Often, to or from his erranding at Larcher's, he would drive the Smuddlemobile along a desert maze spun out of his own spontaneous concocting.

Prodigious gunnysacks of color seemed to open on the mesa tops, and scrolls of it—salsa reds and vivid bunting blues and oolitic earth tones lifted straight from the fundament—unrolled down the seamed, deep-sienna sides.

He watched a lady's beaded bag, a glinting polyp of jet and crimson, suddenly spring and land vigilant: a desert lizard. Some were ruffed, like Elizabethan courtiers. He'd seen them mating. The male had two penises, both barbed. Their eyes are tight black berries, staring out of folds of ancient saurian granulation.

A roadrunner sprinted across the track, a limp snake pinched in its beak. A jackrabbit halted, as still as if it were painted on an old-time tavern sign. Its ears were huge high-standing floral-looking sculls—so thin that, backed as they were by the morning sun, my grandfather clearly saw their filamental networks of blood vessels, ruby on light buff (desert-functional: the air in breezing past them cools the blood).

The creosote bush will grow continuously for 12,000 years—the oldest known living organism. It spreads out from its center, the stems on the inside dying, the stems on the outside ever-pioneering—this can eventually make a green ring up to twenty-five feet in diameter, on the sands. My grandfather stopped the car. There was nobody, only the buffs and the duns and the ambers, and the durable mother-of-all-blues in the sky. There was nobody, only my grandfather. He was the demiurge here, the djinn, he skipped to the center of the circle and whooped, he twirled in place, a feral, energy-spewing creature, spinning to keep the universe on its axis.

Monstrous, wonder-ridden: it may as well have been Barsoom.

"Good." One afternoon at Larcher's he counted out ten cents to an impassive-faced Native American customer shuffling there short by exactly a dime. The Indian's uncracked stoniness was—dignity? anger? My grandfather couldn't tell. "Good" was his only response, then the purchase was made, and the man was gone in a stride. Another white might not have been the recipient even of that single word. But my grandfather gave out the wavelengths of a fellow alien wandering here amid the rows of garden hoses and after-dinner mints.

A world was coming undone by 1912, you could have watched it happen from the vantage of the Larcher's cash register. Recipes for cholla buds, palo verde beans, amaranth greens, the pads of the prickly pear, incendiary mescal, were being replaced by canned and, later, refrigerated grocery goods. This supplantation will increase by the New Deal 1930s (the ethnobotany diet, gone to Cokes and burger patties) with diabetes, hypertension, and chronic obesity its legacy. The principle is Newtonian in lucidity: two worlds cannot equally occupy one point.

Of course, my grandfather wouldn't have known this, any more than the Larcher's cashier or the Indian customer or the well-intended federal food-welfare corpsmen knew it.

But he did know—after all, he was born in a culture where *dybbuks* scrammed from behind the grain trough when you lit a candle—he knew that when he drove through the desert at twilight, spirits skirled in the air, they left their *kachinas* like genies freed for the night from their lamps, they populated the gusts and the thermals and brushed his cheek indifferently, as if to say he wasn't of their tribe, their kind, but neither was he lost beyond the edge of their recognition.

Are these gods? or are these cycles of moisture-exchange in an arid system? He drove, he followed a line of radio-wail and blood-pull that preceded Ur of the Chaldees on this Earth.

It stripped his skin off like old wallpaper. It was magma and thump and theophany in his heart.

And the moon, its bag of bonelight tangled over the mountains.

———✺———

The Arizona moon floats over Krazy's Coconino with such frequency, it's almost a regular citizen of the cast—sometimes as thin as a sickle of cellophane—at others, as rounded and solid as a yellow carnival bump-'em car.

The Navajo night chant, the "Yeibichai," goes:

> *With beauty may I walk.*
> *With beauty before me, may I walk.*
> *With beauty behind me, may I walk.*
> *With beauty above me, may I walk.*
> *With beauty below me, may I walk.*
> *With beauty all around me, may I walk.*

And Officer Pupp soliloquizes:

> Today my world walks in beauty.
> Beneath me a good earth —
> A gracious glebe, lies in beauty —
> Shifting sands dust its cheeks in powdered beauty—
> And now will I turn my eye to the empyrean—
> Where stars' gleam moon's beam
>
> . . .
> So—I'll nap in beauty.

Dat debbil moon. Oh lair of chaste splendor!

———✺———

Varnedoe and Gopnick suggest that "the squiggled needle and mono-liths" and similar vertical structures in the oil paintings of Joan Miró (in illustration of which they reproduce his 1926 painting *Dog Barking at the Moon,* with its ladder reaching from the ground-plane to the sky) have correspondence with "Herriman's great stone fingers"—those monumental, sometimes spirelike lithic formations of the Arizona deserts, that he captured in his own mad manner. "Both devices suggest an enchanted universe where heaven and earth still adjoin, like tenement apartments connected by a fire escape."

Herriman's father "operated a barbershop, owned a bakery, and dabbled in astronomy." So it isn't surprising the son grows up to know how our lathers and doughs can rise alongside our sidereal aspirations.

One Sunday, Ignatz rigs a half-price (lensless) telescope for Krazy, and lifts a flimflam crescent moon on a wire (it looks something like a croissant): "I see a moons, a marvillis moons," she oohs.

But what Herriman also knows is how the "marvillis" is shaped by the "beholda's" eye. Another Sunday, Pupp says to Krazy, "Nice circle around (the) l'il old moon tonight, eh, 'K.'?" "Soikol?" she asks, and looks to see an impressive triangle framing the moon. "Yes—circle."

"He mins a 'try-ankle,'" Krazy explains to Ignatz. So now *he* looks . . . there's the moon, inside a luminous square.

In one panel, it will be rubicond; the next, as green as sweet chilies. Here, as wheezed-out as a flat tire; there, as plump as a bratwurst bursting out of its own rich blotchy casing. Orchidaceously lush or as matter-of-fact as a subway token, it swoops the cockamamie Coconino overspaces in whatever guise is necessary, a small disquisition on relativism, in lunar "lengwidge" as translated by George Herriman: it's a squib of toothpaste or paint from the tube, a penny squooshed on the railroad tracks, a protozoan paisley of Picasso-like conjecture far ahead of its time, a gorgeous thumb-printed pretzel-twist of a moon that could have been baked in a kiln, molybdenum, spongey, amuletic, ping-pongesque, whatever.

> Say a man looks at the moon.
> A woman looks at the moon.
> That makes two moons.

It was silver tonight, so painfully, *sharply* exquisite . . . Keats needed to turn from the cottage's window. He was reminded of the cutting tools he'd seen them use when he was an apprentice in the surgery wards. He felt the moon could enter him that way tonight. "And I've *already* lost my heart," he said.

He was waiting for her, she promised she'd manage to get away from her own enormous gauntlet of household duties by eight—it must have been half-past now, at least. He shuffled a sheaf of pages from *Endymion,* impatiently. "O Moon! Far-spooming Ocean bows to thee . . ." and shuffled again:

> . . . Despair! despair!
> He saw her body fading gaunt and spare
> In the cold moonshine. Straight he seiz'd her wrist;
> It melted from his grasp: her hand he kiss'd,
> And, horror! kiss'd his own—he was alone.

—too true. It must be nearing on nine. And then he thought he heard—he did hear, footsteps, skipping up the rush-strewn gravel path! The heart he claimed he'd lost was doing wild calisthenics in his throat. There was a bashful knock, he hurried to the door and flung it open—

"*Amy?*"

"Well, John," *(puff)* "who" *(puff)* "were you expecting?"

"Amy, please: you know those vile things exacerbate my coughing."

She woke and found herself chuckling, and had the wisdom to carry her dream-chuckle into a hearty, wakeful laugh. Keats, still!—canoodling about in her brain-muck all these years! When she returned to Boston she'd be sure to tell Ada of this, and then they'd both chuckle, lightly holding each other in the ring of sixteen pillows.

Ah, but Ada was many hundreds of miles away now, and the maid, and the maroon platoon of drivers. *This* trip, her first this way, was solo. Somehow it needed to be. She closed her eyes, she imagined the ties of the railroad tracks at such speed that they blended into a single length of excellent parquet-work, the kind in her second-floor study.

She shifted her aching kielbasa body in its seat. A first-class seat!— it could have been a crate for oranges! And some of these other "first-class" passengers!—there was a woman, *foreign,* smelled it, talked it (guttural rollings), dressed it with her three rough-woven scarves worn simultaneously, an *anarchist.* In the darkness, in the aloneness, Amy was sure of it. An anarchist, with an oilcloth bag that might have held bombs. She gave off a mixture of cheap cologne and garlic.

When the porter announced that Providence, the marvels of twentieth-century technology, and seven optional small-town stops that the newlywed engineer had simply ignored in his passion to turn back east, meant they would arrive three hours ahead of schedule, Amy gleamed with relief.

She stared out the window and watched the moon make sterling silver service of the trees. Next stop, Arizona.

"Louis? I merely request an explanation."

Some nights, with a bottle of sugary wine from Larcher's never-failing provender in his pocket, and soon in his blood, my grandfather found himself leaning fraternally (if cautiously) against a great saguaro in the nearby desert, telling it his problems, or singing softly to it, or simply trying to hear the slow green thrum of its own deep-pitched interior life. And this saguaro was as familiar to him as, say, a Hassidic Jew—that is, extreme; but knowable.

Here, though, with the eyes of the pantheon Tolliver, Slipher, Slipher, Lampland, and Lowell upon him, Louie knew that he faced an alien consciousness. "Vahsheenktun, Jafferson, Vahsheenktun," he incanted under his breath. It was all that could come to him in his time of need, an American lucky mantra. Then Tolliver caught his eye. He'd spoken a few times to Tolliver. If he tried, now, to remind this man of their earlier camaraderie . . . ? "Misters. A voman, she meets the bear in the voods. The bear says. . . ."

"Louie: no. Sir," he turned to Lowell, "I've conversed with the man, a little. I believe . . . sir?" Lowell was holding *All-Story*, flipping through its pulp pages. Seminaked Martian paramours, Martian swordsmen. . . . He threw it out the door, into the antechamber, an energetic overhand pitch; for added effect, he walked to the door and carefully, coolly closed it.

"I'm sorry, Mr. Tolliver. You were saying?"

"That I believe this man, who has demonstrated intuitive abilities with mechanical problems, may have . . . may have knowingly. . . . What I mean is, he may have helped us. . . ."

"There is no denying, Mr. Tolliver, that this Louis has helped us." They continued to talk as if he were rooms away. "I should like to determine how accidentally, or how intentionally. And I should like to establish, for this Louis's sake and our own peace of mind, some sets of clearer guidelines for access by the unauthorized to the observatory."

This went on for quite some while. At one point Lowell said to Louie, as if not sure if he were addressing an *idiot savante* or a captured circus ape, "The stars, Louis." Indicating *up* with his forefinger. "What do you know about the stars?"

"Vell, vhen they fall—this means God is closer to the vorld. Then God is lissning to us."

Lowell stared. The staff had never seen Old Ironballs stare this way. He still couldn't tell if he was dealing with pawky ingenuity or idiocy.

But the story of how my grandfather halted the great man in his inquisition, has come down to the family, mixed, eventually, with a version of Einstein's saying he couldn't believe that God played dice with the universe. "See?" someone would say, Aunt Tillie or maybe one of the Pinkuses. "See? *mitt* the stars, *mitt* Gott. He knew, I tell you, chust like Einstein, a *cheenyus!*"

Here, I need to remember that Lowell reads popular detective stories; *The Maulevener Murders,* for instance, is on his shelves. He has his circumlocutious wit. He isn't the worst stuffed shirt the Boston gentry has produced.

But these are tender times. The surer he is of his melt-conducting canals, the more his theories are mocked. And now this—this *bumwipe* of a magazine! And this savvily nitwit floorsweeper! He's exasperated, tired suddenly down to his body's bottommost cobblestone byways. All he can do is stare, and that's how Meacham finds them when he coughs by way of self-announcement and peeks in from the antechamber.

"Sir? Mr. Lowell?"—he's whispering.

Tolliver answers on behalf of his chief. "What, Meacham?"

An orotund stage whisper now: "Them newspaper fellas are—"

Here. With their being a little early, and Louie's draconian questioning running so long. . . . The minions of Mars Hill all are staring as wide-eyed as Lowell now. A beaming, beefy man in a species of derby gives a shake and push to Meacham's hand, as if it were a latch, and Meacham a door; and Meacham, in fact, can't help but act the part, he seems to swivel open. A knot of four of Hearst's reporters enters the room.

"Mr. Lowell! Sorry to barge in early but, well, what good are canals without barges?" Derby barks appreciatively at his own joke. Lowell pales. The other three mean nothing to him, but Derby—! Derby is Garrett P. Serviss, skeptic, and captain of science-column writers for the Hearst chain. It takes only a second for Lowell to see this, to understand the importance of creating a pristinely strong impression, and to realize that the ridiculous situation with this shabby janitorial type now center-stage requires expeditious, subtle maneuvering.

In this same second, Lowell's élan returns. He'll merely dismiss the intrusive Louis for now, and swiftly move to rounds of champagne while Tolliver ably manages to re-shim The Master Unit with something more seemly, perhaps a lacquered cedarwood plaque from the study, perhaps. . . .

But this is a busy second. One of the other reporters, a rumpled sort in a lumpish Stetson hat, has set his bristol board down on the floor, and is dashing excitedly, arms open, to the center of the room, as if greeting a relative at a railway station, but that can't be.

"Lou-boy!" and he's hugging the undercustodian. "Lou-boy, you tickle my buzzum!" He claps him roughly on the shoulders.

"My bosom is also funny from you, mine friend."

"And a lady," Serviss says, with a courtly doffing of his derby, "who accompanied us from town in our taxi."

"Louie!"

"Rosie!" And she drops her bulging oilcloth bag with a thump.

The Master Unit, gentlemen, serves not only Mars Hill but the scientific community on an international scale, as you can see by a small demonstration my staff and I have dribbles away like so much running tapioca pudding, good-bye, it was nice while it lasted, farewell to thee, oh golden one.

Now *everybody's* staring—Lowell, the Lowell subalterns, Hearst's quartet—at Louie, who has some explaining to do.

He points to Rosie.

"Mine luff," he explains.

Herriman grins like a proud proud papa. "Percival, doesn't this call for champagne?"

"Hell (pardon me, ma'am), but any friend of George's" and Garrett P. Serviss gestures expansively toward the Stetson-hatted grinner, "is a friend of mine and a friend of William Randolph Hearst himself, I'll wager, and so is his friend's true lady-love!"

And so Percival Lowell finds himself ringing for Meacham and, by God, five minutes later champagne indeed is flowing copiously, and toasts go around to the reunited couple, who stand there dazed and fitfully whispering phlegmy, gravelly foreign sentiments to each other.

Anyway, *Louie* is dazed. He and Lowell have this, at least, in common. Their stares around the room-at-large resemble the look of mounted deer heads. If anybody here is assured and at ease, it's the foreignest one in the room. But Rosie is happily doing what she'd come to do—reclaiming her man—and doing it quicker, it seems, and in loftier style than she'd ever imagined when the wives of Louie's friends chipped in for her own "first-cless" train ticket to Flagstaff. New in the state by an hour and in the *sanctum sanctorum* observatory by only five minutes, she stands near Louie nodding at the rounds of lifted glasses with regal comportment, as if she were used to the gathered masses bestowing her compliments. The Master Unit backdrops her as if it were constructed with this single purpose in mind: to be the intricate, yea, museum-quality frame around Rosie-from-Cowflop-Poland, Rosie-Come-to-America, for whom the stars and the planets have now been made to stop in their tracks.

My grandmother Rosie, the Queen of the Universe.

And all this while, Lowell—with looks of vague imploration to Tolliver—is hoping their social boil will simmer down, after all it's still possible, and some *soupçon* of factual Martian newsworthiness be broached.

By "all this while" I mean—what? thirty minutes? Enough for the other taxi to finally wind its way to Mars Hill. And it would have been sooner, but first her thirteen suitcases needed gathering up—more than the luggage department at the Flagstaff depot has handled so far all month.

She sees the front door is ajar; Meacham is nowhere about. She spends ten minutes browsing a magazine she finds, *All-Story*; and then, not really caring who she interrupts or why, she opens the observatory door, she peers commandingly over the screwy cocktail scene with consummate Amy Lowell hauteur.

They turn to face a heap of ghee grandstyled in formal diamonded black. "No wonder you see those lines all over Mars, Percy. Offer me a drink and I'll see them with you." She gives them a smile that's won (or at least intimidated) the hearts of kings and philosophers.

And Lowell, stunned by her sudden appearance (he'd planned on having Smuddle meet her at the train at 3 P.M.) but also delighted— his sister, his little sister! *someone who will understand!*—Lowell seamlessly meets the occasion. "Gentlemen: Miss! Amy! Lowell!" and this is what does it: "the Poet." She radiates.

Then he politely corrects himself. "Gentlemen *and* lady," nodding toward Rosie.

Who Amy notices now. "Percy! That woman, her bag—! She has BOMBS!"

It happened this way. It happened in the Barsoomian dimension. I call it "the Syzygy of 1912."

5.

That year, the Arizona Territory becomes the State of Arizona. Chagall completes *The Cattle Dealer*. The R.M.S. *Titanic* sinks: 1,513 drown. The process for manufacturing cellophane is invented by Edwin Brandenberger. Victor F. Hess discovers cosmic radiation. The shaped remains of that charlatan ancestor, Piltdown Man, are found near Lewes (and won't be proved a hoax for forty-one years more). Ravel's ballet of *Daphnis et Chloe* opens in Paris. Carl Jung's *The Theory of Psychoanalysis* appears, as does the new word "vitamin" (coined by the chemist Kasimir Funk).

And Picasso is dabbing away at *The Scallop Shell*, his oil-and-enamel-on-canvas that uses (and so co-opts?) a faithful image of the cover of *Notre Avenir est dans l'air*, a 1912 brochure exhorting France to develop aeronautics for military power. Contrapuntal, squinting-artist-yin and goggled-fighter-pilot-yang, these two zoom into the binary world, here a world, there a world, everywhere a whirled world. . . . It might be as unthinkably large as global war. . . . It might be Wilson's cloud-chamber photographs done in 1912 that lead, at last, to the detection of electrons and protons. . . .

"Kiss my ass," says Larcher to the shipment driver unloading his cases of syrup. This Coca-Cola drink is five cents a glass, as much as a three-egg breakfast with grits, but the thirsty minions of Flagstaff, Arizona, can't get enough of it! And here's this dinkass delivery man who thinks he can drop off *half* a shipment, and credit the store toward shipment-and-a-half *next* month! *Suuure.* What a world!

. . . That's all so far, or seemingly far, away.

The brouhaha's ha'd-out. Elliptic explanations have been offered and accepted; and we find them now, ten men, two women, tentatively stitched together around a common appreciation of Percival Lowell's champagne and Rosie Kaplan's loaves of braided egg-glaze *challah,* that an hour ago were unwrapped from their waxy swaddle in proof that they were balms of a sort, not bombs. They go especially well with the jars of pickled herring she'd brought, and the capers and chutney Lowell directs be excavated from miscellania-level in the pantry.

"EX-cellent bakery goods!" says Slipher the elder a third time, diving into the rick of herrings on his plate, then sandwiching one in a folded *challah* slice. "Still fresh, despite the train ride! You know, Miss Kaplan," and here he brandishes his fork in the air like Liberty her torch, "our friends at Larcher's in the city—Louis, do you know Larcher's?—stock a bread inferior to this as, say, the catfish is to the salmon. If you were to share the secrets behind this with our friends there—for remuneration, of course—I believe the entire Flagstaff community would be in your debt."

A general huzzah of assent from everybody breaks forth, although Louie is half-devoted to studying Rosie's ankles where they're delicately paired beneath her hem; and Lowell is busy with two thin metal rods he's slid from the core of The Master Unit, with which he's demonstrating the employment of chopsticks to Garrett P. Serviss; and Herriman is in heaven, hat tilted back on his head, feet propped up on a pseudo-hassock improvised from Rosie's sturdy hatbox, sketching, sketching!

"Let's see. . . ." Tolliver tries. *"Auntie Rosie's Baked Goods!"* Then he looks at Amy and slips her a wink. *"An explosion of taste in each bite."*

It's evening. He *won't* take "no" for an answer. His distinguished guests from the Hearst empire will stay the night in the Mars Hill baronial guest quarters. Just now, Lampland is beginning the demonstration of The Master Unit—deftly and persuasively, it should be said—having risen in rank to Explainer Supreme, so the sibling reunion can deepen (from its flurried, dramatic afternoon start) in Lowell's study. Suddenly this is vastly more important to him than wooing the flunkies of Hearst or anyone else.

"Oh, Amy, what a vexatious day!"

"These are vexatious times." She's sitting, a living rotunda, on the dragonfoot mahogany sofa (upholstered in red, with fine black striping, it could almost be a design his dearly defended canals have inspired). "Parlous, parlous times," she addends. They each have one of his Cuban cheroots in hand, and they each gaze into its rising writhe of smoke as if an oracle might spell the terms of the future there.

"And this *hell*damn Democrat Wilson who's in office now—! Amy, back east . . ."

". . . are troubles, Percy. The mills are fomenting. The center of our lives, I'm afraid, is coming undone. I'm so scared sometimes, Percy. Not even Ada can coddle me out of it. And my book . . ." her defenses are down in this room, she doesn't need to be The Brass Valkyrie here ". . . what they've done to my book. . . ." She turns her head, so he won't have to be ashamed for her visible weakness.

"Amy!" his lips purse out a raspberry of derision, "Hang the reviewers! Hang the public, too! Hang 'em or buy 'em off, but don't let the dundernoggins stop you. Look, those men out there, from the newspaper—?" and his eyes switch from a lovely bronze-and-polished-rosewood orrery on his desk, to the study door. Does he hear a cabal, even now, tiptoeing up to the other side? "For eighteen years, off and on, again and again, this is what they've tried doing to me." He snaps his cheroot in half.

"Don't go and operatically pluck your nerves on my account, Percy. I'm sorry. You're tired, I can see it, don't fib. Your eyes are red."

"Yes. But it isn't anger or weariness, little Postscript. It's Mars. I swear the color's rubbed off on me, and in me, I probably *piss* red. Amy, I look, and I *look*, I know that planet better than most men know the skin of their wives, and no one believes me. Well, some do. My men here, Flammarion over in France, but . . . Amy, it isn't even my *sight* that goes up the telescope by now, but a connective tissue."

"Look. . . ." he lifts a paperweight (it's Mars, the size of a softball) and flashes a handful of graphs in front of her. "Just from last month. Sightings of double canals, with atmospheric condition at the times of sighting noted. If you knew the moon this well. . . ."

"Now, Percy; there are moons and there are *moons*. I think my darling moon," and here she rummages in her purse, then fishes out the much-crumpled *All-Story* (he's astonished, of course: is he cursed? won't this thing *ever* disappear?) "must be more like *this* Mars than yours." She sees his face. "Don't be disappointed in me. But I don't want to measure my moon with calipers, Percy. My moon was teeming with gnome folk and goddesses long before this urchin magazine was ever birthed into the world." And she holds her hand out to him. He can almost look at the magazine tenderly now, as a unit of what she is, and of the tenderness he necessarily feels for her.

This conversation needs turning around. "Do you remember," she asks, and spreads her arms with thespian overvigor, "the time in the middle of dinner when you and Lawrence started acting out the Lizzie Borden murder trial?"

"Yes! Yes! AND THREE GUESTS LEFT THE ROOM! Remember? Lawrence proved the axe committed the murder all alone, then went and buried itself in the garden. And YOU said—"

"Yes, I said 'Lawrence, stop, the guests are becoming EXAXEperated!'" Giggling. Back there in time. "And I remember the fables your Japanese friend, Tsunejiro, used to tell me. Once. . . ."

They'll do this till the sun comes up. Let's leave the room. Let's linger while one tentative knock at the door interrupts their memory-fest, and then let's leave, let's have them continue this energizing bout of mutual solace in the dignity of private salvation.

"Yes? Lampland?"

"Yes sir."

"Come in. Well! And how did The Master Unit function?"

"Flawlessly, sir—once Tolliver repositioned your pair of chopsticks in the core, and we had the loan of Miss Lowell's tortoiseshell cigar case for a shim."

"Good. Thank you. Tell your guests to sleep well tonight. Tell them it's the closest they'll come to sleeping on Mars herself."

The Martian day is 24 hours 37 minutes 22 seconds.

The Martian day, or *padan,* is ten *zodes* (67 *padans* making a month, or *teean;* 10 *teeans,* an *ord*).

The polar caps of Mars were first discovered by Giovanni Cassini (who later became a French subject and changed his name to Jean Dominique Cassini).

The north polar region is home to both the yellow-skinned people of Okar and the red-skinned people of Pankar; in the south polar region, the black-skinned First Born live in the Valley Dor, and the white-skinned Priests of Issus dwell in the fierce Otz Mountains.

The Viking 1 and 2 explorations of Mars have failed to prove the existence of any life on Mars, not even down to the microbial level.

Mars is Nergal, abode of Nergal, Babylonian god of death and pestilence. Mars is Pahlavani Sipher. Mars is Harmakhis. Mars is Tui (the source of the English "Tuesday"; remember the Rolling Stones song "Ruby Tuesday"?).

Mars is master of the daylight hours of Tuesday. Its metal is iron, its gem is hematite. It rules the liver, the kidney, and the left ear.

Mars invaded Earth on the night before Halloween in 1938, as reported over the radio on *Mercury Theater* (thousands, maybe tens of thousands, of people panic, fleeing on the highways, besieging their local police and churches, falling in fields sobbing).

Mars is just a touch over the size of the Earth (its diameter is approximately 4,200 miles) and Mars is Kepler's key to unlocking the system of planetary orbits and Mars is awash in the blood of the warring green tribes and Mars is close and then Mars is farther away then Mars is close again, with its umlaut of moons, with its emptiness and bounty.

Oh, but Mars is capacious, it will hold all this and, verily, more. Like Earth, it will bear its superfluity selves with the unknowing ease of a pinhead bearing those angels—powers, thrones, and dominions of angels—that the scriptures tally in mystic numbers beyond the counting of humankind.

I don't know what he's like at home, with Mabel. I can only report to you that here, in his baronial guest bed, George Herriman still wears his veteran Stetson. Maybe he thinks he needs the hat to draw. He's drawing, in any case. He's leaned back on his pillow, his legs are up to act as a drawing board, he's humming a sloshy version of "Kissy Kissy Girl" around his thumb-width cigarette.

First, he sketches a few attempts at The Master Unit. Above them goes a dark bowl studded with clustered stars like generals' medals and gumball planets and cymbal moons. In a while, the Kat appears—she's never off his mind, these days—and gambols under this band of astronomical grandiosity. The Mouse appears, a wicked, sulfurous fuming in his breast; he hurls the brick . . . it boinks the Kat's skull . . . so she "sees stars," and they flitter away to join their celestial brethren and sistren. . . .

Now it's a starry canopy, over a wedding. Herriman gives a growly laugh. You see, *he* knows—though Lou-boy doesn't yet, no Lou-boy is lost in a jambalaya of love and fear and indecision and devilish imps in his scrotum—*Herriman* knows, he can see it as plain as his own stained fingers, there's a wedding in the future, he can read the set of Rosie's jaw. She's going to clamp on that boy like a bear trap. She's going to butter him front and back and add a sprig of parsley.

And, before he does let sleep spill its ink through his brain, he tries a portrait of Percival Lowell, an homage to Lowell, there's no line of demarcation where the eye stops and the telescope begins. Perhaps they had an itch in common, and Herriman sensed this; his biographers say, "Obsession is a major theme of Herriman's work."

And just before he sets down the pencil, he places Officer Pupp in the scene. Now Lowell spots the star on that uniformed chest, and the telescope follows it. . . .

Who *is* this man—this serious, sane, astringently intelligent man—who will spend the final twenty-two years of his life insisting he's witnessed a planned-out seine of lines where NASA Mars-probe scientists say they have the on-site photographic proof that none exists?

The question deliquesces away at the edges of thought, leaving only a residue that frustrates us. We may as well ask: who *are* these NASA scientists to say they have the proof no lines exist, where this serious, sane, intelligent man has seen them repeatedly, reading the open russet palm of Mars with probity for the final twenty-two years of his life?

"The point at issue is not whether the things reported were actually happening, but whether they were believed to be happening, and on this point there is not a scintilla of doubt."

That's Edward Harrison, in his fine book *Masks of the Universe*. He says, "The theme of this book is that the universe in which we live, or think we live, is mostly a world of our own making. The underlying idea rests on the distinction between *Universe* and *universes*.

"The Universe is everything. What it is in its own right, independent of our changing opinions, we never know.

"The universes are our models of the Universe. They are great schemes of intricate thought—grand cosmic pictures—that rationalize human experience. *A universe is a mask fitted on the face of the unknown Universe.* Each universe determines what is perceived and what constitutes valid knowledge."

I'd like to think an accurate emblem of this world would be his telescope, an unbent reed angled up at the sky, as the turbulent murmuring currents and mists of the Hopi-Navajo spirit worlds swirl forcefully about it.

Or couldn't it simply be any two people alone together? "Alone" "together." On the oak bench at the milking shed.

"Louie, you made me the promise. You write some letters, very good; but you made me the promise. *Love, Louie* the letters say.

"*Nu?*"

"The night," says Mrs. Kwakk Kwakk, she of duckly mien, "it teems with moon—and promise." (George Herriman, *Krazy Kat*).

The sky is one of Arizona's most opulent effects in a while: velvety indigo, lit with long ribbons of milky incandescence. And speaking of milk: on the other side of the wall, the soft damp huffing of Venus, in some troubled sleep, keeps time. The bell that Satellite wears around her scrawny neck is a fitful counterpoint.

Louie clears his throat. Excited. Uncomfortable.

I'd like to think Rosie is somewhat stern. She's risked humiliation in coming to see him so susceptibly, she's risked the thousand-and-one gentile confusions and degradations in wait around every corner outside of the Lower East Side; she's worn her three good scarves, at once, in staggered layers; she's shared her bread with *meshúgganeh* strangers. All in all, she's earned his deference now.

I'd like to think he offers it. I'd like to believe his time spent on whatever psychic mission the desert represents, was healing time: that the wine and the car and the planet maps and the cacti mean he can step back into his own self now, on Forman Street, with dignity, and direction.

"The cow . . . she was for me to milk, like in Poland."

"Now is not Poland, Louie, now is not Fleksteff, now is New York I think, yah?"

"Yah, Rosie . . . you smell maybe chicken feathers?"

I'd like to think they kiss. I'd like, what the hell, to think they kiss and the whole grand ganglionic burning show-of-shows up there turns fireworks over their kiss, and I'd like to believe their kiss is a contract. Yes, and before we turn our faces circumspectly from this tryst, I'd like to think his tongue is hungrily tracing the question marks that are molded, even before birth, into the human ear.

But what do I know?—this part of the story is buried (since it's never come up) more surely than Assyria or Babylon. I only know that later Smuddle will show Rosie back to the main house: this is 1912, and certain sticky proprieties must be kept. She will sleep, she will wake, there will be a moment of wedding canopy and then many years of depleting labor, these years will pass, she will love, she will ache, she will croon, she will carry my mother.

Percival Lowell will live for four years more. Every night he will break himself like a wave on the sands of that red red planet. Every day he will buzz the buzz of the gadfly in the waking world's complacency.

In November 1916 he will die at the observatory. His body will be buried on Mars Hill in a mausoleum that looks like a small observatory, with a dome of transparent blue glass. His spirit—call it what you want—will ascend, along a line of obsession, to the planet Mars. The natives there will dredge him from one of the Low Canals, and expirate its waters from his lungs. He will marvel: the intricate system of locks (for some are navigable), and the lightsome boating parties!

When Amy learns of his stroke and death, the funeral will be over by a week. She's suffered a month of neuralgia, gastritis, and jaundice—with double the normal dose of morphine fuddling the pain in her body—and the house will keep this news from her until her partial recovery. So much is still ahead! The Imagism wars, and the Spectra hoax, and the Ouija seance, and her book of Chinese translations, the dinners, the roller-coaster reviews of her work, the bold forays and anonymous snipings, every final ovation and snigger, all three operations on her sturdy, hurting, oil drum of a body, every last wrung-out line of a poem. . . . On May 12, 1925, she will look into the mirror and see the right side of her face drop. To Ada she'll simply say, "A stroke." They will gather wagons of lilacs from Sevenels's garden, surround her corpse with these, and then—at her request—she will be cremated, and the ashes consigned to the family plot at Mount Auburn. Her spirit will tunnel loose, her *real* self, a wee transparent flimmer. She's free, at last! And she will hover, a hummingbird, over that posthumous Pulitzer prize, and like a hummingbird she will dart about it, supping from its sweetness. Singing the poet's song: *too late, too late.*

John Keats will consign his memory to the erasure of running water. Edgar Rice Burroughs will publish twenty-eight Tarzan novels and forty-four other books. At Pasadena time 4:53 A.M., July 20TH, 1976, a 1,300-lb. vehicle just about the size of a jeep will land on Mars on the western slopes of Chryse Planitia, 22.3 degrees north latitude and 47.5 west longitude. The sky will be salmon-pink; the soil, uniformly red. The summary Norman H. Horowitz (Emeritus Professor of Biology at the California Institute of Technology) will provide, begins, "Viking found no life on Mars."

Louie and Rosie will live in Chicago. (The New York business will finally fail, after some exhilarating false starts; and distant relatives invite them to that booming lakeshore city.) They will raise (in order) Sally, Regina, Fannie. They will yell out their wares. She will chip Lake Michigan whitefish out of blocks of ice; and he will don his burgundy-and-epauletted organ-grinder-monkey's outfit, lifting the shoppers to toys and fixtures and ladies lingerie. At night the el will rattle their bones like dice in a godly game of chance. They will dance at the *balln.* They will do the two-backed hoochiekoo in bed. She will save the crusts of the bread, he will pick in the alley for rusted scrap and string. The girls will blossom, in their string-bean way (Regina, lost to brain cancer, eating, eating at her, like silverfish in her skull). More weddings. Grandchildren. Time will never press the *stop* switch on its turbines. He will grow hair in his ears ("gray moss!" I yelled, it became a family "cute" joke). She will pluck the bowel from the rend in the chicken one morning and see her hand is shaking. They will sit together on the porch and watch the moon, that great bronze seal of approval on the night. She will teach me to sing "In Jersey City vhere I did dvell," she will buy me a bottle of orange pop and hug me into the florid peeked-at creases of her décolletage—it's heavily shpritzed with dime-store perfume. She will enter her room in the hospital with a cheery wave and leave it without her uterus. She will wail at this all night until the sky tears down the middle like black silk, "Aiy, I'm not no voman no more." He will shrivel. She will die. He will live for a visit a week in the place they call The Home. . . .

But all that's the future. Life is never the past, the present, or the future. Life is moments the size of the Thailand bumblebee bat that weighs less than a penny.

They're at the station now, a week later. Hearst's reporters have gone six days before (with Serviss showily unconvinced of *canali*, but bearing a furtive respect for his host's well-marshaled zeal). Herriman said, "Lou-boy, you're a genuine ring-tailed prodigy," and hugged him and ostentatiously smooched on Rosie. "Here," he gave Louie a piece of paper, folded and taped, "to open later. And here," a separate piece, "my newspaper telephone number. I know a place that seasons its egg foo yung with lightning." But, of course, they never did get together, back in New York.

Then Louie had spent six days at his round of menial tasks while Smuddle searched out a replacement. Lowell took Amy and Rosie picnicking into the desert. Rosie attempted a cigarillo. Amy learned the words to *Bah mir bist du shayn*. Louie had given Lowell a present, a child's toy he'd purchased at Larcher's, that Lowell removed from his briefcase now: a pair of rose-tinted spectacles. Looking around: the sands were red. This is what it would be like.

When the train pulled into the station, there was an all-around formal shaking of hands. Then Louie pinched Rosie's bottom, for show. "Jews," thought Lowell. "You have the monies?" asked Amy. Rosie nodded. (For the recipe, from Mrs. Larcher's private coffers, and gratefully paid out.) "Mine friends," said Louie, clearing his throat and feeling important, "about the good-bye. Ve haff a saying from mine people—" but the train whistle lowed, and they ran off in a rhythm of his duffle bag and her hatbox.

That night, while Rosie dozed, he untaped George's drawing. He was standing under a canopy, holding Rosie's hand, and the sky was crammed with six-pointed Jewish stars.

In the corner, that Coconino feline gave a frolicsome leap and clicked her heels. "Be heppa," she said.

He will kronikle the kanon of the Kat every day until April 25, 1944. Dropsy, migraine, arthritis. "I remember my aunt putting glass tubes in his legs, to draw off the water." He once said that he wanted to end his life in Monument Valley in Arizona "lying down on a cactus leaf until I was shrivelled up and blown away by the wind." In respect of his wishes, his ashes were scattered over the Navajo reservation of Monument Valley.

> *Homeward now shall I journey,*
> *Homeward upon the rainbow;*
> *In Life Unending, and beyond it,*
> *Yea, seated at home behold me.*

"Ve go home now," Louie gratuitously said, by way of indicating his deeply wholehearted endorsement of their confluent travel back to New York. They watched the miles re-ravel back up.

He felt like a monarch. He'd had an adventure! He'd won his woman! And, *ssh*, he had an idea, too, a winner of an idea.

Lenses.

Louie had seen the future.

When they were back, he thought, he'd have a few ambitious suggestions to share with Nate.

Science-fantasy emir Ray Bradbury writes of his coming under the spell of Edgar Rice Burroughs when he was ten: "For how can one resist walking out of a summer night to stand in the middle of one's lawn to look up at the red fire of Mars quivering in the sky and whisper: *Take me home.*"

Coda

Parnassus

Technically I was a man.

This spindly squeaky thing with the Adam's-apple accent was, by virtue of being thirteen and *bar-mitzvahed*, a technical man.

And so the phone call came: they needed a tenth for a *minyan*. Nathan Kaplan—I remembered Mr. Kaplan, didn't I?—needed to say the *yiskor* prayers for his wife, and if I weren't there in attendance, lending my lame but official singsong to these *daveners,* the God Who Demanded a Threshold of Ten would never turn His Ear of Ears to their puff of plaintive Kaplan imploration.

I didn't *want* to; but I went. I *wanted* to—what? Watch television? Play with my willie? Stare at a smear of clouds and wish a burning pinpoint of myself up through them, into the currents of outer space? The angsts and overbrimmings of being technically a man are many. In any case, yes, I went.

There isn't much more to say. They were ancient and stale of breath, and silked and fringed in the ritual synagoguewear, and I stood among them, following their lead and saying *amen* whenever someone's gnarled radish of a finger thumped the word out in my opened book. I loaned my voice, it took its place in a single wing of voice that made its technical way through the top of the ionosphere, and into a realm of shimmering off the scale of human perception.

This is why I believe in the Muses, of course.

There were nine of them.

And ever since, if I've been invited to join them for a moment, to sing along as a tenth—though they may have scraped the bottom of the barrel to get my number, I go.

Notes

These essays were written over twenty-one years, not always with my eye on their being gathered together: each had its separate beckon. Still, I've tried in retrospect to fashion them into a meaningful community. They are ordered now according to perceived demands of design and substance—not chronologically. Because neither the people and places of my personal life nor the curlicues of my prose's surface have remained strictly consistent over these two decades, I've needed to forgive the little inconsistencies from piece to piece, and to find a functional, resonant motif in the little repetitions that result from these essays being collected into one large unit. I'll trust that you find similar empathy.

The readings I've gratefully relied upon are often credited within the text of the essays themselves. Every reasonable effort to credit sources has been made, but twenty-one years is a long time in this unorganized, well-intentioned but haphazard note-taker's life; and I ask understanding for any omissions that have slipped through my mounded ziggurats of scrap-paper records. The following sources were acknowledged when these essays originally were published, and should be recognized—with a grateful salute—this time around as well.

Abstracts of books and articles that inform my survey of the "false memory syndrome" debate, supplied by Dr. Jean Muench; Anderson, *Three Worlds to Conquer*; Anonymous, "Growing Stem Cells" (*Scientific American*, January 1999); Anonymous, "Lion-Lizard Combo Found" (*Discover*, April 1999); Asimov, *The Currents of Space*; Ausubel (ed.), *A Treasury of Jewish Folklore*; Ayrton, *The Maze Maker*; Barker, "Sources for the Dance Historian in the Hoblitzelle Theater Arts Library"

(University of Texas Humanities Research Center); Barks, various issues of the comic books *Donald Duck* and *Uncle Scrooge*; Bartkevicius, "The Person to Whom Things Happened: Meditations on the Tradition of Memoir" (*Fourth Genre*, Spring 1999); Benson, *The Maya World*; Berman, *The Reenchantment of the World*; Bly, *A Little Book on the Human Shadow*; Boorstin, *The Discoverers*; Bosworth, *Diane Arbus* (as well as monographs on Arbus's work from *Aperture* and *Picture Magazine*); Bronowski, *A Sense of the Future*; Brown, *The Story of the Armory Show*; Bush, *John Keats*; Campbell, *The Inner Reaches of Outer Space* (which quotes Natalie Curtis); Carey (ed.), *Eyewitness to History*; Carr, *What Is History*; Casson, "A Mayan City to Buy" *(Discovery of Lost Worlds)*; Casti, *Paradigms*; Ceram, *Gods, Graves and Scholars*; Churchward, *The Lost Continent of Mu*; Clark, *Space, Time and Man*; Connell, *The White Lantern*; Cooper, "The Odyssey of a Synchronic Collector" (*Comic Book Marketplace*, March 1999); Curran, *In Advance of the Landing: Folk Concepts of Outer Space*; Damon, *Amy Lowell, A Chronicle*; Desmond and Messenger, *A Dream of Maya*; Doe-Nimh, *The Lamiph of Mu*; Douglas, *Purity and Danger*; Eclipse Books, *Ignatz and Krazy* (various volumes' introductory materials); Eliade, *The Quest: History and Meaning in Religion*; Eliade, *Rites and Symbols of Initiation*; Eliade, *The Two and the One*; Enfield, "That Mysterious Sound: Pop Culture Epiphany in Albert Goldbarth's Poetry" (M.A. thesis, University of Chicago); Fagan, "What Caused the Collapse of the Maya?" *(Mysteries of the Past)*; Frazer, *The Golden Bough*; Fuller, *Fifteen Years of a Dancer's Life*; Gallenkamp, *Maya*; Gide, *Theseus*; Gould, *Amy*; Green, *New York 1913*; Gribbin, *Q is for Quantum*; Gribbin, *Time Warps*; Grossinger, *The Night Sky*; Hall, *The Dance of Life*; Hansen, *Midwest Portraits*; Harrison, *Masks of the Universe*; Hayes, *Your Memory—Speedway to Success in Earning, Learning and Living*; Heymann, *American Aristocracy*; Hickman, *The Lemurian Stone*; Hope, *The Ancient Wisdom of Atlantis*; Howe, *World of Our Fathers*; Hoyt, *Lowell and Mars*; Huffington, *Picasso, Creator and Destroyer*; Hughes, *Culture of Complaint*; Huxley, *The Way of the Sacred*; Johnson, *The Birth of the Modern*; Jones, *In Parenthesis*; Jung, *Individual Dream Symbolism in Relation to Alchemy*; Kossy, *Kooks*; Kunzig, "A Tale of Two Archeologists" (*Discover,*

May 1999); Laughton, *The Maya*; Leakey, *People of the Lake*; Le Plongeon, *Maya/Atlantis: Queen Moo and the Egyptian Sphinx*; Le Plongeon, *Sacred Mysteries Among the Mayas and the Quiches*; Leshon and Margenau, *Einstein's Space and Van Gogh's Sky*; Lupoff, *Edgar Rice Burroughs, Master of Adventure*; MacCurdy (ed.), *The Notebooks of Leonardo Da Vinci*; McDonnell, O'Connell, and De Havenon, *Krazy Kat, the Comic Art of George Herriman* (which also quotes Gilbert Seldes); Mitchell and Rickard, *Phenomena: A Book of Wonders*; Monroe, *Poets and Their Art*; Nelson, *Popul Vuh*; O'Malley, "Biology Computers" (*Popular Science*, March 1999); Norman, *The Hero: Myth, Image, Symbol*; Petroski, *The Evolution of Useless Things*; Philipson (ed.), *Leonardo da Vinci: Aspects of the Renaissance Genius* (quoting essays by Berenson, Clark, de Santillana, Eissler, Read, Shattuck and Wölfflin); Pizer, *Take My Word For It*; Poncé, *The Game of Wizards*; Porges, *Edgar Rice Burroughs, the Man Who Created Tarzan*; Postman, *Amusing Ourselves to Death*; Postman, *Conscientious Objections*; Quinn, "Krazy's Dad: George Herriman and Krazy Kat" *(Artspace)*; Reid, *Marie Curie*; Renker, "Introduction" to *Moby-Dick* (Barnes & Noble edition); Rexroth, *One Hundred Poems from the Chinese*; Rist, "How to Heal a Masterpiece" (*Discover*, April 1999); Rosemont, "George Herriman (Krazy Kat)" *(Cultural Correspondence)*; Roy, *A Guide to Barsoom*; Rupp, *Committed to Memory: How We Remember and Why We Forget*; Russell, *Beneath the Vaulted Hills*; Sheldrake, *The Presence of the Past*; Shoumatoff, *The Mountain of Names: An Informal History of Kinship*; Stone, "Cloning the Woolly Mammoth" (*Discover*, April 1999); Tedlock, *Popul Vuh*; Thompson, *Maya Archeologist*; Umland, *Mystery of the Ancients: Early Spacemen and the Mayas*; Varnedo and Gopnik, *High and Low: Modern Art and Popular Culture*; Von Hagen, *World of the Maya*; Wallace, *The Fabulous Showman*; Watson, *Beyond Supernature*; Weeks and James, *Eccentrics: A Study of Sanity and Strangeness*; Wilford, *Mars Beckons*; Wilson, *The Occult*; Wilson, *Starseekers; The World Almanac Book of the Strange*; Wright, *Remembering Satan*; poems by Antler, Jon Anderson, Marvin Bell, Elizabeth Bishop, Paul Carroll, Amy Lowell, and Louis Simpson; and about a trillion issues of the *Fortean Times*. The "Krazy Kat" panel by George Herriman is copyright by Eclipse Books and is used by permission. / In the spirit of the essay "Many Circles," one of the books above is my own invention. / In Goldbarthian spirit, none of these pieces was researched or composed on a computer, or was submitted to a publisher on disk.

"What the Boy chiefly dabbled in was natural history and fairy tales, and he just took them as they came, in a sandwichy sort of way, without making any distinctions; and really his course of reading strikes one as rather sensible."

—Kenneth Grahame

Oyf a masse fegt men nit keyn kashke.
Don't ask questions—it's a story.
—Yiddish proverb

ALBERT GOLDBARTH was born in Chicago, Illinois, and currently lives in Wichita, Kansas. He has been publishing notable collections of poetry and of essays for over a quarter of a century, from presses large and small, and is the recipient of three fellowships from the National Endowment for the Arts, a Guggenheim fellowship, and the National Book Critics Circle Award in poetry. His previous collections of essays are *A Sympathy of Souls*, *Great Topics of the World*, and *Dark Waves and Light Matter*; his recentmost volume of poetry is *Saving Lives*.

The text of *Many Circles* has been set in Baskerville, a typeface designed by John Baskerville in the 1750s and cut by John Handy. Book design by Wendy Holdman.
Typesetting by Stanton Publication Services, Inc.
Manufactured by Bang Printing on acid-free paper.

Graywolf Press is a not-for-profit, independent press. The books we publish include poetry, literary fiction, essays, and cultural criticism. We are less interested in best-sellers than in talented writers who display a freshness of voice coupled with a distinct vision. We believe these are the very qualities essential to shape a vital and diverse culture.

Thankfully, many of our readers feel the same way. They have shown this through their desire to buy books by Graywolf writers; they have told us this themselves through their e-mail notes and at author events; and they have reinforced their commitment by contributing financial support, in small amounts and in large amounts, and joining the "Friends of Graywolf."

If you enjoyed this book and wish to learn more about Graywolf Press, we invite you to ask your bookseller or librarian about further Graywolf titles; or to contact us for a free catalog; or to visit our award-winning web site that features information about our forthcoming books.

We would also like to invite you to consider joining the hundreds of individuals who are already "Friends of Graywolf" by contributing to our membership program. Individual donations of any size are significant to us: they tell us that you believe that the kind of publishing we do *matters*. Our web site gives you many more details about the benefits you will enjoy as a "Friend of Graywolf"; but if you do not have online access, we urge you to contact us for a copy of our membership brochure.

www.graywolfpress.org

Graywolf Press
2402 University Avenue, Suite 203
Saint Paul, MN 55114
Phone: (651) 641-0077
Fax: (651) 641-0036
E-mail: wolves@graywolfpress.org